Advance Praise for

UNF*CKOLOGY

"You have never read a book like this in your life. Very few scientists these days pull together the results from diverse disciplines. Very few thinkers give us big ideas. By showing us how to use research from fields like embodiment to change our lives, Amy Alkon has given us two things: new big ideas and balls-to-the-wall hilarity. Amy Alkon is as funny and as wildly inventive as Dave Barry or P. G. Wodehouse and she has established herself with this book as THE top practitioner of applied science."

> —Howard Bloom, author of *The Lucifer Principle*
> and *How I Accidentally Started the Sixties*

"Amy Alkon is such a festive cocktail of funny and brainy! *Unf*ckology* is a hilarious, wise, and amazingly useful 'science-help' for the meek to finally get going on inheriting the earth."

> —Sandra Tsing Loh, host of the syndicated public radio show *The Loh Down On Science* and author of *The Madwoman in the Volvo*

"In this (very funny) book, Amy Alkon explains how not to be a loser. Being socially anxious and desperate isn't fun. And Amy shows you the science behind self-transformation. No shortcuts or thinking your way out—just incremental and targeted action."

> —W. Keith Campbell, professor of Psychology at the University of Georgia and coauthor of *The Narcissism Epidemic*

"*Unf*ckology* is a f*cking good book. The self-help book for people who hate self-help books, *Unf*ckology* is firmly grounded in empirical research and takes a no-nonsense, no-coddling, no-airy-fairy-BS approach to the subject. It's also very funny. Every page sparkles with Amy's irreverent wit and wisdom. Highly recommended!"

> —Dr. Steve Stewart-Williams, associate professor of Psychology at the University of Nottingham

Also by Amy Alkon

I See Rude People
Good Manners for Nice People Who Sometimes Say F*ck

UNF*CKOLOGY
—

A Field Guide to Living with
Guts and Confidence

Amy Alkon

ST. MARTIN'S GRIFFIN
NEW YORK

The Library of Congress Cataloging-in-Publication Data is
available upon request.

ISBN 978-1-250-08086-8 (trade paperback)
ISBN 978-1-4668-9268-2 (ebook)

Our books may be purchased in bulk for promotional, educational, or
business use. Please contact your local bookseller or the Macmillan Corporate
and Premium Sales Department at 1-800-221-7945, extension 5442, or by email
at MacmillanSpecialMarkets@macmillan.com.

First Edition: January 2018

10   9   8   7   6   5   4   3   2   1

For my sister, Caroline Belli,
who makes life better for old people

— CONTENTS —

PART THREE
Putting It All Together

— ACKNOWLEDGMENTS —

This book spent several years trying to kill me.

I am extremely grateful to my editor, Michael Flamini, for believing in me yet again and for giving me the time and support I needed to make this book what it ultimately became. He is wise and kind, full of life and full of fun, and loves pushing the limits in smart ways. I wrote a smarter, funnier book because I imagined him reading it as I wrote it. And after he read what I wrote, his ideas made this a better book and transformed how I write applied science.

St. Martin's Press has been an amazing publisher. Everybody I encounter there cheers and supports me at every turn. Many thanks to Danielle Fiorella and James Perales for designing this book's fabulous cover; to publicity manager Leah Johanson for putting this baby of mine out far and wide; and to Gwen Hawkes, for always making everything okay (and usually much better) and always with sunshine on top.

Some agents just sell books. I have the other kind of agents, Cameron McClure and Ken Sherman, who unflaggingly have my back and have helped me grow as a writer and a human through their wisdom and kindness. Every book I write is better because of them, and it's such a great feeling, as a writer, to know that you are never alone. (I'm so used to Cameron being there to talk me off the ledge that I don't even bother opening the window anymore.)

Amy Dresner edited numerous very scary drafts of the manuscript before it went to Michael, and I'm hugely grateful for all of her meticulous work and for making me laugh with notes like "OMG. This sentence is an abomination."

I was extremely lucky to have grammar ninja David Yontz, who copyedits my column for Creators, as the copyeditor on this book. I'm a better writer because of what I learn from his corrections, and his work made this a better, clearer book. (Any, um, *grammatical license* you see is my doing, per Elmore Leonard's advice, "If proper usage gets in the way, it may have to go.")

Loving thanks to my wonderful boyfriend, Gregg Sutter, who cooked me countless gourmet dinners, read pages, made me laugh, and otherwise helped me hold it together when I could do little else but hammer away at this book.

Thanks also go out to some important people in my life: Christina Nihira ("The Velvet Whip"), Dr. Matthew Pirnazar, Da'Nisha Gibson, Debbie Levin, Kate Coe, Jim Sheridan, Emily and Mark, Caroline Belli, Mari Sunaida, Kate Bergin, Nancy Rommelmann, and Laurent Chalumeau.

Special thanks go to Kaja Perina, who was there for me with friendship, wisdom, and reassurance whenever I sent up a flare. The same goes for Kingsley Browne, Catherine Salmon, AJ Figueredo, Nancy Segal, Sander Greenland, Sandra Tsing-Loh, Virginia Postrel, and Stef Willen.

Many researchers were very generous with their time and thoughts: James Chisholm and Barbara Oakley read and commented on the whole manuscript. Spike W. S. Lee, Norbert Schwarz, and Michael Inzlicht gave me chunks of their time at SPSP, the big social psych conference, transforming my understanding of their areas of research. Sarah Strout, Lee Kirkpatrick, Walter Foddis, and Michael McCullough guided me in essential ways and answered my questions without fail.

Other researchers and science people read and gave really helpful comments on chapters and sections: Andy Arnold, Piotr Winkielman, Sam McNerney, Michael McCullough, Ian Reed, Cristine Legare, Stephan Margolis, Francesca Gino, Richard Harper, and Neil Mc-Naughton.

I'm grateful to my blog regulars who gave me comments, including Ric "Tanukiman" and Purple Pen. Thanks also to Adam Farasati, who commented on this book when it was just a book proposal and to AJ's friend Alan Hieger, who read early chapters.

I'm also grateful to my non-fic lit peeps: Tom Zoellner, Wendy Paris, all of Invisible Institute West, and David Rensin.

Finally, thanks to the late Elmore Leonard, "the poet laureate of wild assholes with revolvers," who's been a big inspiration. I'll always treasure his last words to me: "You have a pert can."

PART ONE

—

You Have What It Takes;
It's Just in Hiding

— 1 —

LOSERHOOD ISN'T DESTINY

You can't order a lightly used spine off eBay. There's no Find My Balls cousin of Find My iPhone. And nobody goes around in a tow truck with a big winch to yank people out of loserhood.

However, there actually *is* a way out of loserhood, and it doesn't involve a therapist—one who's looking forward to finally buying Aruba after decades of listening to you jawing on.

And no, you will not be asked to look into the mirror and recite affirmations. (If you've ever done this, you know how well it works: "I am beautiful. I am happy. I am confident. I am...kidding myself. I am still the same fucking loser I was before I wasted ten minutes doing this bullshit.")

All you actually have to do to change is behave like the confident person you want to be.

I get it—that probably sounds unbelievable—but you'll see in the next chapter that I did this, and I was a particularly hopeless case. I didn't transform myself magically, by bathing my brain in some kind of self-help rays; I did it through the emotionally grubby work of repeatedly acting the way confident people do.

This book gives you all the steps you need to get from point worm (or just mildly underconfident) to full personhood—the point where you aren't always squirming on the inside about what to say or do and whether somebody will approve. Best of all, getting to the point where you go out into the world as the full you doesn't require exceptional intelligence, piercing intuition, or—in case you were wondering— a bullet-deflecting bodysuit with bat ears. You just need to be so sick of living like a human crumb (or just not as fully as you could be) that you're willing to shove your way through your fears and take action.

This isn't to say you won't be afraid—at least for a while. But I'm hoping you'll come to the conclusion I did—that being afraid to do something isn't good enough reason to let yourself duck out of doing it.

While we're at it, I should mention that this is not a "self-help book." (Gross.) This is a science-help book—a self-unfucking science-help book. "Science-help" is a term coined by my science journalist friend David DiSalvo, describing advice that's based on evidence from scientific research. So, no, this book will not advise you to pester the universe to heal you. (The universe isn't listening and doesn't give a shit.)

This book likewise does not contain "The Secret," which is the title of a best-selling book based on the tempting premise that positive thinking works like a giant magnet to pull whatever you want right to you. Supposedly, if you want a new car, you just picture it and think grateful thoughts about it (as if it were already yours) and some pocket in the universe will unzip and out will drop your fabulous new dream ride, right into your life. (Yes, that's right. You only lack that flying Bentley convertible because you haven't put your mind to making it pop up in your carport.)

Ultimately, if *Unf*ckology* does have a "secret," it's that if you get off your ass and do what the science suggests, you can have a far better life.

Not "someday."

Starting NOW.

I call this living by the "car crash principle." People will tell you,

"It was only after I got in that horrible car wreck that I realized I'd better seize the moment—stop wasting my life." The way I see it, why wait? Why not choose to live that way right now—without the twisted metal, disfiguring injuries, and years in rehab spent pushing a ball across a table with your nose?

— 2 —

HATE ME; I SUCK
A coming-of-rage story

I was a loser as a child. I had scraggly red hair and a space between my front teeth you could drive a small car through, and I wet my bed until I was twelve. This was before parents were advised to just relax and wait the bed-wetting thing out. As I remember it now, my mother used to say—in that satanic voice from *The Exorcist*—"You wet the bed again?!"

I had no friends, and the neighborhood kids egged our house, called me "dirty Jew," and told me I killed Jesus. (I was six at the time. I didn't even kill bugs.) I would have done anything to have even one friend. In second grade, I thought I'd hit the jackpot: Two girls came to me and promised to be my friend if I did their math. I did it—during recess, in a dusty, empty classroom—but the moment I put down my fat #2 pencil, they ran out and ignored me, same as before.

Elementary school turned out to be seven long years of getting picked last for everything—except in extenuating circumstances, like when it was time for kickball and the only other kid left had a broken leg. When kids talked to me at all, it was to sneer "The redhead is dead!" or call me "the redheaded hamburger." I was miserable every day, and I sobbed to my mother that I had no friends, but she didn't know what to say.

In third grade, I tried bargaining, silently offering various incentives to God, if only he'd make me look like the other Amy—the pretty, popular honey-blond one our teacher, Mrs. DeMaio, referred to as "Amy long-lashes." Naturally, like all those mean children, God just ignored me.

When I wasn't in school, I had my face jammed in a book. I checked them out of the Farmington Community Library by the laundry-basketful. The stories I read gave me hope that I could someday have a better life, and I learned many things—among them, the dangers of reading while riding a bicycle.

In tenth grade, I joined the youth group at my parents' temple. For the first time in my life, I had friends—but, like some weird weekend Cinderella, only on Sundays, when youth group met. I was terrified that my youth group friends would realize they'd made a terrible mistake, so I tried really hard to be the sort of person they'd find acceptable.

I carefully avoided showing my true feelings—like that my having friends was pretty much the greatest thing since God cut a hiking trail through the Red Sea. I was especially careful to keep mum about how I'd decided the whole God thing was hooey (seeing no reason to let this stop me from playing guitar and leading everybody in Hebrew folk tunes about God's greatitude).

Pretty much erasing myself seemed a small price to pay for finally being liked. However, it meant that I often had no idea what I thought about anything—and not because I didn't think. In fact, because I read lots of novels and loved logic, I was always thinking and reasoning. There was a point of view in there somewhere. But when I was around other people, what I thought was whatever I thought they'd want me to think. All in all, I was a big redheaded empty jar.

HOW MAY I PROVIDE YOU WITH EXCELLENT SERVICE?

At twenty-one, I moved from Michigan to Manhattan. I knew tons of five-dollar and even fifty-six-dollar words from my years of endless reading, but I had yet to learn the word no. This made me a popular guest at many people's apartments—typically when they were moving in or out of them and needed some patsy to pack and haul stuff for free.

Eventually, the guy renting me a bedroom in his loft wanted his place to himself again, and I had to move. I just barely scraped together the rent and security deposit for a tiny dumpy tenement apartment by the Holland Tunnel, or, as I called it, "the rectum of New Jersey."

Hoping against hope for a little quid pro schlep, I called all the people I'd helped move. Nobody was home, or, if they were, they were in bed with a vicious hangnail or just running out the door to their groovy summer share in the Hamptons. "But, hey, good luck with your move!"

I had about four dollars left in my checking account after paying the landlord, so I couldn't afford a moving van or even taxis. Instead, I piled boxes and garbage bags of my stuff onto an old metal-wheeled wooden cart, about six feet long, that a kindly furniture dealer in my new neighborhood lent me for the weekend. I only had to move from Duane Street to Greenwich and Canal—a little over a half-mile— so doing it peasant cart–style didn't seem all that terrible.

This was a desolate part of town back then—especially on the Saturday night I'd chosen to move—so I pushed the cart right down the middle of Greenwich Street. I was pleasantly surprised at how easy it was—until I got to the cobblestoned part in the last three blocks.

Steel wheels and cobblestones are not a good mix. Every inch of that street traveled straight up my arms, hammering itself into the deepest reaches of my brain and making my stomach feel like I'd strapped it to a paint shaker.

This was a far cry from my most recent moving effort: sitting in the plush river-view apartment of an advertising acquaintance, wrapping and boxing a set of her drinking glasses—apparently a little less worshipfully than she would've liked. "Those are from Tiffany's," she snapped. Oh. Sorry.

I considered stopping where I was and carrying everything, piece by piece, to my new place, three blocks away. But, though the streets were empty, it was still New York, and I couldn't just leave the cart and all my stuff.

And even if I chanced that—carrying just my computer and coming back for the less valuable stuff—much like a Tyrannosaurus rex, I have strong legs but arms that are kind of a joke. Carrying everything could have taken hours, so I pressed on, finally making it to the end of the first block.

What was that I felt? Yes, it was sprinkling. I threw my whole body into pushing the cart, hoping to make it to my place before the rain got serious. In the middle of the second block, the cart lurched sideways and stopped, spilling boxes and a garbage bag of my clothes into the street.

I peered underneath the cart. One of the wheels had fallen off. I'd hit some funky "gotcha" cobblestone, probably placed in the street by some mean-spirited nineteenth-century DOT worker. And then, in keeping with my feeling that life was, if not shitting on me, at least peeing pretty much nonstop, the sky opened up and poured rain all over me and all my worldly possessions.

Behind me, there was a *HONNNK!* And then another.

I turned. A taxi. I motioned to the driver to go around me. There was room; he just had to make an effort.

He kept honking. I kept motioning. I moved a little closer so he could see I was trying to guide him. He peeled out on the wet cobblestones and sped around me, hitting a pothole and spraying dirty New York City street water all over me—in my mouth, up my nose, in my eyes.

Looking down on my soggy boxes, my drenched black-and-white TV, and the crippled cart, I burst into big heaving sobs. And there, in the pouring rain, it came to me: "I don't have any real friends."

I GROW A SPINE

The truth is, I had *some* real friends, like David Wallis, whom I met at NYU's off-campus housing office on my second day in New York. We're still friends today, almost thirty years later. In fact, if tomorrow, David called me from the Arctic circle and told me he needed me, I'd hop on the phone to book, oh, three planes, two helicopters, and a team of sled dogs. The thing is, I'm pretty sure David would do the same for me.

Back then in New York, however, many of the people I called friends were just acquaintances or, pathetically, acquaintances of convenience—those people who called me whenever it would make life more convenient for them but never when they had a tip on a great party or just to wonder, "Hey, how are ya?" But, whose fault was this really? I had to admit it: Most of these people weren't bad friends to everyone; they were just bad friends to me.

I'd never noticed this before, perhaps because I was used to the idea of myself as a loser, having been one for as long as I could remember, and probably longer than that. I guess I'd come to accept my Amy Alkon cooties as an incurable disease. Then, it struck me: Could it be something I was doing? Something I could maybe stop doing?

I started paying attention to people everybody seemed to like, and I noticed something extraordinary—how willing they all were to be *unwilling* to please. Here I was, always slaving away to be liked, and here they were, refusing requests and sometimes being disagreeable or bratty.

In fact, they all seemed to feel free to say no—to friends, family, colleagues, even the boss—and not just no but all the variations: "Nuh-uh," "No way," "Not in this lifetime," "Are you out of your fucking mind?" and "Over my dead, maggot-eaten body."

Most amazingly, when they turned people down, they weren't fired, excommunicated, or asked in a low voice to please leave. They were usually just met with "Oh, okay" or sometimes engaged in mild argument. Even if they didn't get things their way, they seemed to garner respect for standing up for themselves—a far cry from the humiliating treatment I got when I showed people that there was no amount of backward that was too far for me to bend over in order to accommodate them.

This—combined with the assholishness about physical risk common to people in their early 20s—made for a weird dichotomy in me. Though I lacked a backbone, I didn't let it stop me from roller-skating fifty blocks to work—in Manhattan traffic, the wrong way up Fifth Avenue. While challenging death like this was just my wacky alternative to the smelly old subway, the mere thought of my testing social boundaries practically turned me into a pillar of salt.

However, the potential reward from doing that—the prospect of yanking down the giant "kick me!" sign posted over my life—had become too tempting. So, little by little—typically when I was around people I perceived to be on the lower rungs of the social food chain— I started squeaking out words of protest: "I'd rather not," "Actually, I can't," "Not this time, thanks." And to my utter amazement, these people didn't tell me off or send me packing. They accepted it; they even tried to accommodate me.

The shift in how people treated me seemed like a fluke—every time. I still felt like the same old loser. I figured that people who didn't treat me accordingly were just a little slow on picking up the terrible stench. I'd eye them, wondering how long it would take before they started sniffing the air and realized that *that smell* was coming from me. Well, not so much coming from me as if I'd farted. I *was* the fart.

Eventually, I couldn't help but concede that people actually did treat me better when I stopped acting like a really big bootlicker. So, I started doing what, these days, I often tell people who write me for advice to do: *acting* like I had dignity, or rather, *acting as a specific person with dignity would act.*

When I did this, I'd mostly be Kathy, the TV commercial producer

I worked for, telling a rock star's manager in her velvety but firm voice that no, he could not have a suitcase of $10,000 in cash. Occasionally, I'd play it as Ed, the big boss producer, sitting at his desk coolly telling some uppity account lady exactly how things were going to be: "Good, cheap, fast—pick any two."

The more I stood up for myself (even while doing it as somebody else) the more I saw it was the right thing to do. It was so beautifully absurd. I was actually impersonating my way to becoming the real me.

I AM BOOGER; HEAR ME ROAR

I won't bullshit you. The road to self-respect is paved with humiliation and setbacks. Most of mine involved my desperate attempts to be loved. We all want love, but I had ulterior motives. In fact, the last thing I cared about was all that lofty crap like shared goals, resonating values, and building a life with another person. I just wanted to be wanted. I saw love as my rescue, the last bus out of social quarantine.

Though, thanks to my "just say no!" experiments, I was beginning to understand the costs of my desperation to be liked, my desperation to be loved was just too deep to be breached by the insights I'd begun to apply at work and with friends. So, whenever I spotted a man I found attractive, I took the subtle approach—subtle in the manner of a starving hyena pouncing on a gazelle.

Eventually, however, I couldn't help but admit that this strategy wasn't working for me, either. This might sound like yet another impressive attainment of wisdom on my part—except that it came to me after I spent a year and a half with a guy in California who verbally abused me and lived off my credit cards (insisting he'd pay me back when the house sold). The house we shared eventually did sell, at which time I learned it actually belonged to his family, who felt zero obligation to make good on Junior's promises to pay my Visa bill.

I had many low points during my time with this guy, but one in particular stands out—the night he lit my copy of *Honoring the Self* on fire. If I'd been a fictional character, those flaming pages would've been just the thing I needed to "see the light" and get out of there, pronto. Unfortunately, this was reality, so I stuck around for months afterward.

It was lust, not self-knowledge, that eventually led me to mend my ways with men. In addition to being achingly lonely, I was hornier than a pack of stray dogs. Despite my blinders about my own behavior, I had some understanding of human nature. I knew women can usually get sex; they just have to want it and get the hint to men.

Distressingly, even that wasn't working for me. Of course, back then, I was kind of on the plump side. I didn't just let my loneliness bounce around inside me; I tried to suffocate it—in an avalanche of sugar. I mowed through cookies, brownies, chocolate Yoo-hoo—just about anything sweet that didn't have a big skull and crossbones and the poison control center number on it. When I wasn't scarfing down boxes of something frosted or making up for it by starving myself and working out obsessively, I engaged in deep self-loathing, which, cruelly, takes a lot of energy but burns almost no calories.

As unattractive as being kind of chunko and miserable must have made me, there are guys out there who like the larger ladies. I couldn't figure out why I seemed to be the exception—especially with the relentlessness I put into pursuing men. In fact, thanks to my "no!" exercises, I'd discovered a well of courage in myself. I used this on men—chasing them, calling them, and asking them out—reveling in how the brave new me wasn't afraid to do that. However, the more I threw myself at men the harder they worked to duck me. I remained unhugged, unkissed, and unfucked.

The clue stick my romantic failures were hitting me with was fast becoming a clue tree trunk, and I again had to admit that I had something to figure out.

Inspired by those "How was your visit?" cards hotels leave out for guests, I drafted a one-page document: "Our Date: A Customer Satisfaction Survey."

There was a space for comments at the bottom, but the survey questions were mostly yes-or-no. My personal hotel room-esque favorite: "Was your date clean and odor-free?" But most importantly, there was "Would you go on another date with this person? Why or why not?"

**OUR DATE
CUSTOMER SATISFACTION SURVEY**

Dear Date,

I would like to thank you for choosing me, _Amy Alkon_ (your name here)----- as your date!

I am aware of the many choices of dates you have while living in the New York metropolitan area, and I appreciate your decision to date me.

I invite you to take a few moments to fill out the enclosed survey as a way to help me better serve your needs in the future.

Call back real soon!

Amy Alkon
------(your name here)------

**Your careful evaluation of the following details is appreciated:
(please include comments on separate page)**

	CIRCLE ONE	
Was your date friendly and personable?	YES	NO
Did you experience any problems or discomfort during your date?	YES	NO
If so, were they resolved to your satisfaction?	YES	NO
Was your date attractively dressed?	YES	NO
Was your date clean and odor free?	YES	NO
Were physical encounters pleasurable?	YES	NO
Was conversation engaging and fun?	YES	NO
Did your date listen to what you had to say?	YES	NO
Were there any problems in the planning stages?	YES	NO
Would you go on another date with this person? Why or why not?	YES/NO/comment	
What is your overall assessment of the date?	please comment	
How might the person you went out with better meet your needs?	please comment	

Assess your date overall on a scale of 1 to 10, 10 being highest:
1   2   3   4   5   6   7   8   9   10

The men I gave this to were mostly horrified by it and declined to fill it out (or ever speak to me again, in several cases). At the big café in

SoHo where I went to write—because it had both ample electrical outlets and an abundance of hot guys—one of my former dates would fumble to pack up his stuff and make tracks whenever he saw me come in.

But, another guy—a young, cute science professor who ended our one and only date by shaking my hand at my door and bolting down Canal Street—took pity on me. He not only filled out my survey but sat down at my table in the café and gave me his take.

The problem, as he saw it, was the way I was all over a guy and did all the work. It made me seem like I had something wrong with me. He also found it kind of exhausting. He explained that he, and men in general, actually like to have a role in the dating process— besides standing around waiting to say yes—and I took that role away with my, um, enthusiasm. Basically, he was telling me the same thing I'd learned from all of the people I *wasn't* trying to get naked with: Desperation un-sells.

HATE ME; I STILL SUCK

After these revelations about my romantic overkill, I made tunneling out of loserhood my top priority. I bought another copy of Nathaniel Branden's *Honoring the Self* and actually read the thing instead of standing by while it went up in flames. I also made myself a little pledge—that, in every area of my life, I would do my best to act like I had a spine for a spine instead of an unusually long piece of overcooked linguine.

Understanding what I needed to do was just a start. After all my years of auto-yes, if I wasn't vigilant, I'd often find my head bobbing into a nod. Also, nobody likes a suck-up, not even the suck-up herself—which made it that much harder to recover from being one.

Every time I said yes when I should've said no, every time I said no but with a little too much hesitation, I hated myself. And then, thanks to the reading I'd been doing about self-respect, which Branden defines on page 4 as a "feeling of personal worth," I hated myself for hating myself.

I probably could've kept this up for years. Luckily, I have a soft spot for the underdog, who, in this case, happened to be me. During a break in my relentless self-flagellation (probably a pause for a change of sackcloth and ashes), I started feeling sorry for myself.

Here I was, putting everything I had into clawing my way out of the primordial pus of loserhood—only to keep shoving myself right back in. And why? Because I made a mistake or two? Well, didn't everybody?

"Ease up, hard-ass," I scolded myself. "You're human. Of course you're gonna say yes when you should be saying 'Fuck no!' Guess what: Tomorrow's a new day. And if you say yes again tomorrow, well, do your best to say 'Fuck no!' the day after."

I'd learned a helpful lesson from repainting my bathroom—after my first attempt at a paint job peeled off almost immediately in long curly latex scabs. Accordingly, I realized that you can't just slap on self-respect without first applying a primer coat, which appears to be self-acceptance. Self-acceptance requires recognizing you're human and therefore fallible.

Say you just returned to that big important meeting in the conference room—with the back of your skirt tucked into the top of your purple thong underwear. When you discover this, what else is there to say but "Anyone have any thoughts on my big white ass cheeks, or shall we go straight to the budget?"

It ultimately took years for me to feel okay with all the parts of me—good, bad, smart, stupid, ridiculous—and even the way I channel all the energy churning inside of me into pick-pick-picking at my cuticles when I'm nervous. Or upset. Or happy. Or excited. Or, to be honest, whenever I'm not in a coma or dead. But I have gotten to the point where I can look at my tortured cuticles with a bit of fondness. Kind of the way you'd look at a scruffy little dog. And my acceptance of that as a part of me is a sign of how far I've come.

This isn't to say that I'm all fixed—that I'm now some superhero of personal growth. At times, I find myself right back where I started. I go to this monthly dinner for writers, attended by some truly interesting people—political writers, novelists and biographers, screenwriters, a prosecutor, and the occasional war correspondent. One night, a few of us were engaged in a rather lively discussion—and then we weren't. Silence. The silence weighed on me, and I panicked. The thought struck me, "I have nothing to say! I should leave!"

But I couldn't leave. Everyone would know I was going home because I was such an emptyhead. This would just confirm what they already thought of me—probably that I have an idiot's grasp of politics, I'm not funny, and I'm kind of a bore. In fact, that's what they'd talk about as soon as I got up.

I glanced around at those who'd soon be commiserating about my aching dullness, and I noticed something important: Their mouths weren't moving, either. That's right; at that moment, just like me, they had nothing to say. I had to laugh. But, before I could, the guy next to me turned and asked me something. And whaddya know, it wasn't "What's a bed-wetting loser like you doing here?"

PARKING SPACE, THE FINAL FRONTIER

I don't mark my life in the usual milestones. I didn't go to my college graduation. I love my boyfriend but feel no need to get married. I find children loud, sticky, and expensive. I also don't celebrate my birthday. (The way I see it, if you are over twelve and not a cancer patient, do we really need to throw a party and give you prizes for surviving another year?)

However, after all my years straining to plant my lips on every ass that crossed my path, I did have a milestone to celebrate. It was the day I got what I consider my unofficial diploma (and what is probably my greatest accomplishment), my proof of graduation from people-pleasing—the restraining order.

This thing was served on me after a company that does sound work for movies and commercials moved in to a building at the end of my residential Venice, California, block. Parking in my neighborhood had become seriously scarce. The sound house had a gated lot with about two dozen parking spaces—many of which remained car-free all day, as if the company were running a sanctuary for bare asphalt. The employees parked on our residential streets, making our already-scarce parking even scarcer. Grrr.

I trotted over to the sound house. In my self-appointed capacity as "block bitch" (or, as I announced myself to the manager of the sound house, "the head of the neighborhood association"), I explained that residential parking was pretty tight and asked that she have her employees park in their lot. The manager, a tiny blonde about my age, said she would.

Oh. Okey-dokey! Cool! Except for how her employees did nothing of the sort.

A week later, one of the company's engineers zipped into the last open spot on our block—directly across from the usual field of pristine pavement—just as my neighbor was returning from Costco with her baby and about a cubic acre of groceries. I called to the guy. "'Scuse me! Can you please park in your own lot?" He put his head down, scurried across the nearly empty parking lot, and slipped into the sound house.

Asshole.

Carrying my wee Yorkie, I stomped over and rang the buzzer. The little blond manager opened the vast steel door. I complained that one of her guys had just taken the last residential parking spot. Her eyes narrowed. "It's a public street," she hissed.

"Well, yes, but it's zoned residential," I said. "And you have all these spaces open in your lot." (I later learned they left all their spaces open because—gag!—they never knew when, say, Tom Arnold might arrive with "an entourage.")

"If you don't like it, get permit parking!" she sneered—a statement that translated to "Go fuck yourself," since it's common knowledge round these parts that the Coastal Commission won't allow it in our neighborhood.

Though I was powerless to stop them from hijacking our parking, I wasn't about to just walk away and let this little blond bully get away with her power grab scot-free. A word came to me—a word that's verbal kryptonite to any woman around my age. And then I said it, quietly—because it's much more powerful that way: "You know... you really are...a cunt."

Her jaw dropped. Her eyes bugged. She turned to the sound house owner, who'd come up next to her. She was trying to say something, but she just made the sounds of someone choking on a small chicken bone.

"Oh, please," I said. "Did your head fall off your shoulders and drop on the floor when I said that? I don't think so."

With that, I marched off, satisfied that though I'd lost the parking war, I didn't let her roll all over me in the process. And then, a week later, it came—the temporary restraining order—or, as I called it back then, the "temporary revenge order."

A few months later, in a Santa Monica court, the little blond revenge-seeker complained to the judge that I was "hostile and unpredictable."

I couldn't help but agree: "I'm both of those things, but I'm not violent."

The restraining order was, of course, dismissed.

And yes, there is a message in this, and no, it isn't that you should go around swearing like a junior Dr. Dre, all the way to a better you.

Here I was, one of the biggest suck-up losers ever to wriggle on the earth. If I could reshape myself—into a person who has not only true friends and a loving boyfriend but a strong enough self to be disagreeable for the greater good—then surely anybody can.

PART TWO

—

The Building Blocks of the New You

THE MIND IS BIGGER THAN THE BRAIN

Meet your new BFF, "embodied cognition"

I know; you want to get right to the de-loser-ification. But in order for you to believe that it works—enough to be motivated to do it—it's important to understand *why* it works.

It turns out that what I ended up doing—overriding my default Amywuss self and responding as my coolly confident boss—was scientifically right on.

I didn't know this at the time. I wasn't some psychological savant, nor did I have a crystal ball with a subscription to all the behavioral science journals. In fact, back then, I didn't have a bent clue about the fuckmountain of science I ended up poring over for this book. But standing in the rain on that cobblestoned New York street, sobbing about not having friends, I was willing to try pretty much anything to claw my way out of social rodent-hood. So, entirely out of teary, snot-faced desperation, I groped around in the dark, and—hellooo, miracle!—it turns out that I accidentally did exactly the right thing.

As for why what I did worked, in 1940, novelist F. Scott Fitzgerald wrote that "action is character"—meaning that what a person does defines who they are. And, more recently, research in a growing area of science called "embodied cognition" finds that action also *becomes* character.

What is embodied cognition? Reread the title of this chapter a few times:

The Mind Is Bigger Than the Brain

Embodied cognition research shows that who you are is not just a product of your brain. It's also in your breathing, your gut, the way you stand, the way you speak, and, while you're speaking, whether you make eye contact or dart your eyes like you're about to bolt under a car like a cat.

It turns out that psychology, with its myopic focus on the brain, has taken a way-too-limited view of what drives our behavior. Recognizing that the body is often a part of cognition—of thinking—is essential to the formation of the new you. Researcher Andrew Wilson has explained the power of embodied cognition: "We might use our movements, for example, to solve problems that we could never solve with just brain power."

This is actually much bigger than he makes it sound. By consistently changing how you behave (down to how you move, breathe, and carry yourself), you can transform how you feel about yourself, how other people see and treat you, and who you are. It's a massive, life-changing shift.

It does help to include some changes in thinking, like coming to understand that "self-esteem" isn't what most of us think it is. (Recent science, laid out in chapter 8, finds that self-esteem actually comes out of how highly—or not—other people seem to think of us.) However, that particular revision in thinking, like the others in this book, leads right back to how essential action actually is in changing yourself—how becoming the new you mostly takes behaving as the person you want to be.

Basically, through repeatedly changing your behaviors, you embed the new behaviors and their companion emotions into your brain—which means that the old behaviors and emotions get pushed to the back and stop being the ones that automatically come up. This, in turn, means that you—like me—can eventually stop thinking about your fucking self-esteem all the time and just *be*.

It probably sounds unbelievable that such a major change in who you are could be accomplished with such simple behavioral steps, but think of it like those Hair Club for Men TV commercials I used to see back in my New York City days. These ads always ended with the owner's Noo Yawk–accented announcement—something like, "I'm not just the president; I'm also a customuh!" Well—likewise— you can see me as walking (formerly groveling) proof that behaving differently is what it takes to stop going through life as a linguine-spined suck-up.

INTO THE WOODS WITH THE MAN
IN THE CHECKERBOARD PANTS

Retiring the lesser you starts with the story of America's first psych professor and a bear. We'll get to the bear. But first, the psych professor.

It was the early 1870s, and William James, a brilliant but depressive eccentric from a society family, was graduating from Harvard med school. The elder brother of novelist Henry James, he was a former art student and a highly creative thinker.

Though the clothing style for men back then is best described as "every day is a funeral," James often tramped around in red checkerboard pants, a top hat, a polka-dot bow tie, and a frock coat, reflecting his idea that a person's clothing should be an expression of their interior and not just a cloth cover to keep from scaring the ladies or the chickens.

James ended up finding medicine kind of a bore, but he'd spent a few years nosing around in the newfangled science of psychology, and in 1875, he started teaching it at Harvard. At the time, the notion still hanging around from French philosopher René Descartes and other thinkers before him was that the mind and body—the mental and the

William James at age 23, in Brazil, 1865. James was
seriously ahead of his time, and not just because he
looks like he owns a hipster coffee bar with artisanal
Wi-Fi. *Houghton Library, Harvard University.*

physical—are two separate and different entities, made out of different stuff.

As Descartes saw it, your thoughts are the real you—a floating
mental you that exists even when your body is gone. Your body is
"just a machine"—a pretty groovy machine but really just a big piece
of meaty machinery attached to the "thinking thing" that makes up
who you are. So, in Descartes's view, the body doesn't play a role
in who you are. It just carries the real you—the eternal mental you—
around for a while, until you die and the body goes bad, like those
leftovers you forgot to eat.

William James didn't buy this notion of the mind and body as separate entities. In fact, it looked to him like they are connected and actually work together. He had been reading Charles Darwin's observations on how emotions in humans and animals are accompanied by specific physical expressions (like how happiness yanks the facial muscles into a smile, not a sneer). And amazingly—nearly a century before I got results from acting confident like my producer boss—Darwin had this sort of thing figured out, writing, "Even the simulation of an emotion tends to arouse it in our minds." (If only I'd read more Darwin and less Nancy Drew way back when.)

Darwin also noticed that the physical expression (like smiling or sneering) that goes with a particular emotion could be used as a sort of volume control for the emotion. Increase these physical expressions and you amplify the emotion; decrease them and you dial the emotion down. That's why, for example, if you're looking to stop feeling angry, "venting" your anger is actually counterproductive. (Notice that you never hear some MMA fighter murmur, "I feel soooo peaceful and at one with the universe now that I've beaten the shit out of that guy.") As Darwin put it, "He who gives way to violent gestures will increase his rage."

Darwin's ideas about the body and mind's working cooperatively helped lead James to think of emotions in a whole new way. Like Darwin, James contended that emotions aren't just thinky things—all in our mind—but that they have a "physical basis," such as the red face, flared nostrils, and clenched teeth of somebody who is seriously pissed off.

But James took this a step further. He began to rethink the order in which we experience and identify emotions. And—radically—he came to the crazy-sounding conclusion that the body is the first responder to emotion-evoking situations and that the mind just comes around in the wake of the body's face-reddening and teeth-clenching, and all to stick a name tag on what emotion the body is going through: "HELLO, my name is Rage!"

I know; this is a little hard to get a handle on. To help you understand what James was getting at, let's bring in our pal the bear.

Imagine that you've stopped your car by the side of the woods somewhere. You're stretching your legs and you go a little bit spaceypants for a moment, mesmerized by, I dunno... the sun on a butterfly's sparkly little wings or something, when—JESUS HELLO KITTY CHRIST ON A ROCKET-POWERED TOBOGGAN!*—there's a big fucking bear.

You break six international track-and-field records running to your car and throwing yourself inside.

As for the sequence of events and emotions here, common sense says it goes like this:

1. You see the bear.
2. You feel afraid.
3. The fear causes you to run.

However, James felt that things go down in a different order:

1. You see the bear.
2. You run.
3. You feel afraid because you're running.

That's right; in James's version, you see the bear and you run, and you feel afraid *because you're running*. In other words, according to James, you arrive at the emotion only *after* you notice what your body's up to.

No—it's not just you. This sounded wacky as hell to me, too.

But the nuances should help. The way James saw it, we don't run from the bear because we're *consciously* afraid; instead, we see the bear

---

*Gratefully purloined from First Amendment ninja Marc J. Randazza, who actually put those words in a legal brief.

and we *instinctively* bolt—*before our conscious mind can make out what's going on*.

As for how this works, James claimed that spotting the bear sends a (split-second) message to our brain's sensory processing system, triggering *automatic* bodily responses (like the pounding of the heart and pumping of the adrenal glands). This goes on in the milliseconds before we are even conscious that there's a bear just feet away from us. According to James, it's only after our conscious mind—arriving fashionably late to the party—notices all this heart-pumping, adrenaline-surging bodily "commotion" that we become aware that we're afraid.

Because that's maybe still a little hard to comprehend, let's take a brief field trip to the offices of the brain. Let's say we've just encountered that bear—though the news has yet to hit our consciousness department. In these (preconscious) first fractions of a second of our encounter, our eyes upload a picture of the bear. It, in turn, gets whisked off to the thalamus, a section of the brain you could basically think of as a security guard manning a desk in front of two corridors.

It's the thalamus's job to simultaneously send the picture down the two corridors. One corridor is short and direct (great for *quick decisions* about the danger you're in). The other is longer and windier (with more detailed fact-checking of what exactly you're dealing with—all the better for *more accurate decisions*).

The short corridor, which neuroscientist Joseph LeDoux calls the "quick and dirty" path, leads straight from the thalamus to the amygdala, a processing center for environmental stimuli that's part of our brain's threat detection system. The amygdala is a set of two lima bean-sized neural bunches that make split-second decisions about what the hell might be going on around us and whether to sound an alarm.

The amygdala works beneath our consciousness, making a rapid-fire comparison of the current input from our environment (bear!) with that from prior situations (from our personal past and our evolutionary past), and then determines the threat level to announce. Meanwhile, up on the longer path, which LeDoux calls "the high road," the sensory cortex—a sensory information processing department—is left to play catch-up. It does its finer analysis of the environmental input—and perhaps determines that the amygdala was a little hasty in jacking you into a mad dash to your car.

The truth is, the amygdala is often wrong. It typically errs on the side of identifying situations as dangerous and preparing you to escape a threat. However, as evolutionary psychologist Martie Haselton points out, this error-proneness isn't a bad thing. You're being pushed to make the least costly mistake, which, for example, would be leaping out of your skin at what turns out to be your asshole friend in a bear suit—as opposed to failing to run from the real deal and ending up the day's lunch special for the bear family.

SOMETIMES YOUR CONSCIOUSNESS IS UNCONSCIOUS

I get it; even after the brain tour, it's hard to buy into James's notion that we're afraid because we run. James himself is partly to blame. He eventually realized that he'd mucked things up, confusing people by using the example of running from the bear.

James then explained that he'd really meant running to be a sort of shorthand for all the "HOLY SHIT!" bodily processes (like an increased heart rate and blood rushing to your extremities) that go on after your amygdala gets wind of the bear.

And (irritatingly!) because some of James's language was less than clear, one hundred–plus years after he came up with his theory, some scientists are still squabbling about whether he got the order right. But, more and more, it's becoming evident that James was onto something. Modern neuroscience research finds that we can have an emotion without even realizing it, because experiencing an emotion *doesn't necessarily start with conscious thought*—and may not involve it at all.

For instance, neuroscientist LeDoux gives the example of research subjects being shown pictures of threatening things "in such a way that they are not conscious of" the stimuli (like when the pictures are flashed too fast for the conscious mind to perceive them). These subjects didn't have any conscious notion that they were afraid. However, the threatening stimuli activated their amygdala, which sounded the alarm, which caused them to sweat, made their heart pound, and made their pupils go wide. This, LeDoux explains, shows that threat detection and response can be "independent of conscious awareness." To put this another way, sometimes consciousness not only is late to an emotional experience but sleeps through the whole damn thing.

That said, the conscious mind has more to do than sit around courtside looking pretty while the body makes jump shots. Consciousness is the brain's verification department, and it does its job by looking at the circumstances surrounding the emotion.

Though James made the claim that we can identify one emotion from another through our bodily sensations alone, in 1962 psychologists Stanley Schachter and Jerome Singer pointed out that a number of emotions have very similar bodily responses. For example, you could be breathing heavily because some hottie is putting the moves on you—or because you're close to learning whether that bear that's chasing you has flossed recently.

Schachter and Singer explain that it's your conscious mind that sorts out the nuances of your heavy breathing. It does this by applying context—like by noting whether you're lost in the woods or lost in somebody's eyes. Your conscious mind then puts the bodily expression (the heavy breathing) in the correct emotional bin—either Terror ("HolyMcMoly...a BEAR!") or Lust ("Rip my fucking clothes off already!"). Most helpfully, this sorting via context keeps you from attempting to have sex with the bear or responding to some rock icon's moves on you by calling for a park ranger to come fast with a tranquilizer gun and a big net.

In other words, though James overreached a bit in downgrading consciousness's role in emotion, he helped shepherd us into the neighborhood of something important: the notion, confirmed by modern research, that *the mind and the body are co-workers in creating our emotional responses.*

This is really exciting, because it means that you can deliberately use body movement to shift how you feel. And by repeatedly changing your behavior—like by taking your rightful place at the table instead of automatically crawling under it—you change the way other people see and treat you. So, yes, you really can hose off that loser stench—for good—by using your body as more than just ground transportation for your brain.

— 4 —

MEET YOUR EMOTIONS
(THE LITTLE SHITS)

More useful than you'd think

We all have emotions, but we don't give them much thought—where they come from, why we have them, and whether they, too, flunked out of Brown or got regular wedgies on the playground when they were eight.

When we do think of our emotions, they can seem overwhelming. This is especially true if you're a person who feels bad a lot of the time. The natural impulse is to avoid your feelings. This works—about as well as sticking all of your unpaid bills in a drawer.

Though ducking your feelings doesn't make them go away, the more you do it the harder it gets to name what, exactly, you are feeling. That's a problem. An amorphous feeling of "shitty" doesn't point you toward any solutions. However, a more specific "I feel ashamed" gets you to the right questions, like "Okay, what is shame? Why is it damaging? And how do I kick its ass out of my life?" (All answered in chapter 9.)

Also, brain imaging research by neuroscientist Matthew Lieberman and his colleagues suggests that putting a negative feeling into words—labeling the crappy feeling that's eating at you—seems to suck out some of its power to make you feel crappy.

It probably seems counterintuitive that digging into some ambiguously rotten feeling—to the point you can stick a name on it—would lead you to feel less of it than if you just did your best to duck it. However, consider that using words calls on more advanced areas of your brain. The Lieberman team's research suggests that the act of labeling kicks off a power transfer in your brain—activating the more advanced part* and, in turn, dampening the activity in your brain's threat detection circuitry (specifically, the amygdala). A less reactive amygdala makes you—ta-da!—feel less stressed by whatever feel-bad thing you're experiencing.

Unfortunately, naming the particular emotion you're experiencing can be daunting because there seem to be so many emotions, all mixed together—much like that mysterious end-of-the-week "stew" the junior-high lunch ladies made out of ground-up leftovers and any textbooks nobody felt like taking to the lost and found.

Well, in 1964, psychologist Silvan Tomkins helped simplify things. He proposed that there are eight core emotions† in humans. (Don't focus too much on his; there are other sets coming right up.)

Interest

Enjoyment

Surprise

Distress

Fear

Shame

Contempt

Anger

Tomkins eventually replaced "contempt" with (love this!) "dissmell"—a word he coined to describe our impulse to push away smelly, gross stuff, like dead animals, sour milk, and poo.

---

* The act of labeling a feeling shifts the activity in your brain to part of your prefrontal cortex—the right ventrolateral prefrontal cortex—that's involved in self-control. Lieberman, in his book, *Social*, calls this area "the central hub of the brain's braking system."

† Tomkins actually gave these longer names, but they're a little hard to get your brain around: interest-excitement, enjoyment-joy, surprise-startle, distress-anguish, fear-terror, shame-humiliation, contempt-disgust, anger-rage.

In the '70s, another psychologist, Tomkins's former student Paul Ekman, concluded, upon researching facial expressions on people around the world, that there are six basic emotions:

> Happiness
>
> Surprise
>
> Fear
>
> Anger
>
> Disgust
>
> Sadness

Building on Tomkins's work, Ekman argued that these are the primary emotions because there's a distinct—and globally recognizable—facial expression that accompanies each (unlike other emotions, like, say, love). His thinking on this makes sense in light of how emotions aren't just feeling-flavored thoughts; they have physiological underpinnings.

Other researchers have come up with slightly different sets, but none of them has entirely persuasive evidence for why their set is more valid. (Ekman himself has wavered on whether contempt should be included as a seventh basic emotion.) That said, for the purposes of emotional transformation, there's a very helpful set—this six-pack by social psychologist Phillip Shaver:

> Love
>
> Joy
>
> Surprise
>
> Anger
>
> Sadness
>
> Fear

Though not all of Shaver's emotions trace to a distinct facial expression, what's so useful about his set is the way he breaks each emotion into its sub-parts—all of the variations that, say, fit in the "Love" drawer or the "Sadness" drawer. *(Check out the chart below to see how this works—along with the goofily helpful psych ward chart on the next page to match your feeling with a face.)*

All of the emotions in Ekman's set can be found somewhere within Shaver's. For example, disgust, from Ekman's model, is there; it's just grouped as a "secondary" emotion under the category of "anger." And Shaver's category of "sadness" most helpfully includes *disappointment*, feeling *neglected*, and *shame* (an emotion I always got a lot of use out of).

CHARTING YOUR EMOTIONS

To help yourself identify exactly which feeling is sitting on your chest and jeering, you may want to dog-ear the page with Shaver's emotion chart—and also the page with the psych ward chart with the little faces.

PHILLIP SHAVER'S SET OF EMOTIONS
(THINK OF IT AS YOUR EMOTIONS' PARK AVENUE
CORPORATE HEADQUARTERS AND THEIR
SUBURBAN SATELLITES.)

PRIMARY EMOTION	SECONDARY EMOTION	TERTIARY EMOTIONS
Love	Affection	Adoration, affection, love, fondness, liking, attraction, caring, tenderness, compassion, sentimentality
	Lust	Arousal, desire, lust, passion, infatuation
	Longing	Longing

Shaver emotion chart courtesy of David Straker, *changingminds.org.*

Joy	Cheerfulness	Amusement, bliss, cheerfulness, gaiety, glee, jolliness, joviality, joy, delight, enjoyment, gladness, happiness, jubilation, elation, satisfaction, ecstasy, euphoria
	Zest	Enthusiasm, zeal, zest, excitement, thrill, exhilaration
	Contentment	Contentment, pleasure
	Pride	Pride, triumph
	Optimism	Eagerness, hope, optimism
	Enthrallment	Enthrallment, rapture
	Relief	Relief
Surprise	Surprise	Amazement, surprise, astonishment
Anger	Irritation	Aggravation, irritation, agitation, annoyance, grouchiness, grumpiness
	Exasperation	Exasperation, frustration
	Rage	Anger, rage, outrage, fury, wrath, hostility, ferocity, bitterness, hate, loathing, scorn, spite, vengefulness, dislike, resentment
	Disgust	Disgust, revulsion, contempt
	Envy	Envy, jealousy
	Torment	Torment
Sadness	Suffering	Agony, suffering, hurt, anguish
	Sadness	Depression, despair, hopelessness, gloom, glumness, sadness, unhappiness, grief, sorrow, woe, misery, melancholy
	Disappointment	Dismay, disappointment, displeasure
	Shame	Guilt, shame, regret, remorse
	Neglect	Alienation, isolation, neglect, loneliness, rejection, homesickness, defeat, dejection, insecurity, embarrassment, humiliation, insult
	Sympathy	Pity, sympathy
Fear	Horror	Alarm, shock, fear, fright, horror, terror, panic, hysteria, mortification
	Nervousness	Anxiety, nervousness, tenseness, uneasiness, apprehension, worry, distress, dread

FACES FROM THE PSYCH WARD

Amy Dresner (featured in later chapters) brought back a withered Xerox of a chart like this one below from her, uh, "visit" to the Glendale Adventist psych ward. I found it funny, but it's also useful.

Since you're reading this book, you probably do what I did—avoid the hell out of your feelings—and you could probably use a little help pairing a feeling with a name.

How do you feel today?

*This version of the faces thing is by graphic designer Ellie Peters (ElliePeters. com), who very kindly allowed me to publish it. Admittedly, feeling "unique" is not an actual emotion, nor is feeling silly, but the rest should help you find a face and a name to pair with your emotions. For a more comprehensive list, reflecting a good many of the emotions from Shaver's chart, google "feeling faces" and click on Google's "Images."

Think of this chart and others like it (see the caption below it) like being in a crowd of strangers and suddenly realizing that everyone has a name tag: "Ohhh...that's Grieving! Wow...she's lost weight! And there's Disapproving! Fuck off already, would you?"

Now that you see that you really have only a handful of basic emotions to wrangle, along with a little train of sub-emotions following each, it's time to get to know the little buggers better. So, next, let's get a sense of what they're made of and why a few of them seem to be working so hard to make us feel like crap.

FEELINGS ARE DYLAN McDERMOTT; EMOTIONS ARE DERMOT MULRONEY

People sometimes have a hard time remembering which Dermot(t) is which.

McDermott and Mulroney don't really look that much alike when you put them next to each other. However, they're two dark-haired white dudes, handsome in a slightly dangerous kinda way, with Irish names with a lot of Dermot(t)age going on—which leads people to confuse the two.

McDermott (left) by Rebecca Dru, licensed under CC by 2.0.
Mulroney (right) via Amazon Studios' "Mozart in the Jungle."

There's a similar problem with feelings and emotions. Neuro-scientists Antonio Damasio and Joseph LeDoux both point out that there's been some long-term sloppiness with language, with people—including researchers—using the terms "emotions" and "feelings" interchangeably.

"Emotions" and "feelings" actually describe two different types of processes that William James highlighted for us—bodily-driven ones (emotions) and thinky-driven ones (feelings).

EMOTIONS

Emotions are your *subconscious reactions* to *physical experience*—to information from your environment that comes in through your senses (sight, taste, touch, etc.).

In other words, emotions are your brain's split-second responses (beneath your awareness!) to the situation you're in that immediately kick off changes in your body. Some of these bodily changes, Damasio explains, are perceptible to other people—like shifts in skin coloration (blushing), body posture, and facial expression. Other changes, like a boom-boom-booming heart, are "perceptible only to the owner of the body in which they take place."

So, for example, say you're in a parking garage and there's the slightest movement in the shadows. It's so slight you don't notice it on a conscious level. But your senses pick up on it. They, in turn, message lower-level, evolutionarily older parts of your brain—like the threat detection circuitry (the amygdala and its policing pals)—before you have the slightest conscious awareness that there may be something to fear. That circuitry, in turn, sets off neurochemical re-actions that push your body to tense up, be on the alert, and get ready to run or serve up some whoop-ass.

It's only then—*after* your body gets into the act—that *feelings* finally come in.

FEELINGS

Feelings are your *conscious reactions*—reactions within your awareness—expressed in *thoughts*. (You can also state them aloud.)

In other words, feelings are your mind's *conscious* interpretation of the environmental input affecting your body; or, as Damasio puts it, feelings are "mental experiences of bodily states." So, for example, when you're outside on an especially chilly-ass day, you might verbalize the *feeling* "If it gets any colder, I'll lose an ear."

However, feelings aren't *just* reactions to environmental input. Memory, beliefs, and associations play an essential role in feelings, bringing *meaning* to whatever you're experiencing (the relevance to your past, your future, and your values, for example).

This meaning-making business happens last in the emotion-feeling sequence. Take that *creepy shadows in the parking garage* scenario. In your conscious mind, in the wake of all the bodily ruckus of emotion—of, say, the goosebumpy heart-pounding of fear—a feeling pops into words: "Eekers, I'm scared!" And then, also in your conscious mind, another feeling may come up—about what the situation could *mean* for you, like, say, "Omigod, it's probably a serial killer, and he'll come bludgeon me with a tire iron, and I'll die a virgin!"

So, just to review, as neuroscientist Damasio puts it: "Emotions play out in the theater of *the body*. Feelings play out in the theater of *the mind*." (Italics are mine.)

But—mea culpa!—beyond this passage you're reading now, I use "emotions" and "feelings" pretty interchangeably in this book. Except when it seems important to highlight conscious versus subconscious reactions (like in chapter 17), I use whichever word seems most understandable in context. This typically means using "emotion" to describe both emotions and feelings. I do feel a little scientifically guilty about this. However, my job here isn't to turn you into a meticulous neuroscientist but to say things in the best way to help you pry yourself out of a lifelong fetal position.

YOUR EMOTIONS ARE YOUR CRUISE DIRECTOR

It's likely that emotions evolved to help us solve survival and mating problems. (No, you don't feel bad when somebody socks you in the ego because evolution thought it would be fun to screw with you.)

Though we think of an emotion as a state of mind—the mental sense that something we're experiencing is, say, sad, exciting, unfair, or sexy—emotions are actually more than mental reactions; they are motivational tools. Emotions push us to take action—for example: Kiss her! Get a lawyer! Hide the body in your freezer!

The motivational job of emotions means that even feeling bad is ultimately a good thing. As evolutionary psychologist and psychiatrist Randolph Nesse puts it, "Emotional suffering can be just as useful as physical discomfort." He's talking about how physical pain provides a most helpful *YOO-HOO! Do something, idiot!* when, for example, in attempting a seductive pose at a party, you accidentally place your hand on what turns out to be a hot stove.

Nesse explains that just like physical pain, emotional pain leads us to "respond adaptively" to opportunities and threats—including threats to both our survival and our social survival. Take feeling crappy about getting socially stomped on. This may lead you to try to guilt your stompers into treating you better—or maybe you'll just lie low, lest you remind them of what an excellent candidate you'd make for Kickball of the Week. The point is that your emotions are pushing you to *do something*.

This motivational work our emotions do comes in two main forms, drive and reverse—pushing us to go toward something or motivating us to pull back from something.

So, for example, "drive" is what's behind "Mmm, chocolate cake?

Don't mind if I do!" or, upon spotting somebody hot, "Would you mind terribly if I mounted you right here and now?"

"Reverse," on the other hand, is the motivation mate of "Eww, gross!" or "Wow, that man approaching us sure is a dead ringer for that parking garage killer on the news!"

In psychology-speak, drive and reverse motivations are called *"approach"* and *"avoidance" motives*, and these impulses are central to the behavior of all living organisms. In fact, it seems that we got them handed down to us from millions-of-years-old wee organisms that actually didn't have hands—let alone minds.

HOW EVOLUTION IS KIND OF LIKE MY GRANDPA JACK

Because the tiny primordial stew chunks we evolved from didn't have minds, they couldn't have emotions. However, they did have what could be considered pre-emotions—physical sensations that pushed them to approach or avoid, i.e., to move toward something survival-enhancing or back away from something deadly. These sensations did the work our emotions do, prodding the wee organisms to take actions that would help them live on and mate (or at least engage in all the hot, sweaty fun that is asexual reproduction).

This relates to us because, well, evolution was not born in Beverly Hills—as in, it doesn't like to go out to Bloomingdale's and buy a whole new gadget when it still has an old gadget that works perfectly well. In this, evolution is like my thrifty grandpa Jack, a seriously early adopter of "upcycling"—now largely known as the practice of reconstituting Salvation Army cashmere into some patchwork monstrosity that sells for $300 on Etsy.

More broadly, though, upcycling involves reusing objects or parts in such a way that the re-creation is more valuable and/or useful than the original. For Grandpa Jack, who immigrated to America from some Poland-adjacent shithole with only lint in his pockets, reuse was religion. If he needed some new machine, he'd start with the base of some old machine, scavenge a bunch of parts to add to it, and cobble together the new thing. Basically, the old machine became the mechanical version of Soup Starter.

Evolution's version of this involves repurposing the approach/avoidance system of these itsy-bitsy organisms and using it as the base for the human emotional system. In research-speak, this repurposing is called "neural reuse." As psychologist and neuroscientist Michael L. Anderson explains it, older brain mechanisms get redeployed for newer tasks—"often without losing their original functions." And once more in English: You've souped up your Dustbuster, turning it into a drone, but you can still use it to vacuum up the Meow Mix that Señor Fluffyface knocked all over your kitchen floor.

Spike W. S. Lee—the Chinese social psychologist, not the African-American movie director—explained evolution's thriftiness to me another way, with the example of a seriously poor community where people can't afford plumbing in a bunch of different rooms. They end up using one sink for everything. ("Excuse me, but can you move your celery so I can wash my feet?")

Well, it seems that our mind and body are also sharing a sink—one that's located in our brain. To understand how this "shared sink" plays out for us, consider Michael Anderson's remark about the brain bits established for one task getting deployed for another—and this is the essential part: "often without losing their original functions."

Now, we are well aware that we can use our thoughts to drive our actions. For example, you can decide "I'm going to flash a gang sign at my goldfish!" and then actually do that. But—probably because of some shared plumbing in the brain created by neural reuse—the thought/action sequence also works in reverse: *We can also affect our thoughts and emotions with our actions.*

For example, psychologist James Laird used action to manipulate people's emotions in a study that was supposedly about measuring the electrical impulses in subjects' facial muscles. Laird stuck phony electrodes on their faces and asked them to squeeze their eyebrows down and together and to clench their teeth. They didn't realize that they were actually being asked to frown, yet they reported feeling significantly angrier afterward. Other subjects were asked to pull the corners of their mouth upward. They reported feeling significantly happier afterward—even though they didn't realize that they had been made to smile.

Another example of how our actions affect our thinking is what I call the "up yours!" study. It centered around giving the finger—the middle finger, that is—that one-finger salute we Americans do when somebody pisses us off. Social psychologists Jesse Chandler and Norbert Schwarz wondered whether this might work the other way around—whether feeling pissed off could come out of unwittingly flipping the bird.

Perhaps out of some desire to make their study sound as boring as possible, they told their research subjects that they were exploring the effect of hand motion on reading comprehension. Some subjects were asked to move their middle finger up and down while reading a story about a guy named Donald (whose behavior could be viewed as either assertive or aggressive). Others were told to move their index finger.

Well, the subjects who had extended their middle finger rated Donald as more hostile—despite their being *unaware* that they'd just done a couple dozen reps of "go fuck yourself!" Yes, amazingly, our body movements seem to drive our emotions even when our consciousness is taking a break—off smoking a bowl or maybe bidding on a vintage Finnish ski jacket on eBay.

As for *how* the body and mind team up, this is revealed, believe it or not, in the workings of metaphors.

METAPHOR! IT ISN'T JUST FOR FRESHMAN ENGLISH ANYMORE!

Metaphors are our mind's little meaning helpers.

A metaphor, in English teacher terms, is a word or phrase used to describe something that it doesn't properly (that is, literally) apply to. For example, there's the metaphor "flea" in "He's a flea among men," which tells you that you can count on the guy to have all the swaggering virility of a tiny darting bug that hides in dog hair.

Typically, a metaphor explains some abstract idea by using some physical action or concrete thing—something that actually exists—to make the abstract idea more understandable. To give you another example, there's the metaphor "zoo" in "The supermarket was a zoo today," which does not mean that you had to shove aside a giraffe and two hippos to get to the organic arugula.

But by describing the supermarket using a place that we can picture—one filled with clawing, screeching wild animals—we get a better idea of what you went through than if you'd used more abstract language, like "busy," as in "It was really busy at the supermarket today."

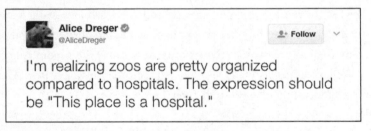

My friend, medical historian Alice Dreger, thinks we're mean to zoos.

Around 1980, metaphors started sneaking out of English class to smoke cigarettes and hang out in the cognitive science department. This started after linguist George Lakoff realized that metaphors aren't just fun language games. In fact, he contends, our human conceptual system—our system for making sense of the physical and social world around us—is "fundamentally metaphorical in nature."

Lakoff, writing with philosophy professor Mark Johnson, goes on to explain that metaphors—and meaning—"arose from the nature of the body." To understand what this means, it helps to recognize that "metaphor" comes from the Greek word *metaphora*, "to transfer."

A metaphor makes an idea—an abstract notion like love or time—more understandable by *transferring it* into our first language, the bodily language that we inherited from the "approach" and "avoidance" motivations of wee organisms. Basically, a metaphor moves a concept over from the fuzzy, harder-to-understand world of abstract ideas to the physical world—the ancestral homeland of our emotions and reasoning.

To understand this, let's look at a statement describing time that doesn't include a metaphor: "Time is valuable." "Value" is an intangible thing—a thing we can't see or touch. If you go to the liquor store, pull on your ski mask, and say "Give me all your value!" they won't know what to do.

However, compare "time is valuable" with this metaphor-driven statement: "Time is money." Saying that time is "money" *grounds* time—explaining it in a way that we understand from our physical experience of the world. It does that by converting time into a physical thing (like a fistful of dollars) that we can immediately picture and unthinkingly understand.

To give you another example of this, let's move on to love. Compare the intangible "love is complicated" to the metaphor-driven statement "love is a battlefield." Or—heh—if your relationship is seriously shitty, "love is a cattlefield." Either way, you can immediately picture the mess. And, in turn, this means that you have a deeper, bodily-driven understanding.

Okay...maybe you're starting to wonder, "What the hell do metaphors have to do with how I'm a guy (or, worse, a girl*) who can't get a fucking date without a credit card?"

The answer? Quite a lot, actually.

---

*This situation is even worse—that is, even more humiliating—if you're a girl, considering that guys, especially those in their 20s, tend to have the "shape and motion" sex rule: "If it moves and it has the right-shaped opening, try to have sex with it."

YOUR MIND IS ALSO IN YOUR ELBOW

Why metaphor matters

If you've been to a therapist and noticed that impressive framed degree from The Freud Factory on the wall, you probably assumed their techniques are based on some sort of evidence that they work. They may be—especially if your therapist uses cognitive behavioral therapy. Unfortunately, a good bit of the advice of many therapists is actually about as evidence-driven as the advice of many witch doctors.

Sadly, insurance won't cover shaking a chicken-foot necklace over you.
"The Secret Museum of Mankind,"
Volume 2, 1935

An example of a dubious therapeutic technique is that "active listening" hooey—therapists telling quarreling couples that they can improve their partnership through repeating each other's words: "So...I am hearing that you'd like to beat me to death with the toaster oven and bury me in a shallow grave..."

Relationship researchers Kurt Hahlweg and John Gottman independently tested active listening, and they came up with similar findings. As Gottman explains, partners have to be so focused on parroting the words back to each other that they aren't connecting or empathizing with each other—which suggests that active listening is mainly effective at making people using it feel like total ass-hats.

This counterproductive technique is just the tip of the therapeutic iceberg. Not surprisingly, much of psychology has spent the past hundred-plus years ignoring the body, advising us to fix our social and psychological problems in a way-too-narrow way—using a "disembodied" brain. Making matters worse, in doing this, psychologists have put way too much weight on conscious reasoning—which, unfortunately, isn't what's driving us much of the time.

I know; this runs contrary to our smug human belief that our behavior is the result of well-thought-out choices, the kind in which we methodically assess our options—as opposed to just taking a wild guess that it's the car and not the goat behind Door Number Two.

But according to neuroscientist Michael Gazzaniga, ninety-eight percent of our brain activity is unconscious. Ninety-eight percent! And this includes a good bit of our decision-making. Which, to be fair, doesn't mean that we aren't reasoning—just that we aren't always doing it with the department that gets all the credit.

In fact, the way we process metaphor tells us something important—that the body is not just a big, somewhat hair-covered piece of meat. The body is an essential participant and partner in a good deal of our reasoning and, through that, in shaping who we are. This goes back to the start of chapter 3—my claim that "the mind is bigger than the brain."

WHY A FREEZING-COLD RESTAURANT MIGHT NOT BE THE GREATEST PLACE FOR A HOT DATE

As Lakoff and Johnson explain it, both our conceptual system and our reasoning arise "from the nature of our brains, bodies, and bodily experience." But they emphasize that they aren't just saying that we need a body to reason. They're making the claim that the actual *structure of our reasoning* comes out of the nature of the body.

In their work, they actually call metaphor "conceptual metaphor" because it reflects how we *conceive* of the world. However, not all metaphors fit the bill. They are not talking about out-there metaphors— like "God is a can opener"—that you need to be on psychedelics to understand. There are also culturally specific metaphors that you have to be, say, Ukrainian to figure out.

Lakoff and Johnson explain that the metaphors that drive a good deal of our behavior seem to be the simplest ones—those universal ones that come out of our bodily experience of the world, like feeling warm, cold, wet, or itchy or perceiving things as loud, soft, high up, or far away.

Take a common (and universal) human metaphor—referring to affection as "warmth."

It appears that "warmth" as a metaphor for affection didn't pop up arbitrarily (say because "pool cue," "pudding," and "tree frog" were off getting drunk at the track). Our temperature is an essential thing our body constantly monitors, seeing that we aren't dangerously hot or cold.

But "warmth" also feels good, so we are physically drawn to warmth—warm bread, warm soup, warm and cozy under the covers. And warmth, as a good feeling, is one that goes way back. Our first experience of it, Lakoff and Johnson point out, is the warmth of our mother's body as she was holding us close as a baby.

Well, right in line with the metaphor that affection is warmth— a metaphor that's consistent across cultures—warming up physically may lead to our warming up emotionally, and vice versa.

In a study by neuroscientists Tristen K. Inagaki and Naomi Eisenberger, subjects were put in an MRI scanner and asked to read sappy (that is, emotionally warm!) or emotionally neutral messages from their close friends and family members.

The warm messages were things like "Whenever I am completely lost, you are the person I turn to" and "I love you more than anyone else in the world." (Awww.) Emotionally neutral messages were statements like "You have curly hair" and "I have known you for ten years." Subjects were also asked to hold a warm object (a hand-warming pack) or a room-temperature object (a ball).

Participants reported feeling physically warmer after reading the positive messages (compared with the neutral ones). And, conversely, after being given the hand-warming pack to hold, they felt more connected to their loved ones.

You could argue, "Yeah, okay...but maybe they knew what the researchers wanted them to say."

Well, check out the results of the brain imaging—which showed "an overlap between physical and social warmth." This means that the researchers were able to see activations for *both social and physical warmth* in the same areas of the brain—the insula (which is thought to be involved in regulating body temperature) and the ventral striatum (part of the brain's reward circuitry).

Interestingly, there was no overlapping neural activity when they gave the participants a task involving "pleasant physical touch"—stroking their forearm with a soft brush. This is important because it supports the researchers' conclusion that the "shared activity in social and physical warmth in this study" wasn't just caused by pleasurable feelings.

As Inagaki and Eisenberger sum up their findings, "These results suggest that a common neural mechanism underlies physical and social warmth."

Hot diggity, huh?

Other studies have similar results. To name just one, in an experiment by social psychologists Chen-Bo Zhong and Geoffrey Leonardelli, when subjects were asked to recall a time when they were socially accepted, they estimated the temperature of the room they were in to be five degrees higher, on average, than when they were asked to remember being snubbed.

In short, it seems that a warm body is likely to lead to warmer feelings toward others, and vice versa. And this metaphorical back-and-forth isn't just reflected in the body. As Lakoff and Johnson point out—and as Inagaki and Eisenberger showed with the neural overlap between social and physical warmth—the workings of conceptual metaphor show up in the brain.

Yes, again, we're looking at that "shared sink," that cognitive plumbing used by both our body and our emotions. The amazing thing about metaphor processing, as Lakoff and cognitive scientist Rafael Núñez explain, is that there's "simultaneous activation" of two or more "distinct areas of our brains, each concerned with distinct aspects of our experience, like the physical experience of warmth and the emotional experience of affection."

Lakoff and Núñez go on to explain that "the coactivation" of these different parts of the brain "generates a single complex experience"— an experience of affection/warmth, difficulty/heaviness, or, for another example, suspiciousness/fishiness.

Suspiciousness/fishiness refers to how "smells fishy" is a metaphorical expression of "social suspicion"—the feeling that somebody's likely to do something underhanded. Social psychologists Spike W. S. Lee and Norbert Schwarz discovered that the "smells fishy" metaphor is used to indicate suspicion in more than a dozen languages, which led them to believe that the pairing was not just a linguistic quirk but an association built into our knowledge structure.

They ran experiments to test for behavioral effects, like whether smelling something fishy in the environment would make a person suspicious to the point where it undermined their willingness to trust another person to behave fairly.

One of their experiments was a two-player investment game with a financial payoff. They predicted that the participants would likely invest more money (potentially making more) if they trusted their gaming partner to reciprocate but would likely invest less if they suspected their partner would screw them over.

This is where the fishy smell comes in. Before the participants came into the gaming area, the place was doctored with one of three different-smelling liquids: fishy (from opened-up fish oil capsules), farty (from a novelty fart spray called Liquid Ass), and "no perceptibly added odor" (from tap water).

The results? Participants who were exposed to the fishy smell invested less money—a whole twenty-five percent less—relative to the neutral smell or the nasty fart stink (which, yes, is a yicky smell but lacks the "suspicion-related metaphorical meaning").

But there's more. The researchers also reversed their experiment— testing for whether "socially-induced suspicion" enhances people's ability to correctly identify fishy smells. And, in fact, when a research assistant "primed" a participant by saying and doing suspicion-evoking things, that person was more likely—72.5 percent more likely—to correctly ID the fish oil.

YOUR MIND IS DOUBLE-JOINTED

A remarkable effect that's showing up in the *social warmth/physical warmth* and *suspiciousness/fishiness* research is what's called "bidirectionality."

I know; that sounds like bisexual acts taking place while you're driving the wrong way down the freeway. But bidirectionality actually describes *metaphorical effects that go both ways*—for example, in how "ewww, fishy" caused suspicion and, in turn, feeling suspicious led to being better able to identify fishy smells in an environment (essential whenever there's an escaped trout hiding out in your den).

In short, it seems that physical experience leads to emotion and emotion also leads to physical experience.

In shorter: Wow.

This two-way street between physical experience and emotion goes way beyond the thinking of Lakoff and Johnson, who insist that metaphor is a one-way deal—"unidirectional." To explain this, Lakoff gives the example of "love is a journey." You *can* see love as a journey—and lovers as travelers, with the relationship as their vehicle, which sometimes brings them to crossroads in the journey. (And yes, I'm gagging, too.)

The thing is, thinking of a journey won't make you more loving, and being on a journey won't cause love. (In fact, when traveling quarters are especially close, two lovebirds can start to seem more like two seriously pissed-off roosters—pecking each other bloody while onlookers bet on which one will live to peck another day.)

But in poring over which metaphors are bidirectional—working both ways—and which are one-way streets, I spotted something important.

Though all the "why the hell is this?" neuroscience is far from worked out, it became evident to me that the metaphors that are at the root of changing who we are seem to be the really basic, body-based stuff—like standing tall to feel taller on the inside (that is, more confident).

Just then, I tripped over what I began to call the "Norbert awareness problem," because it came out of research I read by Norbert Schwarz and his colleagues that—eek!—found that when subjects were aware of researchers' tricks to influence their perception, the effects were eliminated.

To understand this, let's go back to one of the examples from above—the overlap in physical and emotional warmth.

If you're a research subject and you haven't been clued in that warming up physically leads to warming up emotionally—when you lack that bit of information—you are warmer (more generous) in your assessments of a person.

However, once you understand that it's, say, that hand-warming pack that the researcher had you hold that influences how you think of the person, well, *bye-bye, magical metaphorical effect!*

Uh-oh.

Of course, I couldn't tell you to do all this action stuff to transform yourself if you have to be in some sort of walking coma for it to work.

But wait, I thought. Acting like the sort of person I wanted to be worked for me, and not because I thought it would work. (In fact, when I did it, I thought it was a stupid idea, but I was just too desperate not to try it.)

So, though I had no research to back me up—just my own gut feeling—I felt that there had to be some nuance I wasn't seeing.

And finally, after a month of night terrors, I came to realize that there *is* a distinction that matters, and it's in mere perception (like perceiving the warmth of the hand-warming pack) versus action.

Let's look at two studies using facial expressions. First, there's a study in which the subjects weren't clued in on the purpose of the experiments. This is psychologist James Laird's study I mentioned previously—the one using the fake electrodes stuck to people's faces, which they were told were to measure facial muscle reaction. Laird instructed the participants to contort their facial muscles in various ways—disguising that he was actually getting them to smile or frown—and found that they ended up feeling the corresponding emotions.

Next, let's look at a 2002 study by clinical psychologists Charles Neuhoff and Charles Schaefer. Participants were given a sheet of paper explaining their assignment: to rate their mood before and after smiling broadly for 60 seconds and after forcing laughter for 60 seconds. The results? Participants' smiling and laughing boosted their post-test mood—despite their being clued in on the purpose of the study.

To understand why, it's important to recognize that laughter isn't just a sound. Both laughing and smiling are actions—muscular actions. Smiling involves muscles in the face, and laughter involves muscles in the face, respiratory tract, and belly. Laughter also has been shown to have positive effects on the cardiovascular, immune, and endocrine systems, as well as the central nervous system (the brain and spinal cord). To give you just one example, British anthropologist Robin Dunbar and his colleagues found that the muscular contractions of laughter trigger the release of the body's homegrown opiates, endorphins, upping the laugher's resistance to pain.

For another look at how our muscles play into emotion, let's take the Hollywood star route—Botox Avenue. Botox, injected in small doses, paralyzes facial muscles (ironing out those Grand Canyon–like frown lines). But that's not all. It turns out that impairing the ability to frown also impairs the ability to feel the frowny feelings of depression that go with it.

Biochemist/dermatologist Eric Finzi and psychiatrist Norman E. Rosenthal did a study on people suffering from moderate to severe depression, injecting Botox into the area between the eyes that goes wrinkly when a person frowns. Their result? Fifty-two percent of those who got the Botox experienced relief from their depression—compared with only fifteen percent of the unlucky ducks who got jabbed with a placebo.

However, it isn't just the muscles behind facial expressions that we can use to change our feelings. Action matters—metaphorically correct action like "standing tall" in order to feel more empowered. Or even "sitting tall."

Psychophysiologists Vietta Wilson and Erik Peper did a study comparing the emotional effects of sitting upright (versus having a slumpy posture). They found that sitting upright seemed to chase away subjects' gloomy thoughts—making it difficult for many to pull up "hopeless, helpless, powerless, and negative memories" while making it easier for them to recall memories that were empowering and positive.

Their finding—along with many others—is right in line with the metaphor of "up." Happy is up. Hopeful is up. More is up. Progress is up. Success is up. And—most importantly—confidence is up. And what the research suggests is that the more you're "up"—the more you get into the habit of sitting and standing up straight—the more you'll be on your way to the new "taller" you.

ACTION IS THE JOYSTICK OF THE EMOTIONS

Yes, it seems that you can use your body as a joystick to shift your emotions. Again, this isn't what you've heard from much of the "think your way to a new you!" world of psychotherapy. But, as Yale clinical psychologist and child behavioral researcher Alan E. Kazdin explained on my science podcast, "knowing doesn't control doing." In fact, "knowing has very little relationship to doing."

Well, the research from the embodied cognition world suggests Kazdin is right. As I'd put it:

Doing is the key to doing.

And, once again, by repeatedly "doing" over time—by standing, speaking, gesturing, and generally acting like a confident person—you make changes in your brain that reshape your default behavior. At a certain point—as I experienced—you get to the point where you no longer need to *act* like the new you; you *are* the new you. (And hallefuckinglujah to that.)

As for your very first act of doing, well, it's just about time to bury the old you in the backyard.

EAT SHIT AND DIE

The power of ritual

You're probably reading this book because, to one degree or another, you've been eating shit for quite some time. If so, you are long overdue for the second half of that saying—the "and die" part.

Not to worry; I'm fresh out of cyanide-laced grape Kool-Aid*, and I'm almost as creeped out by mass suicides as I am by group hugs. The death I'm calling for is a symbolic one. You need to kill off your shit-eating self so you can have a fresh start in building the new, confident you. This new you is the person who, when handed a Shit Mc-Muffin, will not for a second contemplate eating it just to avoid speaking up.

Better yet, this new you will rarely be handed Shit McMuffins, because—from the way you talk and carry yourself—people will sense that trying to stick you with one of these would end badly for them.

---

*It was actually Flavor Aid (plus cyanide and Valium) that they used in the Jonestown massacre back in 1978, when creepy cult leader Jim Jones instructed his flock to off themselves. Source: Jennifer Rosenberg of ThoughtCo.

YOUR NEURONS CAN HELP YOU STOP BEING
SUCH A LOSER

Unfortunately, your shit-eating self has some serious staying power. That's because any behavior you repeatedly engage in ends up becoming "sticky"—more and more ingrained as one of your go-to behaviors.

This stickiness comes from the particular combination of brain cells (neurons) that fire each time you take a particular action. (Different actions call on different combinations of brain cells.) There's a phrase by neuroscientist Carla Shatz: "Cells that fire together wire together." This is her wonderful little boil-down of behavioral psychologist Donald Hebb's 1949 theory on how behavior links neurons.

According to Hebb, when two nerve cells keep firing at the same time, chemical changes take place, strengthening the connection between them. Hebb's theory—now supported by neuroscientific research—basically says that a behavior gets "worn" into your neural networks, much like a hiking path that's used a lot. The more you take the path the more comfortable and walkable it is and the more you *keep* taking the path—to the point where you automatically take it.

To explain this another way, say you take some action (like, oh, unlatching a cupboard). It requires waking up a bunch of individual neurons and getting them to fire. The first time you do this, Bob Neuron wakes up and fires—which you could think of as the neuron version of driving to the office—and Fred Neuron, a couple of doors down, wakes up and fires, too, off to that same office. You do the behavior again—and a few more agains—and Bob and Fred figure it out: "Dude, let's just carpool."

As for how this "fire together/wire together" thing relates to your changing yourself, consider that you've spent a lot of years getting your neural networks used to reacting in certain ways (à la "Squeak, squeak, I'm a mouse"). You're going to have to retrain them—teach them through repeatedly behaving differently—so mouse mode will no longer be your default. This can be done; remember that I did it. But because this self-remodel requires your fighting years of ingrained behavior and its pathways in the brain, it's helpful to put in a divider—a big, showy rite of passage between "that was me then" and "this is me from now on."

In other words, you need to have a Funeral for the Self—a ceremonial send-off for the doormatty self that you'd like to put behind you.

TURNS OUT THOSE HIPPIE HEALERS WERE ONTO SOMETHING

No, this funeral thing isn't just a hokey stunt. It's a hokey stunt with helpful psychological and behavioral effects that come from the way the brain seems to confuse the real and the symbolic.

There's a "how-to" for staging your funeral at the end of this chapter, and in the next chapter, there are how-tos for emotionally soothing daily rituals you can do. But first, here's the "why-do"—the science showing that rituals can help you dial down your anxiety, feel better about yourself, and have more self-control.*

This emotional composure is essential because a substantial part of this deworming yourself business is calming the fuck down and having some control over yourself when you start using these new confident-person behaviors.

So...let's say you have this fear, "Nobody wants to hear what I have to say," and it keeps you from speaking up in meetings. Maybe you know deep down that you're smart and you have good ideas.

Still, that "nobody wants to hear it" notion keeps popping back up like one of those Bobo the Clown bop bags whenever you contemplate saying something.

---

*The term "ritual" can bring to mind the life-crippling strings of behavior seen in obsessive-compulsive disorder, like checking 26 times to be sure the stove is off before leaving the house. However, the rituals I suggest here are ones you *make an effort to do*, as opposed to rituals a person is *uncontrollably compelled to perform* to maybe get some brief relief from anxiety (as is the case with OCD). Researchers are not yet clear on what causes OCD, but there's some evidence that it has a genetic, neurological basis.

Imagine being able to crumple up that fear like an old gum wrapper and throw it in the trash. Well, using a simple little ritual from social psychologist Pablo Brinol's research, you may actually be able to do that—turn down the power of a damaging thought by treating it as a material object you can get rid of.

Brinol had research participants write down their negative thoughts about their body image. He then had some of the participants rip up the pages and throw them away. This actually served to decrease the strength of these damaging thoughts and diminish their influence on the participants' attitudes about themselves. Conversely, when other participants kept the pages "in a safe place"—tucking them in their pocket rather than tossing them in the trash—the thoughts remained more present, hanging around in their minds like smokers after an AA meeting.

Brinol's experiments are just some of many reflecting how we can make use of the benefits of the "shared sink"—the cognitive plumbing used by both our body and our emotions—and turn ritual into a valuable tool for change.

There are some important elements to a ritual used as a tool for change. We tend to think of a ritual as some behavior we repeat (like, say, somebody's daily coffee ritual—which is actually just a routine). However, a ritual you use to help you change should have both a symbolic element and a goal accompanying it.

Harvard Business School professors Michael I. Norton and Francesca Gino define a ritual as some "symbolic activity" you perform in hopes of making something happen. An example of this is a ritual for "negative energies" removal used by one of their research subjects (and forget for a moment whether you believe this works). The guy told them:

> *I always feel [it] necessary to ground myself to the earth when under stress. I pound my feet strongly on the ground several times, I take several deep breaths, and I "shake" my body to remove any negative energies. I do this often before going to*

*work, going into meetings, and at the front door before entering
my house after a long day.*

Did you notice the metaphorical stuff in there? People's rituals typically contain metaphorical elements. In this guy's ritual, the metaphorical parts are his "grounding" himself and then shaking off and
"cleansing" himself of any bad energies before he goes into work, a
meeting, or his home—same as he'd probably brush crumbs off his
shirt or wipe his feet on a doormat if they were muddy.

Before I read the research on embodied cognition, I would have
had a smug little laugh at this—the hippieshit notion that "negative
energy" is something that sticks to you like cat hair on a sweater and
that it's something you can physically shake off. However, with those
"cleansing" actions the guy is doing—shaking and stomping—he is
both physically loosening up and emotionally relaxing himself. And
similarly, research has found that giving people Valium for anxiety—
for being clenched-up emotionally—also serves to unclench any
muscular tightness they've been feeling. (Likewise, muscle-relaxing
drugs relax people emotionally.)

Granted, we'd all probably see some benefits from doing a little
loosen-up hokeypokey—which is why they had us do this back in
nursery school. But remember that for the guy Gino and Norton describe, this behavior is more than a reflexive physical reaction to tight
shoulders or a knot in the stomach; it's a ritual that he practices with
an eye toward a specific outcome.

Because of this, he boosts the power and positive emotional effects
of his shaking and stomping. As for the benefits he likely experiences, Gino and Norton found that performing rituals led to subjects
having "increased feelings of control." That's pretty important,
because feeling more in control helps you act more in control.

Getting back to the "do you really believe this bullshit?" question,
surprisingly, whether the ritual itself can actually achieve its intended
effect—like whether you can make so-called "negative energies" go

away with a workplace rain dance—is actually unimportant in terms of a ritual's power to shift a person's feelings. Gino and Norton find that this is even the case for ritual-doers who are nonbelievers—those who think some ritual they've grudgingly agreed to do is idiotic and pointless. Yep, even they feel more in control afterward. As this woman did.

LIGHT THE WRONG LOVE CANDLE

When I put out a call on my blog for people to tell me the rituals they do, a woman emailed me, "I did creepy candle-lighting about a guy. And it worked." She wrote:

> I had started seeing this guy long-distance. I really liked him, and I could tell he was really into me. But he'd had a few really awful relationships, so he was afraid to commit and kind of closed off emotionally.
>
> He'd get distant—like not answering a text for days. I would then freak out and call him up, all upset, and act pathetic and clingy. I hated how I felt and how I was acting, but I couldn't seem to take my friends' advice to "play it cool," and I wasn't ready to break it off because I knew we had something really special.
>
> Out of desperation, I decided to try a new tactic—one I thought was super-stupid, by the way.
>
> I went to a witchcraft store and bought a love candle. It wasn't even the "right" one (which apparently would have been a red one). This really cool Australian chick (with red and black striped hair) running the store said they were out of the red ones, handed me a pink one, and said, "Fuck it. Take this one instead."

She told me not to worry about reciting the dumb "love prayer" on the side of the candle. "Just do your own thing."

I'd read online that you can't blow it out—that you're supposed to let the thing burn for seven days straight or something.

"Oh, my God," she said. "Please blow it out if you go someplace. You don't want to burn your house down. The power of this thing is in your intention."

Again, even as I was lighting this thing, I thought it was ridiculous. But I was feeling so bad and so out of control I needed to do something. So, whenever he didn't call or text me back right away, I'd light the candle, visualizing the "flame of love" (gag!) burning up the barriers between us.

A month later, I was back in the witchcraft store, telling the woman, "Hey, he's living with me now."

And no, I am not an idiot. I do not think people fall in love and come together because one of them lights a string stuck in wax.

The feeling that I was doing *something* about the situation allowed me to chill; I didn't feel I had to chide him when he didn't text or call in my time frame. Because I stopped being so demanding and dramatic, I think he felt less pressured and was able to relax and could come to me. And he did.

RITUALS HELP STOP THE KIND OF CHOKING THE HEIMLICH MANEUVER IS NO GOOD FOR

I resent the term "performance anxiety." It's such an *emotionally pruned* way to describe what I suffered from for decades whenever I really needed to be at my best: a huge, suffocating weight pressing down

on me, squashing an otherwise intelligent, articulate adult into a bab-
bling, hyperventilating toddler.

Well, research led by Harvard Business School's Alison Wood
Brooks finds that ritual can be especially helpful in slapping down this
performance anxiety business.

Anxiety is a huge performance killer for a lot of people, draining
short-term memory, squashing self-confidence, and causing shaky
hands, cracked voices, and flop sweat (mmm, sexy!). Suppressing anxiety is difficult because of the role the body plays in it. (You can't treat
your adrenaline rush like a bratty kid and tell it to go sit down.) And,
annoyingly, research by psychologist Daniel Wegner and others finds
that trying to suppress anxiety-provoking thoughts can backfire—
ultimately causing you to feel more anxious than before you tried to stop.

When you are anxious, doing *something*—such as taking *some* positive action with a symbolic spin—rather than trying to NOT do
something, seems to be most effective. So—admittedly—going into
a bathroom stall and repeatedly shaking a hot-pink rabbit's foot over
each shoulder before giving a speech won't actually bewitch the audience into loving your talk. However, you might just be a more en-
tertaining and commanding speaker after your ritual helps you feel a
little calmer and less like a giant turd with a face.

ARE YOU THERE, GOD? IT'S ME, FLOTSAM

In addition to the awful physical sensations that come with performance anxiety, Alison Wood Brooks notes that the psychological fun
also involves uncomfortable feelings of uncertainty—a sense of powerlessness over the ultimate outcome. So, given the findings that ritual increases feelings of control, it isn't surprising that anthropologists
observe that rituals often pop up in situations where there are high
levels of uncertainty.

Anthropologist Bronislaw Malinowski explained in *Magic, Science
and Religion and Other Essays* that the Trobriand Islanders engage in

"extensive" ritual when venturing off into the "danger and uncertainty" of deep-sea fishing. However, they don't bother doing any rituals before heading off to their version of the corner fish store— the neighborhood lagoon—where "fishing is done in an easy and absolutely reliable manner."

Ritual is also an important element in the Trobrianders' preparation for combat. Malinowski explained that in warfare, the Trobrianders are very clear that *skills* such as "strength, courage, and agility play a decisive part" in whether they win or lose; however, they do rituals beforehand to manage the uncertainty—"to master the elements of chance and luck."

Back here in our world, there's a similar need for a combo platter of skill and uncertainty management in professional sports, which is probably why a number of athletes use pre-performance rituals. Take former Boston Red Sox third baseman Wade Boggs. Chris Giblin writes in *Men's Fitness*:

> Boggs had an insanely regimented pre-game routine— reportedly, he would field exactly 150 ground balls in the infield, start his batting practice at exactly 5:17 PM (during night games), and run wind sprints at exactly 7:17 PM. Then, of course, there was the chicken he would eat before every game, earning him the nickname, "Chicken Man."

Tennis champion Rafael Nadal is another with pre-competition rituals. Giblin reports:

> Nadal takes a cold shower 45 minutes before every match, he towels down after every point (even for aces and double faults), he points the labels of his drinking bottles toward the end of the court he's about to play from and he never stands up from his chair before his opponent.

Nadal's cold shower has significant bodily effects (such as constricting blood vessels and releasing mood-invigorating hormones). There are also bodily effects from some of Nadal's and Boggs's other behaviors—in addition to the emotionally soothing, uncertainty-reducing effects of performing a ritual.

LET THEM EAT (LESS) CAKE

The most exciting finding about ritual is that beyond making you *feel* you have more self-control, it may improve your actual self-control. Consumer behavioral researcher Ding (Allen) Tian and his colleagues recruited female gym members who were trying to lose weight and asked them to cut their net calorie intake by about ten percent (over a five-day period) through both eating less and exercising more.*

The researchers (sadists for science, it seems) had fun with some of the subjects, telling them that they had to complete a three-step "ritual" whenever they ate to help themselves cut calories:

1. Cut their food into pieces.
2. Arrange the pieces on the right and left sides of a plate so they were perfectly symmetrical.
3. Press their fork against the top of the food three times.

Those who performed the three-part ritual did cut their caloric intake—showing a net calorie intake of 1,154, compared with 1,413 for those who had no ritual.

There is a caveat from this research, dovetailing with the findings that trying to suppress an unwanted behavior is very hard and sometimes even counterproductive. Tian explains that rituals don't "unconditionally increase all forms of self-control." They are more

---

*This research was still unpublished as this book went to press.

likely to improve the self-control that comes with taking *positive action*—like doing rituals to support healthier eating—instead of trying to avoid doing something like, oh, diving into a chocolate frosted sheet cake (and then waking up from the sugar coma four hours later covered in shame and smudges of frosting).

WHY THIS WEIRD SEMI-SUPERSTITIOUS CRAP WORKS

As for why rituals work, researchers still have very little idea. (Sorry. I was hoping for something more definitive, too.)

What's important is that rituals *do* seem to work—to help you feel less negative and anxious and more in control, and to actually have more self-control. I suspect the reason for this has something to do with "expectancy," which neuroscientists Lauren Atlas and Tor Wager define as "the belief that something will happen." It turns out that what you expect to happen after you take some action influences what you actually feel *has* happened.

The placebo effect is an example of this—sick people reporting feeling better and sometimes even getting better after they take what turns out to be a sugar pill. But the placebo effect isn't limited to the medical world. Wine snobs fall all over themselves about the "exceptional bouquet" of some grape swill when they're told they're drinking the pricey stuff rather than Chateau de Cardboard Box.

Getting back to rituals, it might seem hard to believe that merely expecting an effect can lead to an effect, but remember that in performing a ritual, you're taking some purposeful action. You're doing *something*.

In fact, as noted previously in this chapter, it doesn't even matter if you think a ritual is stupid and won't work. The expectancy effect— believing that something will happen—takes hold of you because of the way our minds leap to the conclusion that we don't take action for no reason whatsoever.

Your conscious mind and your unconscious mind might even have a little argument over this:

Your conscious mind: "This is fucking stupid."

Your unconscious mind: "Well, she's doing something. There must be a reason. Sit down and shut up."

Yes, even if your mind spends a good deal of time going all mean girl on you for what a loser you are, it ultimately refuses to believe you're a total dumbshit. If you're doing that thing with the hot-pink rabbit's foot, it's sure there must be some productive outcome expected from this. And there actually will be—because the feeling that you're taking meaningful action will help you relax and feel less anxious.

TODAY IS THE FIRST DAY OF THE REST OF YOUR DEATH!

Looking at societies around the globe, anthropologist Arnold van Gennep found that there are three phases to any big life change: *separation* (from the person you were), *transition* (adapting to your new role and the behaviors that go with it), and then *incorporation* (the merging of the new identity into who you are).

However, before you can take on new behaviors, you need to get rid of those that aren't working for you. You can do this with a rite of passage, a ceremony used around the world, throughout history, to mark changes in a person's status in their society.

This is the ceremonial form of stripping off old paint before painting a car—stripping off the old you so you can have a fresh base for your new identity. If we lived in a tribal society, the ceremony might involve head shaving, teeth pulling, or scraping off the fun parts from your lady bits. But not to worry—I stand especially firmly against tribal dentistry and home clitoridectomies. I do, however, think you might get a lot out of a ceremonial death rite—throwing a funeral for your soon-to-be former self.

This funeral thing is something you should do in the company of at least one friend or family member. Yes, you really do need an audience. Funerals are not one-person affairs. (I even had a small gathering—okay, my little sister and my Barbie—for the solemn backyard service after my hamster, Squeaky, died when I was eight.)

Because we have an evolved concern for reputation—for other people to think well of us—having those who are close to you witness the ceremony is a powerful form of reinforcement to help you stick to your goals in becoming the new you. Feeling that other people will be monitoring our behavior motivates us to behave better. This is why there are public weigh-ins in weight-loss groups and support groups for stopping all sorts of behaviors, from smoking cigarettes to smoking crack.

PLANNING THE FUNERAL FOR THE LOSER YOU

Your funeral should be a simple, tasteful affair, with just a few steps:

1. Create some symbol of you—maybe a photo of you on a page with all the behaviors that you no longer want to engage in. Create a companion page of the behaviors that you want to make up the new you. Fold up this new-you sheet and put it somewhere safe.

2. Invite mourners. Have at least one person present—somebody supportive. Ideally, you and anybody else in attendance should dress appropriately. (Fashion ideal if you're a woman: the Italian widow from the movies—black dress, black gloves, black veil.) At the very least, wear black.

3. Read a eulogy you've written: "(Your name here) has lived for many years as a suck-up..."

4. Put an end to the symbolic old you by lighting the "you" page on fire in a bowl and scattering the ashes in nature. Or, if you prefer, crumple up the page and bury it in the backyard next to the late Chairman Meow. (If you're an apartment dweller, you could rip up and flush the old you down the toilet like a dead goldfish.)

5. Give the old you a final wave goodbye. Then walk through
   a doorway to symbolize going off into your new life. As you
   do, say something inspirational, like "Farewell forever—to
   being gum under life's shoe!" "You're dead to me, old self!
   Dead! Dead! Dead! Yahooooo!"

You can now celebrate your very first success. You put some loser
out of their misery and didn't even need to make it look like an accident.

SOUPLANTATION FOR THE SOUL
Make your own daily rituals!

Obviously, you can't step out of the conference room and slaughter a goat whenever you need a boost of confidence to speak up in a meeting.

A confidence-improving ritual has to fit into your daily life, with simple, unobtrusive steps, like twisting some symbolic item around in your pocket. But have some fun coming up with your ritual. Use a weird heirloom. Paint a rock. Grind up a superhero action figure so you can sprinkle some of it on your clothing before you leave for work.

There are also a number of elements you can add to your ritual to increase its power to dial down your panic and discomfort in social situations—especially those with an unpredictable outcome, whether it's asking for a raise or asking some fucknugget on the bus to stop kicking your seat.

PETE AND REPEAT WERE WALKING DOWN THE STREET

Doing a bunch of "reps" seems as helpful for your rituals as it is for your abs.

Psychologists Cristine Legare and Andre Souza have studied Brazilian rituals called simpatias. They find that people who use them perceive them to be more effective when they have a bunch of different steps, some of which repeat, like sticking a knife in a banana tree not just once but four times in a row.

Legare explained to me that repetition increases our sense that our effort will work. She gave the example of how we'll often press an elevator button a bunch of times—just in case our message that we want the elevator didn't get through on the first press.

Chances are, repetition also feels good because patterns are comfortable for us. We are pattern-seekers and -noticers, and patterns of action are what make up those well-worn (verging on automatic) pathways in our brain—those brain cells that "fire together" and ultimately "wire together."

IT'S A RITUAL, NOT A THINGYDOOEY

Interestingly, simply calling a set of gestures a "ritual" seems to have an effect—reducing anxiety and improving the ritual-doer's performance in some fear-inducing task.

Harvard Business School's Alison Wood Brooks and her colleagues discovered this when they had two groups of research participants go through the same wacky-ass steps before doing some math problems. One group had the steps described to them as a "ritual"; the others were told they were "random behaviors" they were to complete:

> *Please count out loud slowly up to ten from zero. Then count back down to zero. You should say each number out loud and write each number on the piece of paper in front of you as you say it. You may use the entire paper. Sprinkle salt on your paper. Crinkle up your paper. Throw your paper in the trash.*

The participants who were told this was a "ritual" did better on the math problems and reported feeling less anxiety. This, the researchers explain, suggests that the specific steps included in a ritual don't matter as much as "performers' belief that those steps constitute a ritual."

In other words, when you're doing a ritual, for maximum effectiveness, be sure to identify it that way to yourself (as opposed to "a bunch of crazy shit I got out of Amy Alkon's book").

METAPHOR POWER

Your rituals will have more psychological power if you ground them in metaphor. To give you a little refresher from chapter 3, a metaphor makes some abstract idea more understandable by converting it into some concrete thing—something that actually exists—or some physical action. (So, for example, in Metaphorland, shame is ducking and hiding; pride is standing tall.) And because embodied cognition research shows that our actions shape our emotions, grounding your ritual in metaphor simply means choosing the ideal physical actions and elements—those that align with the emotional effects you're going for.

For example, remember the "approach" and "avoidance" motives (chapter 4) that are the underpinnings of our emotions? Behavioral science researchers Yan Zhang and Jane Risen found that incorporating "avoidant actions" into ritual—like throwing salt or a ball away from the body—seems to lead to a "mental simulation of having avoided harm." And amazingly, going through the motions of avoiding harm seems to ease a person's mind as if they'd actually avoided it.

Yes, with the assistance of the appropriate metaphor, there's a good chance you can trick your anxiety into submission about as easily as you can fool a toddler into thinking that small change comes out of their ears. So, before you have to present stuff in a staff meeting, maybe write the words "all my silly fears about my ability" three times on a page and then scratch each line out, crumple up the paper, and throw it in the trash. (Fuck you, fears!)

When your mind is hammering you with regret about something you've done, another simple metaphor you can take advantage of is the notion of cleaning up—washing away that regrettable behavior (and any forensic evidence that could lead to your retirement on an island called Rikers). This comes out of a study by social psychologists Spike W. S. Lee, Lady Macbeth,* and Norbert Schwarz. As Lee explained it, if people are feeling bad about a decision they made and they wash their hands, "it removes the dissonant feelings that they made a bad choice."

Another metaphor that can be applied in a ritual is moving out of a bad situation and into a better place. Say you've screwed up at your job and it's weighing on you. You could use a doorway to create a quickie ritual—simply by going through the doorway of the room where you messed up and into another room or the hallway.

And yes, this actually seems to have a positive effect. Research by psychologist Gabriel Radvansky found that passing through a doorway moves us from one "event horizon" to another, weakening our memories of things in the previous "event horizon."

As for why simply crossing a threshold seems to eat up our ability to remember, Radvansky suspects that the shift from one room to another creates an "event boundary," triggering our mind to separate and file away whatever was in the room we left.

MIX YOUR OWN METAPHORS

Just like Souplantation, this chapter offers a buffet—metaphors you can pick from to add power to the rituals you create. (Sorry. No ranch dressing or bacon bits.) Below are a few metaphors I pulled from linguist George Lakoff's *Master Metaphor List* that relate to becoming more confident and the problems that come up around it.

To use these, first figure out what your problem is—what scary

---

*Awakeness check!

situation you'd like to feel better about or what goal you're looking to achieve. For example, say there's some daunting task that's being added to your duties at work and you're afraid you don't have what it takes. To put this another way, you've got a difficulty. What's a difficulty? Well, translated into metaphorical terms (that is, into a physical thing or action), a difficulty is a drag. A pain in the ass. A *burden*.

First, using the metaphor "difficulties are burdens" (from Lakoff and Mark Johnson's *Philosophy in the Flesh*), consider what it takes to make a burden carryable. One thing you can do is to break it down into smaller parts.

Second, think of some way to represent your task—like as a slab of food. Okay—so maybe you cut it up and eat it as part of your ritual!

I get it. That sounds seriously goofy. However, you've seen the evidence that this works psychologically. And, very importantly, this is also a ritual that fits seamlessly into your day. (Nobody's going to know you're cutting up your chicken Parmesan because you're terrified of being fired; they'll just assume you weren't raised in the woods by a family of wild dogs.)

Here's another example, using a metaphor from Lakoff's list: "Progress is forward motion." When I'm writing my weekly advice column and notice that I've rewritten a single line thirty-six times in a row (yet failed to improve it in the slightest), I'll do my "get out of stupid" ritual: I put on my symbolic superhero shield—uh, that is, those huge wraparound sunglasses worn by eclipse watchers, glaucoma patients, and elderly Asian power walkers—and I walk to the bank at a pretty good clip to get $20 out of the ATM. (The $20 isn't relevant; it just gives me enough of a reason to go to the bank.)

This ritual always makes me feel better, both because I'm getting my heart, limbs, and blood moving and because I'm doing *something*—something besides feeling stupid and incompetent while slaving over a hot computer. Also, because of *bidirectionality*—that back-and-forth between action and emotion—the physical action of moving forward moves me forward emotionally. (The break from writing also allows my brain to do a little background processing on the stuff I've been obsessing over.) So, typically, when I go back to my writing, I'll see a way to fix the problem—and not because the secret of writing well is taking brisk walks to the bank.

THE METAPHOR BAR

(Try not to bump your nose on the sneeze guard)

METAPHORS TO CREATE YOUR OWN RITUALS,
FROM LAKOFF'S MASTER METAPHOR LIST

Success is up.

Important is big.

Important is heavy.

Light (the kind you can see, not lightweight) is knowledge or goodness.

Value is size.

Progress is forward motion.

Harm is physical injury. (So protecting from harm would be shielding.)

More is higher, heavier, or bigger.

Competition is a race, physical aggression, or war.

Opportunities are objects (things to seize).

Reasoning is following a path (being *led* to a certain conclusion).

Ideas are objects. (You can *find* an idea in a book or *trade* ideas with someone.)

Beliefs are clothes. (You can *cast off* or *outgrow* a belief.)

Beliefs are pets or plants. (You can *adopt* a belief like you can a dog, and you can *cultivate* a belief like you can a plant.)

Desire is hunger.

Fear is cold.

Euphoric states are up (like being really *high* on an idea).

Morality is a straight path (being on the *straight and narrow*).

Morality is cleanliness (having a *spotless* record).

Moral is up (being on *the up and up*).

Immoral is down (*stooping* to something *underhanded*).

Good is up.

Bad is down.

A problem is a target.

You may have noticed from my examples that I don't do a bunch of steps or repetitions. You don't necessarily have to, either. Just do what works for you and what seems most believable, helpful, and— ideally—fun.

OM DEPOT

There's a kind of meditation that involves a ritual aspect…

Hey! You there…reading this book! Don't skip this part!

I'm just saying that because I would have—before I read the re-search and discovered that there's a form of meditation that doesn't require you to close your eyes and sit cross-legged for hours in swami-wear. In fact, what I love about this kind of meditation is that it fits right into your day—like that thirty-five seconds when you're wait-ing for your boss to get off the phone or when you're standing in line at 7-Eleven behind some guy paying for a beer in pennies.

All you have to do is repeat a word or short phrase a bunch of times in a row—silently, in your head—in those moments during your day when there's a lull in the action. Even for twenty or thirty seconds.

By the way, the particular word you choose to repeat is what brings the symbolic element to the ritual, which otherwise could be argued to be more of a "practice"—like doing 20 reps on the lats machine at the gym. Technically, this word you repeat is a "mantra," and this is "mantra meditation." But don't let that chase you off, either. The word "mantra," in Sanskrit, translates to "tool for the mind." So you could think of this as giving your mind a hammer or—better yet—one of those $3,000 massage chairs.

It seems that the purposeful repetition done in meditation helps soothe the ravaged mind—and the body right along with it. Research on meditation by cardiologist and Harvard med school professor Herbert Benson finds that focusing on and repeating a word, a phrase, a sound, or even a movement a bunch of times in a row "breaks the chain of everyday thinking" (like ricocheting worries). This, in turn, seems to reduce your blood pressure and heart rate and diminish stress. Benson calls it the "relaxation response."

As for how this plays out "under the hood," neuroscientist Daniel Lowenstein notes that brain imaging studies find that concentrating on repeating a short phrase activates the frontal and parietal lobes. These are the areas involved in selective attention, meaning the ability to maintain a singular focus in the face of distracting stimuli.

Research by nurse scientist and professor Jill Bormann finds this sort of repetition helps with both symptom and stress management in veterans with post-traumatic stress disorder. With practice, she explains, it can become a useful tool "to interrupt automatic or negative thought patterns at any time or place."

Bormann, like Harvard cardiologist Benson, believes that by repeating the word or phrase, you develop a conditioned (automatic) relaxation response to it.

She compared each repetition you do to "putting money in the bank" for when you're in a stressful situation. Then, she says, you can " 'cash in' by drawing on your ... reserves"—repeating your meditation word or phrase in your thoughts and calling up its calming effect on you.

Bormann calls it "a Jacuzzi for the mind."

The way I see it, since it seems to help chill out badass soldiers who did multiple tours of IED disposal, it just might help you calm your ass down enough to ask the cute girl in the evening gown and the Doc Martens to coffee.

INNER PEACE FOR THE IMPATIENT

HOW TO MEDITATE

Meditation is easy and—surprise!—does not require you to be good at concentrating.

According to Harvard cardiologist Benson's research on meditation practices throughout history, meditation requires only two steps:

> Step One: repetition—of a word, phrase, sound, or
> movement.
> Step Two: thought herding.* When a wandering thought
> rudely cuts in front of whatever you're repeating, just
> disregard it and go back to the repetition.

Regarding Step One, you just repeat the word silently, in your mind; you don't walk around repeating it out loud—assuming your goal isn't a complimentary stay in the psych ward.

Step Two is especially important to note if, like me, you assumed you couldn't meditate because—"attention defici—ooh, shiny!"—staying focused isn't exactly your mind's bestiest skill. Mind-wandering is actually to be expected. Your thoughts aren't jumping around because you're a failure at meditation; they're jumping around because you're not dead.

CHOOSING YOUR WORD OR PHRASE
TO REPEAT—RELIGIOUS OR SECULAR:

Not to worry, there's something here for everyone—even if you're a godless harlot like me.

Nurse scientist Bormann, whose research was inspired by the practices of meditation teacher Eknath Easwaran, favors the repetition of

---

*My term for it.

a "sacred" phrase, like "Namo Butsaya" ("I bow to the Buddha"), or
a word with some sort of sacred or sacred-ish connotations, like Rama,
Jesus, Allah, or shalom.

As a post-Jewish atheist, using god words makes me a little uncomfortable. The good news, fellow heathens, is that you can also use a
secular word, like "one" (the word I chose).

Harvard cardiologist Benson reports that when he and his colleagues instructed their research subjects—Harvard med students they'd co-opted—to meditate using the word "one," the
benefits were "indistinguishable from those of transcendental
meditation."

Benson noted that religious people thought it was really wonderful that they went with "one," reading it as "the oneness of God and
the oneness of the universe." Benson came clean: "Well, in truth, it's
because Harvard medical students couldn't count to ten."

HOW OFTEN DO YOU DO THESE REPETITIONS?

Bormann advises doing these "as often as possible" during your day—
whenever you can grab a minute—and also before you go to sleep at
night.

Personally, I'd find incorporating this into every spare moment annoying. However, if you're a ball of anxiety—practically turning to
stone at the prospect of asking the waitress for a salt shaker—well, at
least for a while, perhaps more is more.

HOW MUCH TIME SHOULD YOU PUT INTO EACH SET OF REPS?

Maybe a better question is, "How much time do you have?" You can
do it in the elevator or while you're waiting for the copier at work.
Or, "for example," Bormann wrote me in an email, "while sitting at
a stoplight and waiting in traffic, you could repeat a sequence . . . for
one to three minutes (or more)."

Personally, I just do my "one" thing sometimes for the thirty seconds or minute or so it takes me to fall asleep.

WHAT ABOUT BREATHING?

Bormann told me that you don't need to "purposefully think about breathing" or force it; she says you'll begin breathing more slowly just by repeating your meditation word or phrase. Personally, however, I purposely do my "one" repetitions to big, slow, diaphragmatic inhales and exhales, because this kind of breathing activates our calming parasympathetic nervous system (the body's Department of Chillaxing).

HEY, DUDE, WHERE'S MY CHANGE?

Bormann also told me via email: "Don't expect a thunderbolt of change or difference, but over time (and that differs for everyone), you will notice a change in your 'reactivity' to events that would ordinarily 'push your buttons.'"

LIKE ALL RITUALS, MEDITATION COMES IN TESTER SIZE

Think of meditation simply as something you're trying, not something you're committing to doing from now on. The same goes for any other rituals you might create or new habits you're trying to instill.

Making a big change in your life often feels like too big of a commitment—one that can cause you to avoid even starting. Nobody understands this like a diet doctor—for example, my friend Dr. Mary Dan Eades, a pioneer in advocating low-carb eating and co-author of the *New York Times* best-seller *Protein Power*. To get around patients' psychological stumbling block to making a change, she asks them to commit to eating low-carb (or to some other healthy new behavior) for just three weeks.

Her "just three weeks" request is really smart. This amount of time is not *so much* of a commitment, and after a few weeks of some new practice, I suspect that people see enough benefit—fatwoman looking a little more like Catwoman!—that they're motivated to continue.

Accordingly, maybe commit to *trying* these repetitions for a set period of time—like three weeks—and mark a date on your calendar to check in with yourself to see whether you've noticed a change. Chances are, with regular repetition—of meditation and/or other rituals—you'll start seeing that you're no longer anxiety's bitch.

SELF-ESTEEM IS NOT WHAT YOU THINK IT IS

The irrelevance of whether you like you

As you read in chapter 2, I had an extremely painful childhood. It was an accepted fact that I had a virulent, incurable case of cooties. I was anguishingly lonely, and when I was bullied (whenever kids got bored with just ignoring me), I felt even worse. I often wondered what I could do to break loserhood's apparent death grip on me.

I sometimes did this wondering aloud, leading adults to advise me (using that annoying singsong), "Sticks and stones may break my bones, but names will never hurt me!"

I now wish I could go back and punch every person who said that to me.

How other people see us is actually deeply important to us—and, contrary to what we've been told, it drives what we call our "self-esteem."

WHY THAT "STICKS AND STONES..." SAYING IS A BUNCH OF CRAP

Obviously, sticks and stones can leave you seriously messed up. But "names will never hurt" you?

Wrong-orama.

Recent research finds that name-calling isn't so benign. In fact, those names will kick you in the teeth and then hold your head down in the toilet and give you a swirly.

It turns out that what researchers call "social pain"—the emotional hurt you feel from bullying and rejection—hits you in the same regions of the brain as physical pain (like the dorsal anterior cingulate cortex and the anterior insula, in case you were wondering).

Yes, once again, it's that "shared sink" in our brain between the emotional and the physical, and once again, its workings show up in metaphor. As one of the researchers, UCLA neuroscientist Naomi Eisenberger, explains, "When people feel rejected or left out, they often describe their feelings with physical pain words, complaining of '*hurt* feelings,' '*broken* hearts,' or 'feeling *crushed*.'"

By the way, this finding is more than an interesting science factoid. It leads to some seriously good news.

Consider what you do to relieve physical pain, like if you twist your ankle really badly. Maybe you pop a few Tylenol to dull the throbbing, which allows you to sleep at night and maybe even hobble to the bathroom without waking the neighbors with your screaming.

Well, a team of researchers, led by social psychologist C. Nathan DeWall, discovered something amazing: Tylenol also diminishes *emotional* pain. The researchers had subjects take 500 milligrams of acetaminophen (the generic of Tylenol) twice daily for three weeks. The subjects reported that it reduced the pain they felt from social exclusion—more and more over the course of the study. Brain imaging also showed an effect: decreased activity in the regions where pain shows up (compared with that of the unlucky fucks who got the placebo).

However, it seems that it doesn't actually take three weeks for the Tylenol to alleviate the pain of rejectionitis. In another study, psychologist Daniel Randles and his colleagues found that a single "acute dose"—1,000 milligrams of acetaminophen—worked as an existential angst-reliever, muting subjects' uneasiness after the charming exercise of writing about either the fun of dental pain or what will happen to their body after they die. ("Welcome to the Million Maggot March!")

Because of their finding, I've made Tylenol my drug of choice before I do a speaking engagement. These days, when you're speaking to a group, you look out onto at least a handful of people with their eyes locked to their wireless devices. I suspect the Tylenol dulls my flash of "Eek! I'm boring them!" anxiety while also making me care a little less that the guy in the front row is probably tweeting upskirt photos of me from his iPhone.

But before you start popping Tylenol daily like Tic Tacs, a caveat: A study led by Ohio State University doctoral student Geoffrey Durso found that acetaminophen didn't just blunt negative emotion for their research subjects. It shut down "extremely positive" emotion by twenty percent, as well. In fact, the more intense the emotion— whether positive or negative—the more the acetaminophen shut it down.

And another warning against daily use for those who'd like to keep the internal organs they have: Regular use of acetaminophen can lead to liver damage. Kidney damage and even kidney cancer can be a problem for people who drink alcohol while taking it. (Happy hour tends to be a little less happy when it may lead to weekly dialysis.)

However, neuroscientist Naomi Eisenberger told me that she suspects that aspirin would have an effect similar to that of Tylenol, as both decrease inflammation. Inflammation is commonly thought of as an immune system response to getting physically sick or injured, but Eisenberger and her colleagues have also observed that it gets jacked up in response to emotional wounds.

And, right in line with findings that support the notion of the "shared sink" in the brain, the researchers speculate that "social rejection may trigger inflammatory activity to manage the possibility of injury." (Think of it like having the fire department waiting on your porch while your cooking-challenged girlfriend follows through on her threat to make you a romantic dinner.)

As I wait for somebody to run a study on the effects of aspirin, the essential takeaway remains—the amazing finding that an over-the-counter drug that blunts the pain of a sprained ankle seems to have similar effects on a sprained ego.*

Again, I wouldn't take one of these pills daily (unless the VIP list you're looking to get on is the one for organ transplants). However, for the occasional emotionally stressful event like a presentation you have to give, it may be just the thing to keep a lid on your social anxiety: the difference between a colleague saying your ideas are "a breath of fresh air" and shouting, "Slow deep breaths! The EMTs are on their way!"

THE EMOTIONAL/PHYSICAL PAIN OVERLAP
ISN'T JUST A COOL PARTY TRICK BY YOUR BRAIN

Understanding what's behind this emotional/physical pain overlap and how to make use of it starts with a little refresher on evolution.

Evolution works through a process of "selection"—selecting traits to pass on to the next generation that best help an organism "adapt" to its environment, meaning manage the problems and opportunities that the environment serves up.

Consider the trait of skin color. Some people have very dark skin and others (like me) have skin the color of fresh Wite-Out. If the environment is Africa, well, please come visit me as I'm dying of melanoma. If, however, the environment is often-overcast eastern Europe, the dark-skinned person had better go get tested for vitamin D deficiency before they're in the hospital getting treated for rickets.

Africa and the European backwoods are, of course, physical envi-

---

* Departing the pharmacy for the farmacy, social psychologist DeWall and his colleagues found that pot blunted the emotional pain of lonely people. (Bong hits for rejection!) Yay! Oh . . . wait . . . except for how pot can also blunt your will to do anything but stare at the coffee table and wonder why it doesn't jog off on its stubby little legs to get you more Doritos.

ronments, but there's also a social environment. Whichever it happened to be—physical or social—organisms with the traits best suited
for it would out-survive and out-mate the others, allowing their traits
to prevail in future generations.

At least that's how evolution worked until we got, as they say, *all
modern and shit.*

In modern human society, innovations over the past few
centuries—and especially medical advances—have helped many
people survive previously deadly diseases, life-threateningly moronic
behaviors, and myriad sucky traits that would have offed them in short
order in Paleolithic times.

Also, for most of human history, women didn't *decide* to have
children; they passed on their genes (and their environmentally winning traits) simply because they had sex. Today, however, modern
birth control methods allow women like me to answer the cocktail
party question "So...do you have any children?" with "Not unless
one broke into my house and is hiding in the attic."

And finally, you'd think our human psychological operating system
would, oh, check its Apple Watch and notice that it's the twenty-
first century and—whoops!—upgrade human psychology accordingly. However, evolution doesn't work that fast. In fact, anthropologist
Donald Symons explains that "natural selection takes hundreds
or thousands of generations to fashion any complex cognitive
adaptation."*

So, while it will probably be only a matter of decades until we all
have not only self-driving but self-flying cars, we're stuck with bodies and a psychological operating system that are seriously antique—
and thus mismatched for our current environment.

As for how this plays out, take the adrenaline-fueled fight-or-flight
response that would help you escape a pack of feral hogs (surely a

---

*Generations are considered to be 20- to 30-year periods, with 30 being the estimate for modern
generations.

common experience when you're going to the grocery store in your motor vehicle to buy a package of shrink-wrapped pork chops). It turns out that *a mere verbal attack* (perhaps a wee bit more likely in modern society) triggers this same fight-or-flight response. However, in the wake of mere harsh words, there's none of the physical release of bolting the hell away from a marauding pack of monster pigs. This means that the flight-or-flight stress hormones released when we're afraid or angry just pool and poison us instead of being burned off.

Evolutionary psychologists Leda Cosmides and John Tooby sum up our problem: "Our modern skulls house a stone age mind" with "stone age priorities."

Some of these "stone age priorities" still driving us come out of how we evolved to be a social species—to live cooperatively with other people in small, consistent groups.

In ancestral times, especially, our lives hinged on what the other people in our group thought of us—whether they saw us as valuable to the group's welfare, a drag on resources, or, worse, a shameless freeloader. Social rejection—being booted from the group and made to go it alone—would very likely have meant death back then, before the invention of Motel 6, couch surfing, or even couches. And even for social outcasts who didn't get cast out—who just got put on the ancestral equivalent of the D-list—there were survival costs, like being shoved to the end of the line for food, perks, and favors.

Alas, our dumbass antique psychology is under the impression that we're still living in the sort of ancestral hunter-gatherer environment in which some or many of us would be lucky to see a hundred people in our lifetime. Back in that environment, according to separate estimates by anthropologists Robert L. Kelly and Irven DeVore, it's possible that a person would be stuck with pretty much the same twenty-five people until he or she kicked off.

In other words, it makes sense that social pain would jack up activity in the same brain regions as the physical kind. Neuroscientist Naomi Eisenberger describes the emotional/physical pain overlap as "a common neural alarm system" warning us to "prevent the potentially harmful consequences of social separation." In plain English, the ouchie we get from emotional pain tells us, "Hey, dumbshit! Do something before we're out on our ass alone in the Serengeti!" (Never mind how, these days, we're actually living in a vast and highly mobile modern society and if somebody important in our circle decides we suck, we can easily move to another city, get another job, or just start hanging out at a different bar.)

YES, THAT'S CHARLES DARWIN PICKING YOU LAST FOR KICKBALL

Studies from behavioral science and neuroscience show us *how* we behave. Applying evolutionary psychology—how certain behaviors would have served us in an ancestral environment—explains *why* we behave as we do.

No, evolution isn't all "Hey, let's throw some random behavioral shit up on the wall and see what sticks." Likewise, your emotions didn't evolve to make you feel crappy because they're bored or sadistic or they lack hobbies. ("Yo, Sarah. It's 12:35, and it's been at least two hours since you worried that you'll die alone and your cat will eat your face.")

Recall that emotions are motivational tools. They evolved to push us to act in ways that ultimately help us survive and mate, which is how we pass on our genes. So when you're trying to understand some behavior—yours or somebody else's—it helps to look at it through these two main evolutionary objectives:

SURVIVAL: escaping the guy in the loincloth with dessert plates in his earlobes who's coming at you with a bloody spear.

MATING: persuading somebody to, uh, come up and see your cave paintings.

Not all behaviors lead so obviously to survival and mating—but they're all attempts to get there. Take generosity—and, more importantly, being seen as generous by others in your hunter-gatherer band. If you're a guy, this helps you get the girl, since women evolved to look for men who are willing to fork over resources to support them and their little Neanderbrowed whippersnappers.

However, being considered too generous—a pushover—will work against you. Women will see you as a wimpy suck-up who won't be able to defend them. And, thanks to the antique psychology still driving us, no, the ladies do not take into account that these days, a four-foot geek could bring down some cauliflower-eared MMA gorilla with one sweaty little finger, squeezing off a shot from his Ruger.

What's essential to note from these examples is that our generosity or pushoverhood is measured in other people's eyes. In all of our interactions, we are acutely aware that we are playing for an audience. This makes sense, since what has truly mattered for our mating and survival is not what we think of ourselves but what other people think of us.

And this is precisely where psychologists have gone wrong on the very-much-misnamed "*self*-esteem."

THERE'S NO GOOD EVOLUTIONARY REASON FOR YOU TO LIKE YOU

Throw away everything you think about self-esteem.

Psychologists have long defined self-esteem as your overall evaluation of your own worth—basically, how good or bad you feel about yourself.

This led to the self-esteem industry, which led to books, seminars, grade inflation, participation trophies, and personal theme songs like "I Am Special" (sung to the tune of "Frère Jacques"). Yet, countless people found themselves feeling about as crappy about themselves as they did before they limped onto the self-esteem assembly line.

It turns out that this "I like me!" state we've all been told to strive for—the one we've been told is primary to our well-being—*makes little functional sense.*

Psychology researchers and therapists far and wide failed to ask the "why?" question that evolutionary psychology demands: Why would it be evolutionarily advantageous for you to like yourself—for you to sit around saying, "I'm fabulous! Kiss the royal hand!"?

What actually would have helped our distant ancestors survive and mate is for *other people* to have liked them—meaning respected them, maybe wanted to have sex with them, and wanted to pass them that extra piece of meat.

Sure, there is the argument that feeling confident helps you lead other people to believe you're worthy (of whatever you happen to be pitching yourself for). And, sure, there are those unconfident people who can fake confidence well and others who are, um, *a little generous* in how positively they see themselves. They may get a little boost in other people's eyes because of that—at least until they get found out.

However, confidence is not the same as self-esteem. True confidence is not just a feeling; it is action-driven. It is your prediction of how you'll do in some situation *based on your prior performance* and how you feel and act in light of that. In other words, the "I got this" feeling of confidence is not something you can fake, and it's very different from the baseless "I like me!" that's been sold to us by self-esteem peddlers as the feeling we simply must have.

What's especially nutty, however, is the self-esteem industry's dogma that caring about what other people think of you is a sign that, psychologically, you're a broken toy.

Again, we are people who evolved to care very much about what others think—because our survival depended on it.

SELF-ESTEEM SHOULD REALLY BE CALLED
"WHAT OTHER PEOPLE THINK OF ME-ESTEEM"

The International Court of Mean Girls in The Hague, also known as junior high school, doesn't come to an end when you graduate.

Like chickens, humans have a pecking order—a social hierarchy, perpetually ranking and re-ranking each person relative to the others in a particular group. And, again, because ancestral humans in a motel- and 7-Eleven-free environment needed to retain the protection of living in a band, it was vital for them to keep tabs on how they were fitting in, which would allow them to make any necessary repairs or adjustments to their social status.

Recognizing this, anthropologist Jerome Barkow observed that we humans seem to have an *internal monitoring system* to tell us where we stand with our peeps. Barkow concluded that this monitoring system tracks our social status through our levels of *dominance* and *prestige*.

Dominance is the fear-inducing "I can kick your ass"-ness—the brute way to stay on top. Cultural anthropologist Joseph Henrich describes dominance as *forcing deference* out of others. It's more of a factor in nonhuman societies, though it also shows up in human society, in playground bullying, prison, street gangs, and bar brawls. However, in humans, social status is more often about prestige, i.e., earned deference from others—*deference that's freely given* to a person out of, say, respect and admiration for their talents, smarts, generosity, or even sparkling good looks.

Though humans tend to be pretty driven to scramble up the ladder of social standing, whether through dominance or prestige, Barkow notes that this drive is not the "sole human motivation" and that it does not dominate us all equally or even consistently throughout our lives.

What we all do feel throughout our life span is a fundamental need to belong. Noting this, social psychologist Mark Leary broadened Barkow's notion of a dominance/prestige monitor. The way Leary sees it, we have an internal tracking system that helps us keep tabs on "the degree to which other people accept versus reject" us.

To name this inclusion/exclusion tracking system, Leary took the prefix "socio"—which means "relating to society"—and stuck "meter" on the end, coming up with the "sociometer." But since that sounds more like a rectal thermometer for social scientists than a thing that determines much of your future happiness, let's call this social monitor thingy what it is: the accepto-rejecto-meter.

This accepto-rejecto-meter is basically a barometer measuring how much other people think we suck (or rule!). It does this by monitoring the social environment for *cues* about where we stand. It's especially sensitive to negative cues—like indifference, dislike, and rejection—indicating that others' acceptance of us may be on the skids.

However, monitoring how others see us is just the first part of the process. The information the accepto-rejecto-meter picks up gives rise to *emotions* in us—the positive or negative feelings about ourselves that we call "self-esteem." Predictably, you'll feel good when you perceive that you're liked and appreciated by your crew, and you'll feel pretty bad when you sense that they've banished you to Yousuckville.

These feelings that arise are not just there for decoration; they have a very important purpose: pushing you to take *action*—to do some repairs on your social standing (or, when you're doing well, encouraging you to keep on keepin' on).

Again, though these feelings—what we've long understood as "self-esteem"—*result* from the social monitoring process, they are just one part of it. Self-esteem is ultimately an emotion-driven behavioral guidance system—one that likely evolved to help us avoid getting kicked off the social island.

In short, self-esteem is *our perception of what other people think of us*, which gives rise to *feelings in us*, which motivate us to try to *fix or maintain our social position*.

By laying this out in steps, you can see that self-esteem has three parts:

1. A *cue* telling us about how we're doing socially.
2. Our *emotions* in the wake of this information.
3. Emotion-motivated *action* we take to fit in better (or to stay where we are).

And finally, here's how the cue-emotion-action sequence might play out:

CUE: I notice you sneering at me.
EMOTION: I feel shitty that you're sneering.
ACTION: I sniff my pits to make sure my deodorant hasn't taken early retirement.

SELF-ESTEEM IS BASICALLY A HOME
SECURITY SYSTEM FOR THE SELF

Now that you understand how self-esteem actually works, consider the stupidity of articles like "10 Ways to Raise Your Self-Esteem!," advising you of ways to change how you feel about yourself. This is idiotic, since how you feel about yourself *isn't the problem*; it's just your reaction to your social report card—and the midway point in a three-part *system* to monitor and fix your social standing.

Accordingly—and rather revolutionarily—evolutionary psychologists Lee Kirkpatrick and Bruce Ellis point out that low self-esteem is actually not "bad" (nor is high self-esteem "good"). Your level of self-esteem is "adaptive," meaning it's a response—like a home alarm going off when a burglar smashes a window, pushing you to do something before you're tied to a chair and having the combination to the safe beaten out of you.

In other words, as Kirkpatrick and Ellis explain, attempts to merely help people feel better about themselves are treating the symptoms of an illness "without treating their underlying cause." Yes, that's right; the advice countless therapists have been giving for decades is genius on the level of "counseling drivers to feel better about the fact that their car is overheating, rather than stopping and adding water to the radiator."

WHY SELF-ESTEEM AS A MONITORING SYSTEM
MEANS YOU AREN'T PERMANENTLY FUCKED

The fact that self-esteem should rightfully be called "what other people think of me–esteem" means there's hope for anybody looking to crawl out of their social shitcasserole.

Contrary to what countless therapists have advised, this doesn't take years of mental calisthenics. To shut off the pain of social rejection, you need to change the way other people perceive you— get them to stop seeing you as such a loser. And this just takes *behaving differently*—acting like the sort of person that other people think highly of.

Best of all, your new behaviors will lead people to like and even respect you—which will be reflected in how they treat you. You, in turn, will observe that you're being treated better and then feel better about yourself—which will reinforce your continuing to behave in these new ways.

Also playing a part here is the "neurons that fire together wire together" thing, describing how behaviors you repeatedly engage in become increasingly automatic. Accordingly, these new things you're doing, repeated over time, will start to feel more like they're yours— to the point where you won't need to think about them; you'll just do them because they've become who you are.

So, sure, right now, in the words of Johnny Rotten, "you got a problem; the problem is you." But you also have a solution, and that's also you.

JEER PRESSURE

What shame actually is and how to beat it

Gregg, my boyfriend, is a guy's guy from Detroit. He was the literary researcher for the late crime writer Elmore Leonard, whom a London mag called "poet laureate of wild assholes with revolvers."

Gregg has a dark sensibility and sense of humor, which I'm pretty sure come out of his suspicion that we're all doomed. He's built like a bear, and he once described himself as "disheveled in an employed sort of way."

Gregg's job was not for the squeamish. When we first met, he was going out with the Detroit cops to some crime scenes. One was a triple murder, with three charred, chopped-up bodies lying on the floor—you know, like giant shish kebab bits without the sticks.

Not long afterward, at another "scene," as he and the homicide detectives stood over the body, what was there to do but pass around a baggie of the dead guy's miniature Snickers bars? As Gregg put it: "We were just being practical. It was Christmas. It was kind of festive. It was like we were visiting with the guy, except he was dead."

Gregg does have his weaknesses, and they have names like Skipper, Scout, and Lucy the Lonely Pit Bull. Yes, Gregg is dog mush.

He's especially mushy for my dog, Aida, a six-pound Chinese

crested—a breed that's best described...well, you know how dogs supposedly descended from wolves? Aida looks like she descended from My Little Pony.

Early one evening, I came back from visiting a neighbor, and there he was—my big, Detroit-ornery boyfriend, crouched by the sofa at doggy-snout level, cooing in this disturbingly Muppet-esque voice: "You are so cute, little dog, it should be a crime! Yes, it should be against the law!"

He looked up, disturbed to see me there doubled over in silent laughter.

"NO," he said. "You cannot tweet this."

Yes, though it appears Gregg's very much in touch with his cuddly-wuddlier emotions, he prefers that the world believe they're quietly estranged.

"You don't want guys to know about your behind-closed-door habits with little doggies," he explained. "They wanna know that you're playing fetch with your golden retriever, not that you're a slave to some glamorous little micro-geisha."

Gregg's wanting to preserve his man-branding makes evolutionary sense. Psychologist Joyce Benenson, who researches sex differences, explains that men evolved to be the warriors of the species, and this plays out in the acceptable ways for men to express themselves. In fact, there are actually life-or-death reasons for men to be stoic. As I explained—citing Benenson's work—in my syndicated column:

> When you're a warrior, revealing your feelings—like
> having a good cry on the battlefield—puts you at a
> disadvantage. (Kind of like going out in a T-shirt with a
> big arrow and "Your spear here!")

"So," I said to Gregg, "why are you letting me use this story for my book?" (My sneaky way of "asking.")

"Ultimately," he said, "it's a cost-benefit analysis you have to do when you're in a relationship with a woman. What is the cost? An egg-head in Australia is going to read this book and go, 'He likes little dogs. What a sap.' And then there's the benefit—a goodwill bump with you or just not having to deal with the greater cost: 'Why won't you let me use it?' or, worse, tears. Are we done here?"

WELCOME, FUTURE LOSERS OF TOMORROW

The way a Hollywood publicist spins some star's no-show with "Oh, she's in the hospital for exhaustion" has a long legacy.

Because we evolved as a cooperative species and a good reputation was essential to our being allowed to remain in our ancestral band, we're emotionally programmed to read threats to our public image as threats to our survival.

So it makes sense that we care deeply about how we're seen by others—and feel bad when others witness us or hear about us engaging in some less-than-admirable behavior.

But considering this—along with how self-esteem is really "what other people think of me–esteem"—a question occurred to me: Why do we feel like shit about ourselves when there's nobody around but the cat?

Well, it seems that we're deeply affected by the mere *possibility* of others' judging eyeballs on us—like if they could see us eating that whole sleeve of cookies, get a glimpse of that gross mold in our shower, or learn that we haven't washed our sheets since cell phones looked like submarine sandwiches with dial pads.

Recall, from the previous chapter, the *internal monitoring system*

On a bad hair day, a hat will usually suffice. Really.
Photo by Gregg Sutter.

tracking where we stand with our peeps? Well, a system needs software to guide it, and the software for this monitoring thingy appears to be the *internalized standards* for what is and isn't acceptable behavior.

One example of these is our standard for keeping ourselves and our living environment spick-and-span. Evolutionary psychologist Joshua Tybur and his colleagues point out that we evolved to feel disgust at unclean people, places, and things. This feeling leads us to keep our distance from yicky people and stuff, which protects us from disease.

Of course, even the suspicion that a person was carrying some disease would—rather obviously—have an impact on how welcomed they were by their crew. In other words, our feeling bad about having bad hygiene is a preventive measure—an internal alarm that gets sounded to help us guard against the social rejection that would likely come if somebody pointed a finger at us for it.

To explain this another way, our accepto-rejecto-meter, the sociometer, seems to have a *predictive policing function*—a sort of pre-crime department—causing us to respond to threats to our social standing that have yet to be made.

Lovely, huh?

Just the fact that somebody *would* think badly of us if they knew—if they saw or heard about that shameful thing we're doing—is enough to make us feel bad about doing it.

This brings us to shame.

Shame—like Kanye West, factory farming, and starchy carbs—gets a lot of bad press. In fact, we've been schooled by numerous therapists, books, magazine articles, and pop-sci sites to, basically, feel ashamed about feeling ashamed.

This comes out of how shame has been made out to be the maladaptive (as in, damagingly unuseful) emotion of psychologically unhealthy losers.

The problem is, the definition of shame that we've been going by for decades—since the 1970s—is wrong.

The largely unquestioned (and, yes, incorrect!) popular "wisdom" on shame comes from a researcher, Yale clinical psychologist Helen Block Lewis. In 1971, she contended that shame involves a negative evaluation of the *self* whereas guilt stems from a negative evaluation of an *action* a person's taken.

You've probably heard the shorthand version of Lewis's shame-versus-guilt definition—the notion that shame is *"I'm* bad," in contrast with the supposedly "healthier" feeling of guilt, "I *did* something bad."

Granted, a persistent feeling of shame *is* associated with a number of negative physiological and mental health effects—including depression. And of course, feeling shame is about as fun as breaking a bunch of toes or getting electrocuted awake when you flip the switch on your coffeemaker.

But the notion that we would have evolved to believe that we suck (that "I'm bad" thing) just doesn't make evolutionary sense.

Let's check Lewis's definition of shame against the evolutionary "why?"—as in: In an ancestral world, what helpful function would this "I'm bad" belief have had?

Why would feeling that we suck and probably don't deserve to take up space on the planet help us to survive, mate, and get better cuts of bison?

Umm...umm...

Oopsy, huh?

TARRED WITH THE SHAME BRUSH

Shame is actually neither good nor bad. Like self-esteem, shame seems to be a reputation management tool. As evolutionary psychologist Daniel Sznycer and his colleagues put it in a paper, shame is an "emotion program"—a "defensive system" that evolved to keep us from getting "devalued" by others in our social world (which, again, in an ancestral environment, would've been a serious drag on our welfare and possibly even fatal).

Sznycer and his team explain that the feeling of shame is *information-*

driven—brought on by the sense that others could find out about our yicky, dishonorable, or unfair behavior and downgrade us because of it. So, another way to see shame is as a sort of inner crisis PR specialist—urging us to keep unsavory facts about ourselves from getting out and tanking our reputation or, if that happens, urging us to take steps to minimize the damage.

Shame comes in two flavors—universal and local. Though humans around the globe evolved to be (universally) disgusted by disease-carrying stuff (like boogers and rotting corpses), cultures vary, and so do some of the *specific behaviors* people in them find shameful. For an example in the table manners department, as an American, using your left hand to pass the potatoes is beyond unremarkable. However, you'd probably gross people out if you did that in India, where the left hand is the one traditionally used for post-poo duties.*

Understanding cultural nuances like this, the Sznycer team came up with twenty-nine *general* shame-evoking scenarios—involving theft, infidelity, stinginess, and other behaviors. They gave these to subjects in three countries—the U.S., Israel, and India. In each country, they divided the subjects into two groups—with one group answering as if they'd done the shameful things and the other responding as if they'd witnessed them.

The results in each culture corresponded in an essential way: The level of shame people said they'd feel for engaging in some behavior closely tracked the degree of devaluation others would assign for that behavior. This shows that the amount of shame we feel for a particular act is neither personal nor arbitrary, and in turn, it supports the notion that we evolved to have internalized standards that dissuade us from behaving in ways that will get us kicked down the social totem pole.

---

* Sznycer and his colleagues note that though the particulars of shame vary by culture, the subject matter ought to ultimately be the same, like disease avoidance, showing loyalty to parents, and being a trustworthy group member. So, though we don't have the left hand as the poo hand in the U.S., the prospect of poo getting near food yucks us out, same as it does people in India.

Sznycer explained to me that it's "a basic design feature of defensive systems" to "activate in proportion to the threat they defend against." This is true of defensive systems across the board—like in the military domain, law enforcement, and pest control. As for an example of proportionate response, consider that the Orkin man doesn't bungee a nuclear warhead onto his pickup truck when you need to rid your house of termites.

Close calibration of the defense level to the threat level is a way to "avoid the twin errors of overshooting and undershooting," Sznycer says. "So you can say shame is nicely engineered, because it has this design feature."

The really remarkable thing from their findings was a universality to the shame and devaluation—with U.S. shame for a particular act tracking the devaluation in India and Israel, and vice versa. As Sznycer explains, "This suggests that the things that audiences devalue (and people find shameful) are very similar across cultures."

Getting back to shame's colleague, guilt is also powered up by internalized standards, but it's different from shame. Sznycer and his team explain that whereas shame involves your avoiding being devalued by others, guilt comes out of a feeling that you've shortchanged somebody you value—motivating you to try to right the balance.

Sznycer explained to me that there are people in our lives whose welfare we have a stake in. These include children (who are passing on our genes), people who share our worldview and thus act in ways that benefit us (fellow Democrats, fellow Republicans, fellow communists), and good friends (who value *our* welfare). You want to treat these people well, Sznycer advises, "because if you harm them, you are harming yourself (to some degree, of course)."

So, for an executive summary:

Shame is image-oriented: You don't want to *be seen* as a
   doucheberry, and this may motivate you to avoid acting
   like one.

Guilt is relationship-driven: You don't want to *be* a doucheberry to somebody you care about, so you're compelled to act in their best interest, even when you can get away with screwing them over.

The Sznycer team has a helpful comparison in their paper, using guilt and shame in infidelity.

Say you're cheating on your partner.

If you feel guilt *and* shame, you may be motivated to stop. You could get found out (shame!), plus you start having pangs about how your loving boo deserves better from you (guilt!).

But say you feel shame *but not guilt*. Uh-oh. In this case, you're more likely to keep cheating. You'll just work harder to hide it—like by meeting your fuckhoney at out-of-the-way motels, paying in cash, and signing the register with a name from *Scooby-Doo*.

CONFORM FOLLOWS FUNCTION

If I were a crow on a wire, I'd be the hot-pink one on the end.

At twelve, when everybody was wearing polyester vests and pant-suits, I started going around in a floor-length tiered skirt I made out of a light-pink cotton bedsheet my mother was giving to Goodwill.

Though my fave item of clothing was about as goth as cotton candy, my humor has always been very dark. At fifteen, in my high-school ceramics class, I made dozens of little people trapped in clay jars. Each had their tongue sticking out, bulging eyeballs, and other signs of choking for air. I found this hilarious, but I suspect that if a shrink had seen these, I would have ended up a bed over from one of those kids who hurt pets.

Clearly, despite my deep longing to escape my continuing pariah-hood, there was a part of me that just wasn't willing to do the stuff to be like everybody else. In fact, I think I even enjoyed sending the message, "I've gotten the social marching orders, and I'm going to thumb my little freckled nose at them."

I'm telling you this because it's easy to make the leap from understanding shame as a reputation defense system to assuming that we need to conform to make it in the social world.

And sure, there is a stack of social science research papers (starting with psychologist Solomon Asch back in the 1950s) that suggest that humans are conformist creatures. And sure, we all need to hit the marks to some degree, like by bathing with some regularity and not bringing Silly String to job interviews or Shetland ponies to funerals.

But once again, an evolutionary understanding is essential. Why would conformity have helped us survive and get laid in an ancestral environment? (COME ON! What woman doesn't want to have sex with the crowd-following yes man?)

Though we evolved to live cooperatively—and conformity is often a part of that—evolutionary psychologist Sznycer explains that the human mind is designed for *resisting devaluation*, not for conforming. In fact, Sznycer observes that there appears to be "pervasive design for resisting conformity."

A good deal of research supports this notion, like psychologist Jack Brehm's work on "psychological reactance," which finds that the more we're pressured to do something or to adopt a certain view or attitude the more we'll try to resist being controlled. We also tend to respect people who are independent thinkers and who have the guts to stand up for their beliefs.

The truth is, though conforming is *often* in our interest, sometimes, being the outlier—taking the original or oddball way out—pays off better for us than following the pack.

When you're facing a decision on whether to conform, there are a couple of questions to ask yourself:

- Is going your own way a smarter strategy in the situation than going with the herd? (I was tempted to drop out of college three years in. I was impatient to get out into the

work world, plus it seemed stupid to hang around and pay
to do what I do anyway—have my face in a book half the
day. But, recognizing that some businesses won't hire you
without a degree or will use it as an excuse to give you
suckier pay, I stuck it out and graduated.)

- Can you *afford* to go rogue—as in, do you have the social
  and emotional capital to shrug off the costs of flying your
  freak flag? Or...is the potential benefit so worthwhile that
  you're willing to accept the costs?

BEATING SHAME

There's that famous Watergate-era line: "It's not the crime that gets
you; it's the cover-up."

The truth is, it's sometimes the crime. However, if you own up to
what you've done instead of getting found out, you'll often be viewed
much less harshly.

Take author and former comedian Amy Dresner.

As a drug, alcohol, and sex addict, Dresner was something of a late
bloomer. Dresner grew up privileged in Beverly Hills—a good girl
who excelled in school and didn't even try drugs or have sex until her
early 20s. But then, making up for her late start, she became an addiction overachiever—at one point staying up for seventeen days on
meth and feeling sure she'd come up with the mathematical equation
for god. One day, while shooting cocaine, she had a grand mal seizure,
nearly cracking her head open. This did send her a message—no, not
to stop but to wear a bike helmet while shooting up...just in case.

If there were a museum of shame, Dresner's two decades of addiction would be in it. She repeatedly violated numerous societal
standards—and no, not by littering or parking in the handicapped
space while running to the ATM. She did IV drugs, got committed
to psych wards on four separate occasions, and gave herself permanent brain damage in the form of epilepsy. She also notes that some

of her history is "especially stigmatizing for a woman, like sex addiction and being arrested for domestic violence" after waving a knife at her now-ex-husband while high on oxycodone.

Once Dresner got sober, she needed to take control of the damaging facts about herself—facts that could be unleashed on her at any moment and mess up the post-addiction life she was trying to lead.

She decided to "flip shame"—to "just completely own" everything she'd done and put all the shameful stuff out there herself. She started writing a regular column for the addiction/recovery site The Fix and speaking publicly about her experience, and she eventually wrote a memoir, "My Fair Junkie: A Memoir of Getting Dirty and Staying Clean." As Dresner explains it, "Instead of worrying that people would find out, I made sure they knew."

Dresner's stock in trade is merciless honesty and in-your-face humor. Instead of downplaying her domestic violence, she details it, announcing to a packed room at an addiction treatment center, "Being arrested really took the shine off handcuffs for me—even the furry ones."

She ultimately sees her openness as a way to "rejigger the power structure"—the power other people could have over her. "The value of gossip is that it's secret info that somebody's passing along. It takes the charge out of it if you've already revealed everything. And then," she said (referring to her column), "if the information is in an article you write on a website that's getting millions of hits, it's not gossip anymore; it's journalism."

WHEN BAD IS GOOD

Discovering that somebody's struggled with addiction—especially to the degree Dresner has—typically leads to their being dinged with what Sznycer, in academic-ese, describes as "reduced social value." After all, as Dresner puts it, " nobody says, 'I'm just looking to settle down with a nice IV drug user and sex addict with a criminal history.' "

Though there are people who will always look down on Dresner, she's won many over. Her strategy—"owning" behavior people consider shameful instead of hiding it—is effective because it's what anthropologists and animal behaviorists call a "costly signal." This describes an extravagant or risky trait or behavior that comes at a high price—one that handicaps a person or critter's chances of survival and/or mating. This, in turn, suggests that it's a reliable signal of their strength or other valuable qualities.

Israeli zoologist Amotz Zahavi, who calls this "the handicap principle," gives the example of a little show gazelles put on for hyenas.

Hyenas have a name for gazelles: "Lunch." So when a gazelle spots a hyena on the horizon, it goes, "Holyfuckamole! Time to bolt!" And some gazelles do take off—the weaker ones. But the strongest ones often stick around and do this weird thing called "stotting"— bouncing up and down in place, as if to say to the hyena, "Look, bro, I am gonna finish my espresso and maybe have a cigarette, and then I'll consider taking off."

Well, it turns out that the gazelles that the hyenas typically go after are not those that hang around and stot but those that are quickest to skedaddle—in other words, the gazelles showing that they have reason to be afraid.

The message here? If you're one of the, um, scrawnier gazelles, stotting (as in, putting on a brave show) may sometimes work for you. It is a risk, because others may see through it, but if the cost of failing isn't ending up having your arm gnawed off by a hyena, it might just be a risk worth taking.

WALK THE TALK

We should all be a little more Italian.

I speak almost no Italian, but when I stayed with friends in Rome for a month, I managed to understand a good deal of what non-English speakers were saying because maybe thirty percent of any conversation was carried on by people talking with their hands. (Yes, I know this is a stereotype—and, worse, a cliché—but it didn't come out of thin air.)

When you have something to communicate, expressing yourself shouldn't be something you do only by moving your lips. Consider that Amy Dresner is a powerful speaker—and successful at winning people over—because her refusal to "hang her head" isn't just a figure of speech. Dresner stands tall and marches people through her drug, sex, mental hospital and rehab humiliations like she's leading a tour, making sure they all get a good view of her low points (and the low points on her low points). For example:

> "These days, I've gotten very picky about what I put in my body...I'm all 'I don't eat dairy or gluten, blah, blah, blah...' but I'm just waiting for some old friend to go, 'Wait—didn't you used to smoke meth made with Drano and shoot cocaine cut with laundry detergent into your neck?' "

Dresner's physical presence—taking up space like she owns the place (along with taking over the airspace with her big, Lauren Bacall–husky voice)—is the embodiment of her refusal to accept the shame she's "supposed" to feel. This is essential, because our body language (including our tone of voice) can either confirm or undermine the words we're speaking.

The problem is leakage. Because emotion is expressed by the body, you may not do such a great job of communicating "I'm confident that...!" when dew (aka flop sweat) is forming on your upper lip and it feels like your rib cage has become a bouncy house for your heart.

To get your body to behave, what you can do is practice—before you get into a situation—using the body language of confidence. This means standing tall, speaking in the voice you'd use to tell somebody some important truth, and taking up space when you're talking (like Dresner) instead of standing all scrunched-up like you want to disappear or die.

Your goal should be getting used to standing and carrying yourself in these new ways, in hopes that you'll get to the point where your body just automatically "assumes the position"—of confidence, that is—without your having to think about it.

What you don't want to do when you're speaking is to be all up in your head about how you're standing or sounding or what your body parts are doing. Sian Beilock, who researches performance anxiety, finds that this tends to cause a person to "choke."

Accordingly, it should help to pair this walking-the-talk business with techniques for calming the fuck down—as seen in the chapters on ritual (chapters 6 and 7) and the one on not letting your feelings boss you around (chapter 11).

Initially, despite your trying to show the bodily signs of being confident, be prepared for some of the wrong body language to pop up (like those syphilitic showgirls, fear and doubt). That's okay. In fact, it's to be expected. When this happens, try to view it as part of a larger process—your project to change how you walk, talk, and act. Ultimately, you're on your way—working toward approaching life's little battles more like Julius Caesar ("I came; I saw; I conquered!") than the salad kind: "I came; I saw . . . I hid under a big crouton."

YOU SUCK. OR DO YOU?

Confidence, assertiveness, and the Self sisters
(self-compassion, self-acceptance, and self-respect)

I've been rejected a lot in my life—by both people and houseplants.

Yes, while other people successfully raise families, I can't even successfully raise a fern. Though I follow the directions on the little plastic tab that comes in the pot, it sometimes takes a week; it sometimes takes a few months; but there's one thing all plants that come into my life have in common: They commit suicide on me.

Being abandoned—even by something with leaves and a stem—feels pretty bad.

But rejection by people—friends, lovers, employers, or even strangers—can drag you into a really dark place. It says you aren't worthy; there's surely nothing you can do to be worthy; and you should probably do the world a favor and follow the lead of my plants.

Right? That's how it feels, anyway.

Then again...maybe, just maybe, rejection is whatever you *say* it is.

That's how my author and professor friend Susan Shapiro plays it. It started early on in her career as a writer, when she'd amassed quite a collection of rejection letters from magazine editors. But being Sue, she didn't dump them in a drawer or use them to clean up cat puke. She pasted them all over her walls and threw a party.

I was at that first rejection-letter party, back in the late '80s.

Sue now throws these parties regularly for her writing students. A rejection letter for an article or book is the ticket to get in. She makes her students tape theirs to her walls—next to her own. She explains to them that "a rejection from an editor (is) a great sign, because it (means you're) out there, trying." It's just a process you go through— "a rite of passage." She adds, "I especially loved the ones from publications who later bought my work."

In Sue's book *Only as Good as Your Word: Writing Lessons from My Favorite Literary Gurus,* she further explains the thinking that keeps her so intrepid: "In this biz, no never means no. (It means rewrite, retitle, respin, add a more timely lede, and resend it to the hopefully nicer editor at the next cubicle.)"

She's right; however, it isn't just in the writing biz that this is true. In life, what happens to you happens to you, but you retain some control—over how you see it and what you do about it. With a little help from these buggers just below.

SELF-ESTEEM HAS A FEW COUSINS

Self-esteem doesn't quite have a family tree; it's more of a family shrub.

On it are a few branches of Selfs—Self-confidence, Self-acceptance, Self-compassion, Self-assertiveness, and Self-respect.

We tend to see all of these as feelings we can do little about. And that's where we're wrong.

Self-confidence, self-assertiveness, and self-respect come out of what we do—which means we can have more of each simply by doing things differently. Yay, right?

And though self-compassion and self-acceptance *are* feelings, they're feelings we can choose to have. For example, you can just choose to accept yourself. Decide you're going to do it, and then do it. And really, you need to—because you can't very well expect other people to be nice to you if you aren't willing to lead the way.

SELF-CONFIDENCE (STREET NAME: CONFIDENCE)

Confidence—the feeling of "I got this!"—popped up in the previous chapter. Recall that confidence is action-driven. It's our prediction that we'll do well at something *based on our prior performance.*

Though we tend to perceive people as having overall confidence (what researchers call a "global" quality), confidence actually varies depending on our chops in a particular area. As evolutionary psychologists Lee Kirkpatrick and Bruce Ellis explain, our performance-based evaluation of ourselves is "domain-specific," meaning that we can have very different levels of confidence in different areas of our lives. In ancestral terms, this means you might be a guy who's gangbusters at bringing down a bison (fantastic in the "work" domain) but socially, kind of dim. So, based on your history, you'd be a very confident hunter and a rather unconfident lady-hunter.

Confidence, however, is not just a feeling; it's a form of advertising for the self. Personality psychologist Tomas Chamorro-Premuzic explains that we tend to read people's confidence as *competence*, making the assumption that confident people have the skills and ability to back it up. They don't necessarily—but they may not be trying to put one over on us. Sometimes they're just good at self-deception (aka "believing your own bullshit").

But because confidence is performance-driven, you can increase yours through practice—that is, by becoming more competent at something. You might also invite self-acceptance and self-compassion to sit in on your practice sessions, which should make you less likely to follow them up with one of those long, luxurious baths in self-loathing.

Of course, a big change you need to make can seem overwhelming—too big to even start. But I've learned to make even the biggest changes feel doable by taking them on bit by bit, step by step. I also take my own advice above and apply self-acceptance and self-compassion, which help me avoid hating myself for failing to become an expert in the time it takes to bring Cup Noodles to its full chicken-, beef-, or shrimp-flavor(ed) promise.

Take how I de-suckified my TV and radio persona. I was getting booked for TV and radio somewhat infrequently, which made every appearance seem wildly important—like it would be THE END OF THE WORLD!!! if I didn't slay. This, in turn, made me terrified of screwing up or not being interesting or funny—which made me screw up and not be interesting or funny.

Hoping to either practice or bore myself out of being scared, I signed up to do a $40-a-month podcast on Blog Talk Radio. (P.S. That's $40 I paid them, not the other way around.)

I was kind of excited about my little weekly show, so I sent a link to one episode to my Los Angeles radio pro friend, news reporter Michael Linder. Looking back, I'm guessing his initial reaction could probably be described as "silently horrified," but he emailed me something tactfully supportive, like "Great you're doing this." He then took me out for a drink and gently told me all the things I needed to change. (Apparently, in addition to talking about twice as fast as is comprehensible to a normal human brain, I was saying "you know" and "um" about twenty-eight times a minute.)

I posted a fluorescent Post-it on my wall: "No 'you know' or 'um.'" On a vase across from my desk, I stuck another Post-it: "SLOW! Clear!" (My boyfriend left a companion Post-it: "FAST! Indecisive!")

Week after week, I tried to do better. Sometimes I did; sometimes I didn't. But I kept at it.

After three years, my little homegrown weekly podcast—which I recorded while pacing in my underwear and a tank top in front of my home computer—won an honorable mention in the Los Angeles Press Club Awards for best radio documentary, beating out finalists from the pledge-driven public radio powerhouse KCRW. And these days, there's a new Amy on radio and TV—one who sometimes goes a little speedy but who, for the most part, isn't leaving the audience wondering whether the search-and-rescue chopper will get to her before her walkie-talkie battery craps out.

SELF-ACCEPTANCE

Self-acceptance is best understood in contrast with self-*unacceptance*, which is basically seeing yourself as a wheelbarrow of crap with credit card debt.

Self-acceptance is a sort of default "I'm okay"-ness. It's an acceptance of all the raw material that is you (including your feelings and doings—the good, the bad, the boring, and the "holy shit, that's ugly").

Accepting yourself in this way doesn't necessarily mean liking or even approving of all of you. It just means understanding that simply because you exist, you have a right to exist—to be on the planet and to try to scrape up some happiness for yourself.

Many of us wait for self-acceptance to come to us, like it's some traveling salesman who'll knock on our door someday. Bad strategy. You need to work your way to self-acceptance. As for a timetable, an ideal one comes from the rabbi-philosopher Hillel: "If not now, when?"

For a starting point, consider the sunblock term "broad spectrum." That's how you need to look at yourself—by putting yourself in context with the rest of humanity. We humans are all flawed and make assholish errors. But, in every one of us, that stuff goes with the good stuff about us. It's a package deal.

Take me, for example. I have ADHD—attention deficit hyperactivity disorder, or, as my boyfriend puts it: "Do I have your divided attention?"

ADHD is idiotically named, because we who have it don't have a deficit of attention; we just have problems controlling where it goes. And where it goes, in me, is all over the fucking place, all at once.* This attention-to-everything business is problematic because, if you are paying attention to sixteen things at once, you aren't really paying adequate attention to any of them—which is to say, when I need to go somewhere, I should first check the freezer for my keys.

Yes, this is a pain in my frighteningly white ass. Still, I see ADHD not as a disorder but as a feature—because I'm pretty sure I'm vastly more creative and funny than I would be if my brain weren't making all the wild connections it does by bouncing around like a carpet beetle having a panic attack.

With my ADHD also comes this bursting energy. (Think five-year-old on a sugar rush.) This is great when I need to get things done, but it often needs to be held in check, like if you're talking to me in a less-than-rapid-fire way—as in, slowly and thoughtfully. Slow-speed speech is hard on my brain, which, like autocomplete in a web browser, has already predicted the end of the sentence you're... TOTALLY ANNOYINGLY meandering toward.

I, of course, can't just cut you off and get on with telling you what I think—much as I'd like to. But all of that energy I have needs to go someplace, so I channel it downward—into the oh-so-classy habit of pickety-pick-picking my cuticles.

I hate the way my hands look. But because I accept myself—as a person with kind of a cool brain that imposes some costs along with the benefits—I can say, without hating myself, "Well, I *could* find some other form of stress reduction, but I really don't care enough to put in the effort."

And sure, there are times it would be better if I had the hands of an accomplished adult woman instead of an angsty teenager. Luckily, for these occasions, there are full-length black satin opera gloves—

---

*Having ADHD is like trying to think while being attacked by a flock of crows.

which make me look fascinating instead of like a woman whose fingers seem to have been gnawed by a dog.

SELF-COMPASSION

Self-compassion is basically calamine lotion for the red, itchy self— self-soothing kindness and understanding as an antidote to self-hate, self-pity, and other fun forms of psychological cutting.

Self-compassion is helpful in looking at both your shortcomings and your life so far—especially the parts you'd like to shove under a rock. It's a big part of how Amy Dresner comes to grips with her years of addiction and relapse. "For a while," she said, "I did feel like a bad person—a weak, broken person. But then I realized, I'm not a bad person. I did some shitty things. And I have to forgive myself and move forward." She does this by putting things in perspective: "If I could have done better, I would have done better. I did the best I could at the time."

Understanding self-compassion starts with understanding compassion. Compassion, as I defined it in *Good Manners for Nice People Who Sometimes Say F*ck*, is "empathy with an action plan." Upon noticing that "shit, this person is really suffering," it's the desire to make things better—to do something to ease their suffering. This desire comes out of a belief in someone's dignity—the sense that they have value as a person and that their feelings matter.

Applying self-compassion simply involves taking the compassion hose and turning it on yourself when you fail, screw up, or notice things you don't really like about yourself.

Psychologist Kristin Neff, who studies self-compassion, breaks it down into three parts:

1.   Treating yourself with kindness.
2.   Recognizing your "shared humanity."

3. Being mindful when you're considering negative aspects of yourself.

Neff lays out examples of these in her "scale" to measure self-compassion:

> Self-kindness: "I try to be understanding and patient toward aspects of my personality I don't like."

> Shared humanity: "I try to see my failings as part of the human condition." As with self-acceptance, this means cutting yourself a break for being "mortal, vulnerable, and imperfect" (as Neff puts it)—just as you'd likely do for other people.

> Mindfulness: "When something painful happens I try to take a balanced view of the situation." This means standing back a bit from your negative thoughts and emotions, naming them, and then observing them—as opposed to judging yourself for having them or trying to push them away.

Neff notes that many people are reluctant to be self-compassionate because they confuse it with mindless self-indulgence. But, she says, "self-compassion is not a form of positive evaluation." It also doesn't mean ignoring, accepting, or excusing bad behaviors, à la "Yeah, so I strangled my boss, but the copier was broken, and it's my second day without caffeine."

Neff explains that self-compassion just means relating to ourselves with kindness and concern—whether we're living up to our ideals in the moment or seriously sucking at it. Extending this kindness to ourselves, as we would to others, comes with many benefits, including feeling happier, more optimistic, less depressed, and less afraid of failing. Also, self-compassion sure beats the alternatives—self-hatred and -contempt—which, in my experience (and probably yours), are not exactly feelings that have us leaping out of bed in the morning all "Carpe fucking diem!"

SELF-ASSERTIVENESS

Self-assertiveness is the "I've grown a pair!" cousin of self-esteem.

Being assertive simply means standing up for yourself and what you value. This may not come naturally to you, but you don't have to let that be the guideline for how you act. (It might help to talk yourself into being a little mad about whatever's been done to you.)

I learned something about assertiveness when my car was stolen. It was my first car—an absolutely adorable powder-pink 1960 Rambler. I'd bought the thing in a fit of "It's PINK!" when I'd moved from New York to LA, not quite understanding that the reason for having a car is to get places, not to look fabulous while waiting for tow trucks.

My Rambler was an ever-surprising source of mechanical problems and thus a source of unexpected wealth for mechanics around Los Angeles. After all I'd put into it over the years—including my stupidity in thinking that nobody would be dumb enough to steal a pink car—I was outraged that anyone would dare take it from me. But there I was, walking out of my house one day and finding only a few oil spots in its place.

My rage at the indignity of this fired me into a months-long Nancy Drewing to track down the hipster muralist asshole who'd stolen it. One night, when I got a tip from a car parts guy about the whereabouts of the thief, I called the cops, thinking that this would work like it does on TV—that they'd go nab the guy, jail him, and then reunite me with my car. Instead, the desk officer's response: "None of the detectives are here right now. Can you please call back tomorrow?"

Having only the phone number of the thief, not his address—and not knowing what else I could do—I called the number. I yelled into the phone, telling him that I knew everything about him, mentioning his high-school girlfriend and some FBI guy. I yelled some more, promising that the FBI guy would find him and throw him in jail for the rest of his life, and demanded that he bring my car back that evening. Which—rather amazingly—he did.

My little experience with do-it-yourself justice made me feel pretty powerful. And though I won in the end, I realized that even if I hadn't gotten my car back, what mattered—what made me feel so good—was that I had refused to roll over and just take it. You, likewise, may not win in every challenge you take on, but the way to not feel like a victim is to refuse to act like one (assuming whatever you do isn't likely to get your naked dead body dumped in a shallow grave).

SELF-RESPECT

Self-respect isn't some mysteriously occurring feeling. You don't get it from a wizard. It comes from shining your shoes. Hosing down your porch furniture. Washing those dishes scattered all over your house instead of leaving them for the archaeologists to find.

In other words, self-respect is an action. It's something you do—acting self-respectingly; that is, like you have value. Out of that action comes the *feeling* of self-respect.

Understanding self-respect as something you do is exciting, because it means you have control over the level of self-respect you feel. Simply by behaving as the self-respecting you that you want to be, you affect your feelings. Which affects your behavior. Which affects your feelings. Which . . . (you get the drill).

Yes, it's "bidirectionality" popping up again—that back-and-forth between behavior and emotion. Another example of bidirectionality at work comes out of a study on "enclothed cognition"—a term coined by organizational behaviorist Hajo Adam and social psychologist

Adam Galinsky describing the influence our clothes have on our emotions, perceptions, and behavior.

Take a simple white coat. It could be worn by a doctor or by an artist (like a painter). Consider that doctors are supposed to be precise and scientific. However, we see artists differently—as wild, creative, and free-spirited.

In one of Adam and Galinsky's experiments, subjects were given an attention test while they wore either a doctor's lab coat or their street clothes. Those in the doctor's lab coat made about half as many errors. In a subsequent attention test, some subjects were told the white coat was a doctor's lab coat, and others were told it was an artist's (a painter's), and those who thought they were wearing doctor garb showed far more attention to detail.

Once again, this reflects the power our actions have to affect our emotions and our perceptions of the sort of person we are. And this again emphasizes how essential it is for you to see—and treat—self-respect not just as a feeling but as something you do.

This may sound like a big order. And behaving self-respectingly does involve tougher stuff, like refusing to let some office bully take advantage of you. However, you can seed the ground for standing up against the workplace SuperDick by acting self-respectingly in many small ways, every day. As for ways you might incorporate that into your daily life, just consider how you'd treat somebody you respect who's paying you a visit. I'm guessing you'd put out the nice towels. Well, okay. Now start doing that for yourself. And then you'll glance over and be like, "Oooh, look at them fancy towels! Who's the guest of honor? Oh ... right ... ME!"

YOUR FEELINGS ARE NOT
THE BOSS OF YOU

It's not what you feel; it's what you do

There are people who keep their writing "pure" by doing it only when they feel inspired. We call these people "independently wealthy."

For the rest of us, there's the daily terror of the blank page. Come anywhere near it and it sneers, "You suck. You're not interesting. You have nothing to say to anyone. But hey, go ahead and type something."

Truth be told, the fear this provokes can be motivating. For me, it typically leads to a burning desire to clean my refrigerator—a task I usually reserve for when some long-abandoned bowl of leftovers starts growling at me as I open the door.

Unfortunately, my lack of inherited wealth is accompanied by a lack of practical job skills, such as the ability to do more with tools than hold them while smiling flirtatiously. So, I really, really do need to write. Luckily, I've found the perfect way to make myself do that, and it's by *refusing to let my feelings be in charge of my behavior.*

I do this by writing with a timer—fifty-two minutes on and seventeen minutes off. So there's no stalling to the tune of "Whoa . . . I don't think I can pull this piece together"; there's only that bitch, the clock. I turn it on, and no matter how horrified I am by what I've put down on the page, I keep at it until there's that "ding!" of the time running out.

Just to be clear, this clock—a digital timer in the upper left corner of my computer screen—doesn't change my feelings an iota. It simply tells them to fuck the hell off.

This is a beautiful thing—allowing me to earn a living as a writer, and not just of cardboard signs to hold up at the freeway exit asking for spare change. It does have its downsides, but mainly in the housekeeping department. My refrigerator is often a hostel for developing life-forms, and with all the books and research papers piled on any remotely flat surface in my home, my Venice, California, shack is best described as a "walk-in fire hazard with a bed and an oven."

Sure, this can sometimes make finding the dog difficult, but there is a simple (post-book deadline) solution—timed tidying jags! Yes, by bypassing my hatred of the housekeeping arts with that ticktocking Stalin, the clock, I will eventually open my home to visitors who don't come to the door with a search warrant.

FIGHT THE COWER

What I'm saying is that you may *have* a feeling—like the urge to dodge some scary, ego-filleting challenge—but that doesn't mean you have to go all "Yes, your lordship!" in response.

And sure, I did explain in previous chapters that feelings are "motivational tools," but they aren't necessarily motivating you in the right direction, right now. Say there's some person you should talk to—some Hottie McBody or somebody who'd be really good for your career. But—whoops!—up come your feelings, singing their usual tune: "Quick! Find somebody portly to hide behind!"

Your feelings are *trying* to act in your best interest by protecting you from rejection. Unfortunately, it's your *evolutionary* best interest. Yes, it's that annoying mismatch between our evolved psychology and our environment popping up again.

It would have been important for you to "know your place" (and stay in it) back in an ancestral environment, where not showing a sufficient level of deference to the Stone Age quarterback and cheer-leaders could have led to your lonely death by starvation on some rocky outcropping. But these days, the crushing fear driving your so-cial submissiveness no longer makes sense. The worst thing that's likely to happen to you from overstepping is getting humiliated; and "died of embarrassment" is only a figure of speech, not something they write on the forms at the coroner's.

This fear keeping you from going after what you want has a co-conspirator—your "automatic" behavior, i.e., your habits. Because "neurons that fire together wire together," creating behavioral grooves, all of your *ducking* instead of *doing* has turned ducking into your thing. You have become *predisposed* to duck.

Earlier in your life, your nasty ducking habit may have served you—maybe even keeping you from getting your kiddie ass kicked by playground bullies (back before children were monitored like prisoners who've tried to garrote themselves with dental floss). How-ever, being preprogrammed to take cover is not helping you now. In fact, it's doing just the opposite—keeping you from getting up on your hind legs and having the biggest life you can.

The solution is to do what I did: Tell your feelings to beat it, and then get on with doing whatever needs to be done. (Which isn't to say you won't be scared, terrified, nearly shitting your pants, or other-wise ill at ease about it.)

To give you an example, a friend of mine—a fellow author—was chatting with me in the green room at a book festival, when she spot-ted Mr. Famous Agent strolling in, followed by a small entourage. She got excited—and then bummed. She explained that she was afraid to just go up and talk to people—unlike me.

She thinks that way because we write at the same café and she sees, well, the me that I've become—always talking to strangers—so she assumed that I was all cool and comfortable with that. Hah. Au fucking contraire, I told her. I'm often at least a little afraid to strike up a con-versation; it just doesn't seem a good enough reason to avoid doing it.

RETHINKING OUTSIDE THE BOX

You've got your assignment: Blow past your feelings, and act with the confidence you aren't quite feeling.

But wouldn't it be great to have a smaller pile of feelings to blow past? After all, the smaller things are the easier they usually are to manage. It's the principle behind those steel-belted sports bras that compress massive boobage (boobs so top-poppingly enormo that each should get a delegate at the U.N.). And it happens to be a principle you can apply to your fears and other big, ugly emotions.

A technique called "cognitive reappraisal" is really helpful for shrinking your looming sucky feelings to a more manageable size. It simply involves changing how you interpret a situation to change how it impacts you emotionally.

Let's say that you—like my author friend—need to introduce yourself to some important stranger. At the thought of this, a lightning bolt of fear comes down and slices you in two. Now, you could just lie there on the floor in pieces, still smoking slightly, until the stranger goes away—or you could do a little rethinking.

That rethinking would go something like this: *No, this is not a fearsome experience; it's an opportunity.* In fact, you could see it as multiple opportunities. It's an opportunity to show your courage. And it's an opportunity for opportunity. As I say about why I regularly strike up conversations with people I don't know: "Be friendly; magic sometimes happens."

Psychologist James J. Gross, who's done much of the research on reappraisal, finds that reappraisal is most successful when it's done early on in the emotional process—as an emotion is first bubbling up. This helps keep your cognitive resources from getting hijacked, which helps keep you from freezing in place like a pillar of salt.

Cognitive reappraisal does take some mental work, so it's tempting to just try to shove your feelings in the drawer with all the Chinese takeout menus so you can't hear their nasty little whispers about what a big pile of suck you are. However, you read a bit about the late psychologist Daniel Wegner's work in chapter 6. It turns out that emotional suppression—trying to forget, ignore, or shove away thoughts, especially anxiety-producing thoughts—brings them right back up, like one of those bloated dead bodies in New York's East River.

Wegner famously told research subjects, "Try not to think of a white bear"—thus dooming the poor dears to fail at this task right from the start. Trying to *not* do something is a cognitive energy-hogging procedure. Thought suppression is a particularly counterproductive one. It turns out that your mind sweeps around to check on your progress—i.e., whether you're succeeding at not thinking about the white bear, which, of course, involves thinking about the damn bear. (In fact, it pretty much turns your head into a traveling white bear circus.)

There is a trick you can use to prevent those pesky white bears and other unwelcome thoughts from pawing at you. Psychologists Jens Forster and Nira Liberman found that you can keep yourself from endlessly revisiting a thought if you simply admit that not thinking of it is hard.

This solution probably sounds too simple to be for real, but it actually makes sense. Removing the need to patrol your thoughts also removes the mental sticky note that tells you to keep going back into Thoughtland with a flashlight to see how well you're doing at it. So, sure, you still might go back to some unwanted thought from time to time, but not nearly so much as if you told yourself that you absolutely, positively need to avoid doing it.

TURNING NOJO INTO MOJO

Below are some of the cognitive reappraisal techniques I think are the most helpful. But you can also use these as guidelines for coming up with your own, for those times when some social challenge you're facing leaves you feeling like the terrified kid on the business end of the high dive.

GIVE YOUR ANXIETY A NAME CHANGE

There's a whole big section in this book—in chapter 4—about how hard it can be to know exactly which emotion you're feeling. Well, it seems you can use this to your advantage when performance anxiety's got you by the throat.

Harvard Business School's Alison Wood Brooks points out that anxiety is "signaled by increased heart rate"—but so is excitement. Her research suggests that reappraising your pre-performance anxiety as excitement actually helps you feel excited—and less nervous— and perform better because of it.

I do this anxiety-as-excitement reappraisal whenever I'm about to go on the radio for a short segment. Short segments are particularly tough because having only a few minutes puts a lot of pressure on me to be smart and funny in an extremely concise way. Sure, simply telling myself to calm down would be a great idea—except for how my typical pre-media adrenaline surge could be an alternative fuel source for NASA's next rocket launch.

JUST ADD ARETHA

What's scarier for me than the need to be concisely smart and funny on the radio? Well, either being chased down the street by an angry mob armed with flaming pitchforks or being asked to go on some TV show and talk about the science of something or other.

On TV, I need to sound smart and make sense, just like when I'm on the radio. But TV adds the visual element. This means that I have to wrangle my wriggling hands, do my best to look sane, and try to sit at an angle that doesn't make me look like Mr. Ed. (The perils of the long-faced Jew, what can I say?) This pressure combo pack does not make for cool confidence on the air.

So, in addition to telling myself that I'm *excited* to go on the air and *excited* about what I have to say, I increase the power of my reappraisal by bringing in my body and metaphor—the metaphor "happy is up." As for the body part, I make myself do what we do when we feel really "up"—smile big and dance. In dancing, I use big expansive arm movements—"Own it, baby!"-type moves—because research on posture suggests that these broad moves may increase feelings of confidence. (See chapter 15.) I also choose songs that always make me feel excited, happy, and (dare I say) *empowered*—songs belted out by large black women or large black women who are also men named RuPaul.

(To do this one-person dance party thing discreetly in the workplace, go in a bathroom stall with your phone and headphones, and then do your best not to dance your phone into the toilet.)

DON'T TAKE IT PERSONALLY—EVEN IF YOU'RE PRETTY SURE IT *IS* PERSONAL

You can also use this "tell a better story" technique to reinterpret others' behavior toward you. You just make up a little tale about them that involves a less ego-trashing reason for whatever they're doing.

Say somebody hasn't responded to your email. Tell yourself that they're probably slammed at work and really tired, not really tired of you. Picture them disaster movie-style, heroically fighting an onslaught of paper and flying file folders and a paper clip hailstorm.

Of course, you are well aware that you just made up that "slammed at work/really tired" explanation; you can't know for sure that it's the actual reason. Fortunately, that doesn't seem to matter. Energywise, like suburban McMansions, our brains are "expensive" to run. So, as psychologist Daniel Kahneman explains it, they like to take shortcuts whenever they can—going on autopilot instead of going to the trouble of thinking everything out. Or, to put it another way, our lazy-slob brains are suckers for a story, and once you give yours one that's at all plausible, thanks, it'll go with it, and screw the fact-checking.

Most helpfully, providing yourself with a less degrading story to explain somebody's behavior could keep you from prematurely dashing off some resentypants follow-up: "Can't even spare that precious two minutes while you're on the fucking john to email me back?"

That's important, because you'll really feel like an asshole if you get the reply (no joke!) that my journalist friend Joseph Menn eventually sent to an obnoxiously persistent publicist: "Sorry I didn't respond to your pitch; I was in a coma."

WIN SMALL

A natural part of putting yourself out there is getting shot down. When that happens, there's a way to put your loss or failure in perspective—and even make it motivating—and that's by reappraising it as a "small win."

Yes, there really is a tiny victory you can fish out of your loss, and it's that you, a person who's spent years defaulting to social servitude, bucked your psychological system and stood up for yourself for a change. That's really something.

This "small win" idea is actually pretty important for motivation when you're trying to make a big change in yourself. It comes from a classic social science paper by organizational psychologist Karl Weick, exploring what motivates people to take action on social issues.

When a problem is vast—GLOBAL HUNGER!!—we are overwhelmed and feel we can't possibly make a difference, which stops us from doing anything at all. Weick explains that we can overcome this effect by "changing the scale of the problem"—breaking it down into manageable chunks and taking on some tiny part of it. For example, if we address global hunger by bringing a sandwich to a homeless guy, we immediately make a difference, see it right then and there in our own little world, and feel good. And feeling good—feeling we've accomplished something—motivates us to go accomplish more.

CALL A MEETING OF THE LOGIC BOARD

You should also keep in mind that our fears are often overblown and seriously irrational. Because of this, psychologist Albert Ellis, the late co-founder of cognitive behavioral therapy, advocated using reason to reappraise our fears—to help us see how absurd many of them actually are.

Ellis was influenced by the Stoic philosopher Epictetus, who said that it is not things or events that disturb us but the views we take of them. In other words, it isn't what happens or could happen that makes us feel so bad; it's our interpretation of it.

Say we flub a line in a presentation we're giving to a bunch of co-workers.

The ridiculously irrational interpretation:

> "I am a rotten, worthless, accidentally employed turd who
> is only still working here because I'm too insignificant for
> anyone to remember to fire me."

The rational comeback to that:

> "I'm human; humans screw up all the time. I've seen
> colleagues stumble over a word. They just laugh and get
> back to what they were saying. They aren't dragged out of
> the building past a jeering mob of co-workers."

Ellis explains that it's okay to want to do well—to *prefer* to do well. The problem comes when we "awfulize"—engaging in drama-queenie generalizations, like telling ourselves that failing at something will be "awful!" or "horrible!"

Take the unhelpful mental chatter, "It'll be *horrible* if I go ask that girl out and she blows me off." Well, it won't be a birthday party for your ego, but "horrible"?

Give yourself a wee timeout from hyperventilating, and ask yourself something:

> "What is the *worst-case scenario* ... the worst thing that is
> likely to happen if she says no—or even ignores me
> altogether? Will there be a firing squad at dawn? Will a
> wizard appear and turn me into a hairball? Or... *will I feel
> like crap for a few minutes and then get on with my day?*"

If your answer is that last one—that "feel like crap for a few minutes" thing—remind yourself that the worst possible outcome from hitting on a woman (or whatever it is you're doing) will not actually be "horrible." It will merely be kind of a bummer—and a temporary one at that.

USE YOUR WORDS

We typically see our feelings as these abstract mental states. But that's a rather dignified view, and dignity is power. So, instead, think of your feelings—and maybe even talk to them—like they're rotten children: "Really, Fear? Throwing yet another tantrum? Lovely. Yes, go right ahead—dump your applesauce on the floor. You're still not getting your Lego out of toy jail."

Beyond how fun it can be to berate the little shits, as I noted in chapter 4, labeling what you're feeling may be helpful in dialing down the roar of your fear and anxiety.

Using language requires you to put your mental weight on your brain's higher reasoning department, the prefrontal cortex. With that increased activity up there in the front office, there's less activity in your brain's alarm center, the amygdala, which likely means less anxiety coursing through you.

There are actually a number of ways you can use language to cool the jets of your amygdala.

PEN FOR YOUR THOUGHTS

When you're facing a challenge, right before you take it on, writing down what's worrying you may help you yank yourself off the negative-thinking hamster wheel.

Psychologist Sian Beilock has tested this in an area rife with dread for many—math tests. She and her colleagues found that students taking math tests who wrote about their worries for about ten minutes before the test were less anxious and performed about fifteen percent better than those who, say, sat around staring into space and hoping for a miracle.

Beilock explains that the mental processing that goes on in writing may allow a person to tame distracting emotions—shrinking anxiety so it no longer takes over so much of what's called "working memory." Working memory is kind of like a mental whiteboard— a temporary workspace for information you need to keep accessible so you can kick it around in the moment.

Memory researcher Nelson Cowan explains that you need working memory to remember something while engaged in some other task—for example, so you can hang on to partial results while you're solving a multi-step math problem or recall which ingredients you've already added when you're baking a cake. In conversation, working memory is what you'd use to, say, combine premises in your argument for why somebody should hire you—so it isn't exactly ideal to have it temporarily flattened by the fearasaurus.

HISTORICAL FRICTION

While Beilock looked at writing as emotional prep *before* going into some intimidating activity, you can also write about painful experiences that have already happened.

This is called "expressive writing," and it also seems to keep stress and anxiety from taking such big bites out of you.

In psychologist James Pennebaker's first study on expressive writing, back in 1986, students did fifteen minutes of writing, for four days in a row, about the emotional impact of a traumatic experience (such as a loved one's death, childhood trauma, or sexual abuse).

Trauma leads to stress, and stress—especially prolonged stress—can cause all sorts of medical problems. However, in the month after the study, those who'd written about their experience (along with the emotions that went with it) had a fifty percent drop in their visits to the university health center.

Pennebaker explains that the benefit from expressive writing seems to come from reinterpreting and making sense of what happened. In fact, Pennebaker found that the more people who wrote about their trauma used what I'd describe as "explainer" words—words like "because," "reason," and "caused"—as well as insight words (like "understand," "see," and "realize"), the more improvement they saw healthwise.

Interestingly, the writing medium seems to matter, and it may have something to do with the interconnectedness of body and emotion. Using a pen and paper (rather than a computer) seems to be the most beneficial way of doing expressive writing—perhaps because it incorporates the body as part of the mind, without any electronic intermediary.

What seems important in reinterpretation is finding meaning. We toss around that term—finding meaning—but we often don't stop to consider what it, well, really *means*. Meaning is "significance," yes. But, as I see it, the essential thing to understand about meaning is that it is future-oriented. You make meaning out of something that happened in your past by turning it into an action plan—how you'll see and/or do things differently in the future.

So, for example, if you have a bad relationship, you don't go around boohooing, "I'm going to have my vagina bricked up!"; you admit what you didn't look at when you were diving in to your thing with Mr. Bad Guy and then conclude, "Hmm, maybe I shouldn't date men with a long criminal history who claim that they 'only smoke crack socially.'"

Pennebaker had a "quibble" with my contention that meaning is future-oriented. He explained to me that "in theory, meaning *should* be future-oriented, but in practice," it often isn't. "For example, a person may put two and two together by realizing that their health problems stem from a particular early life experience. This discovery may have no direct future implications, but just resolving that puzzle can be helpful."

I see his point—and agree with him. However, I would say that his example—the meaning-making without future-orientation—is still future-oriented in a way. It allows people to go forward without the "why?" or "why me?" weighing on them so much (and possibly causing unhealthy rumination). So, ultimately, I do think it's helpful to look for future-oriented meaning in the insights we come to about our life—or at least give them some spin that offers some comfort to us going forward.

SPEAK EXPERIENCES

Writing as a form of stress reduction isn't for everyone—or, as a writer friend of mine put it: "Writing for no pay? I'd rather blow a homeless dude, then suck his toes for afterplay."

If you feel similarly—or just aren't a big writer—not to worry. Just tap that record button on your phone. Experiments by happiness researcher Sonja Lyubomirsky, among others, find that the benefits of recording your feelings for fifteen minutes are pretty comparable to those of writing them down.

Lyubomirsky and her colleagues point out that perhaps because both writing and audio recording our thoughts involve an "external source"—either a piece of paper or an electronic device—they tend to involve a level of organizing, integrating, and analyzing problems that mere thinking does not. Also, the thinking required to create a narrative on the page or in a recording often leads to searching for meaning and enhanced understanding about what you're going through.

EXPRESSIVE WRITING FOR LAZY PEOPLE

Spilling your guts onto the page for fifteen minutes a day for four days in a row is a chunk of time. But good news! Research by social psychologist Chad Burton and personality psychologist Laura King finds that just two minutes a day of expressive writing for two consecutive days may do the job to ease your emotional load. A month after their subjects did the writing, they showed fewer physiological symptoms of stress.

But wait. Two minutes? That barely seems to be enough time to write much more than "once upon a time" and "the end." Not surprisingly, Pennebaker and his colleagues speculated that writing for only two minutes left these participants with "unfinished business." However, that actually wasn't a criticism. When you aren't focusing your brain directly on some problem, your brain's "default mode" processing takes over. This is basically background processing—like when you give your computer a software program to run and then go out to dinner. The work gets done—but without you sitting there for an hour screaming about all the horrible things you'd like to do to Bill Gates.

As for how much time to put in and which method will work for you, Pennebaker told me, "My belief is that people need to be their own scientists in figuring out the best ways to write. There is no true way." He said that sometimes, "writing for two minutes works." Other times, a person will need to do it "multiple times." He also explained that we shouldn't be too rigid about the writing medium. It may work for you to write on a computer or by hand, "and even just writing with your finger in the air can work." (Of course, the finger-in-the-air thing could have an added benefit—getting people to give you a little extra space on public transportation.)

RUMINANT WITH A VIEW

There is a caveat about expressing your feelings. Consider what goes on for a certain set of ladies who lunch—ladies who happen to be cows.

Cows are called "ruminants," a Latin word that means "chewing over again." Your friendly neighborhood cow chomps up some grass, swallows it, gives it a mini-vacation in her rumen (the upper-level stomach and fermentation center), and then—gross-out alert!—upchucks some of the bigger particles of this grassy yumminess and gives them another chew.

This is probably why cows are not considered good cocktail party guests.

It's also a poor model for feelings management.

The late psychologist Susan Nolen-Hoeksema studied the mental rechewing in humans, known as "rumination." This is a form of overthink that involves obsessively running your mind over your feelings, problems, or shortcomings. Maybe that doesn't sound like such a bad thing. The problem comes in the ultimate pointlessness of this—as compared with the helpful act of expressive writing.

Consider that expressive writing doesn't just involve expression; it's "Let's hash this out—find some meaning in it—so we can move on." The essential element here is forward motion—in your feelings and in your life. Rumination, on the other hand, is the repetitive no-hope route: "Let's crawl into the corner and snivel about it. And then, after a brief bathroom break, let's crawl right back and snivel some more."

Not surprisingly, ruminating tends to make negative feelings worse, increasing stress and pessimism and even leading to depression. If that's not bad enough, Nolen-Hoeksma found that rumination can also lead to a loss of "social support"—kind of understandably—because who wants to be around somebody who's put some fear or problem on endless repeat?

HELLO, DALAI LAMA

Emotions are grabby little fuckers—fear, anger, and anxiety especially. They jump out from nowhere, get you by the neck, and start dragging you down some gully.

The thing is, you don't have to go with them. You can say no. It might help to remind yourself that *you* are not your feelings; your feelings are *happening to you*. They are your knee-jerk reaction to something in your environment.

You can surely understand this intellectually, but what's much more helpful is getting to the point where you can look at them with a little perspective, a little distance—as if you were standing across the street watching yourself go about life rather than drowning in the quicksand of you.

Earlier in the book, you read about mantra meditation—repeating a word like "one" for a minute or a few minutes here and there, which might make you less angrily or anxiously reactive. Because this kind of meditation doesn't require stopping your day and lying down, I think people are more likely to do it. I certainly am.

As I mentioned in chapter 7, I do that "one" thing for maybe just thirty or forty seconds in my head as I'm taking deep slow breaths to fall asleep, at night and in my daily between-writing naps. (Recall that slow deep breathing engages the parasympathetic nervous system, calming us down.) Just guessing here, but I suspect that when there have been opportunities for me to hop the crazytrain, this mantras-before-napping thing has helped me get to "uh, thanks, but I think I'll walk."

Well, mantra meditation has a relative; it's called "mindfulness meditation"—and, sneeringly, "McMindfulness" because it's become so trendy. Mindfulness meditation simply entails sitting or lying quietly, scanning your body with your mind, and observing your thoughts and bodily sensations nonjudgmentally—kind of like they're scenery you're passing in a car.

The end goal of this sort of meditation is different from that of the mantra kind, which is supposed to help you get out of yourself—transcend obsessive and damaging focused attention so you can, at least for a little while, float in some Neverneverland of you.

Mindfulness meditation is, instead, about being engaged and aware—bringing more attention to the present moment and getting used to feeling your bodily sensations and feelings. People who do this regularly seem to become more able to stand emotional and physical discomfort—which could be seen as a low-level form of superpowers, since it allows a person to persist where they might otherwise have wimped out.

For how many minutes a day would you need to do mindfulness meditation? "Long enough so that you get really bored and antsy and learn how to make room for unpleasant moments," molecular biologist Jonathan Kabat-Zinn told science journalist Maia Szalavitz in a *Time* magazine interview. Kabat-Zinn, who researches mindfulness and created the "Mindfulness-Based Stress Reduction" program at UMass med school, advises meditating for at least fifteen minutes daily to start.

Now, there are a lot of claims made for this sort of meditation—and a lot of loosey-goosey, low-quality research. But an analysis by two doctor-researchers—Madhav Goyal, M.D., and Sonal Singh, M.D.—of the better-quality research out there found moderate evidence for "small improvements" in levels of anxiety, depression, and pain. They also found small improvements in stress and distress levels, though from lesser evidence.

Still, their upshot was that "meditation programs can reduce the negative dimensions of psychological stress." In fact, they found that meditation seems to be an anxiety and depression reliever on a par with "what would be expected from the use of an antidepressant" but "without the associated toxicities" (and the fun orgasm-killing side effects).

However, the main reason I think this form of meditation might be worth doing is that it could help train you to approach intense negative feelings more like a tourist—observing what's happening instead of just impulsively reacting to it. This gives you something important—time—so you can decide what to do. Standing back from an emotional issue in this way gives you your best shot at a cooler response—ideally allowing you to observe that you're experiencing some unpleasantness, realize that you can tolerate it, and wait for it to pass.

Think of this like peering through your front-door peephole at Girl Scouts hawking boxes of those satanically good caramel/coconut/chocolate Samoa cookies*—at the end of your first successful day on a diet. You don't have to come out with a BB gun: "Get off my fucking property!" You don't have to come out at all. They'll ring your doorbell a few times, and if you don't answer, they'll go try to fatten up your neighbors.

WHAT IF YOU'RE ONE OF THOSE PEOPLE WHO JUST CAN'T MEDITATE?

I kind of said this in chapter 7, but I'll say it again in case you are, oh, on the porcelain Barcalounger at your friend's house, picked this book up, and randomly opened it to this section. (Hi there! Welcome! Don't forget to wash your hands!)

Now, maybe you are convinced that you can't meditate. Well, you're wrong. I always thought I couldn't, either, given how my mind wanders like a feral cat in heat. The thing is, a wandering mind doesn't

---

*@Popehat tweet about a new kind of Girl Scout cookies: "I thought they were kind of meh at first but by the third box I ate in the garage they were growing on me."

mean you can't meditate or aren't doing it right. Wandering is just what minds do. And there's a way to deal with that.

Don't judge the wandering. Just notice it: "Oh, there goes my mind, drifting over to that mole that I'm sure is cancer." Then just refocus— bring your mind back to, say, your fingertips or your ear...until your mind runs off again, which it will.

What's great about this—this practice of nonjudgmentally yanking your wandering mind back—is that it's a form of self-acceptance. You're noticing your thinking rather than flogging yourself for the subject matter. This may help you get in the habit of witnessing your feelings—as opposed to panicking that you're having them, which gives them full run of the place.

JUST DO IT (AND THEN DO IT SOME MORE)

You should also recognize that even if you're determined to change— even if you're determined to keep your feelings from calling the shots—you probably won't wake up every day thinking, "Hmm, it's Tuesday...yet another great day to stick my head into the lion's mouth!"

Consider giving yourself the assignment of taking one social risk—one social flying leap—a day. This should just involve putting yourself out there in a way you wouldn't have before, like by nuh-uh-ing some line-cutting jerk or chatting up some delishy stranger.

Doing this at least once daily is essential because studies—by psychologist Phillippa Lally, among others—find that repetition leads to habit acquisition, to the point where the new behavior becomes automatic.

Getting to the point where self-assertiveness is your default behavior is what I call "Roboconfidence." I now have it. This means that my go-to behavior is standing up for myself. And this is pretty fucking amazing, considering that my response to conflict for much of my life was wishing for an alien shrink ray to zap me so I could instantly be small enough to duck behind the leg of the nearest coffee table.

Granted, it isn't always appropriate to go all confrontational. But if you're using this book for more than steadying a sofa with a limp, chances are you have an IQ over the highway speed limit. So...I'll trust that you ladies have the smarts not to exercise your assertiveness by throwing a drink in some bruiser's face and that you dudes know better than to offer him an instructive counterpoint, such as, "That's not what your momma said when I was bending her over the trunk of my car."

BE INAUTHENTIC!

Screw the real you; be the ideal you

Be *in*authentic?

Yes, I'm serious.

"Be authentic!" is one of the stupider bits of advice we all keep getting. What if the real you—the default you—is a liquor store robber or a baby-seal clubber or enjoys Ritual Sacrifice Wednesdays?

Authenticity has varying definitions in the psych literature, but it basically means having your outer self—your behavior—match your inner self (your thoughts, feelings, desires, and values).

Social psychologists Michael Kernis and Brian M. Goldman, in their research on authenticity, call this inner self your "true self" or "core self" and define authenticity as the "unimpeded operation" of it in your daily doings.

That's problematic, and we'll get to why.

But first, here is the helpful stuff from Kernis and Goldman's work.

Kernis and Goldman break down what it means to be "authentic" into four separate but related parts.

Their big four are: behavior, self-awareness, "unbiased processing," and "relational orientation."

I explained the *behavior* thing above.

There are three other parts to their model, each of which is important to practice.

There's *self-awareness*—being tuned in to your entire self (your emotions, motives, likes, and dislikes, down to your preferences in vegan cheesefood and nipple clamps). This means connecting with and continually trying to learn more about all of the stuff that makes up you—not just the parts that make you seem fabulous.

Next, there's *unbiased processing*—being objective in assessing information about yourself. This involves being willing to look at yourself—even when the view seems dark and ugly—so you have a realistic picture of who you are. (It helps to wear protective eyewear—in the form of self-acceptance and self-compassion.)

The final part of their model is *relational orientation*—the "Who are you when you're around other people?" element. This just means that you're open and genuine with people you're close to—letting friends and romantic partners know who you really are and what you really think.

However, a caveat to that: If you'd like to *keep* your friends and romantic partners, it's important to be mindful that there's a difference between honesty and brutal honesty. (Sometimes the naked truth needs a bit of a back wax before it gets presented to somebody you care about.)

All in all, these practices from Kernis and Goldman are essential parts of the foundation for going about life with guts. They're linked with all sorts of personal and social goodies, like better relationships and increased autonomy, personal growth, and purpose in life. Also, you really have to figure out who you are and where you're coming from to understand who you wanna be and where you need to go.

But, again, there's a problem with Kernis and Goldman's thinking, and it's this "core" or "true self" business.

ALL OF MEH

Kernis and Goldman's calls to have your "core" or "true self" leading the way are right in line with that Shakespeare quotation "To thine own self be true." I know, that sounds so beautiful and noble and poetic. The problem is, Shakespeare was not a neuroscientist.

Modern neuroscientific research reveals that there actually is no core "self"—no singular, stable "this is me!" complete with consistent standards, preferences, and practices. Instead, there seem to be various brain parts and processes grabbing the controls and having a turn at being in charge.

The idea that we don't have a singular self is hard for us to understand or believe. In fact, most people will probably insist that they have stable preferences and that they make the choices they do because they are logical and rational.

And sure, we each have some pretty steadfast personality traits (like how extraverted or conscientious we are), and we have some likes or dislikes that are unlikely to change. If, say, you are terrified of brown recluse spiders on Friday, you probably aren't going to spend Saturday morning googling the nearest brown recluse spider rescue so you can try to adopt.

Despite these constants, a good deal of neuroscientific and behavioral research suggests that each of us is a big buzzing hive of inconsistencies, with competing brain parts and circuitry. We will often have no idea why we behaved in a certain way on one occasion and not another—which won't stop us from sticking a completely lucid-sounding reason on our behavior if someone presses us for one.

We do this because the drive to be consistent is a powerful one in humans, as social psychologist Leon Festinger discovered in his research on "cognitive dissonance." This is Festinger's term for the very uncomfortable feeling we get when we're holding two inconsistent beliefs or attitudes. An example of cognitive dissonance is when a cigarette smoker has two competing "cognitions": "Smoking will lead to a horrible death" and "I really love having a cigarette."

When we experience a clash like this, we are driven to reduce the discomfort it causes by smoothing out the inconsistency in our thinking ASAP. But, going back to the case of the smoker, instead of their admitting that they've been wrong in continuing to smoke—a knock to the ego—they are likely to comfort themselves with some thought like, "Well, there are all those toothless old people in Russia who smoked and were still chasing their goats around at the age of 116."

This sort of self-justification reflects what social psychologist Elliot Aronson later discovered in researching cognitive dissonance— that we tend to iron out the inconsistencies in our thinking in ways that are ego-serving or -preserving, like with the option that doesn't say, "Hello, I am a huge idiot buttknuckle for smoking!"

The idea of the singular self seems to be one of our mind's comforting illusions—a mental crutch we use to feel that we have a grasp on who we are and that we are in control of our thoughts and behavior. However, in the 1970s, neurobiologist Roger Wolcott Sperry, working with his then-grad student Michael Gazzaniga, found that different parts of our brain can act in ways that are brattily independent. They were doing research on "split-brain" patients—epileptics who'd had their brain's left and right hemispheres surgically severed to stop their seizures.

I know; this brain-splitting business sounds very "Welcome back, Dr. Frankenstein!" However, the surgeons don't go in with a tree saw and hack down through the whole brain, all the way to the brainstem. They just do a little delicate work at the top, snipping what I think of as a bundle of phone lines linking the two hemispheres. By doing this, they stop this wiring—the bundle of neural fibers called the corpus callosum—from transmitting information (and seizure-causing electric discharges) from one hemisphere to the other.

Now, our eyes are hooked up to our hemispheres, with the left eye transmitting to the right hemisphere and the right eye transmitting to the left. (Don't worry about remembering the *which eye goes where* business.) When the hemispheres are connected, information from the right and left eyes basically goes into the same, uh, mental stewpot for processing.

In these split-brain patients, however, if you block off one eye— say, pirate eyepatch–style—from seeing what the other sees, you get some pretty wild results. What happens compares to having one version of a magazine sent to your house and a different version sent to your neighbor and then being asked to explain what's in his version and having to bullshit your way through it.

It's like this for these split-brain patients (when one hemisphere is in the dark about information the other has gotten) because the left hemisphere and the right have different specialties.

Left: Language is primarily centered in our left hemisphere (except in a few left-handed people). Our verbal left hemisphere is also the part of the brain that Gazzaniga calls "The Interpreter." It's tasked with making sense of the information our brain takes in, which it does by coming up with stories—coherent or seemingly coherent explanations and justifications for our behavior.

These stories allow us to see ourselves as sensible, consistent, and rational instead of as randomly acting idiots. The Interpreter is also behind our mind's creating what Gazzaniga calls a "unified sense of self"—a unified self that Sperry and Gazzaniga's research found does not actually exist.

Right: The right hemisphere, in most of us, is the thinking-in-pictures side—or, as researchers put it, the "visuospatial" processing specialist (in charge of tasks like facial recognition).

So, in short:

> Left hemisphere, words: the Literary Department—the side where the verbal explanations come from.

> Right hemisphere, pictures: the Art Department—home to our brain's facial recognition software and other visual processing.

Again, in people who haven't had split-brain surgery (most of us, that is), the two hemispheres work together as a team, sending information across the phone lines—the corpus callosum—that connect them. So what one side knows, the other side knows pretty licketysplitski.

However, Sperry and Gazzaniga took advantage of how split-brain patients, with their severed "phone lines," can't toss information from one hemisphere to the other like the rest of us. The researchers projected images in such a way that either these patients' right hemisphere (only) or their left (only) had visual access to them.

Something fascinating happened.

When the researchers showed an image—like a spoon—to the subject's verbal left hemisphere only, the person would be able to name it. If, however, they showed it to the nonverbal right brain only, the person could subsequently point to the spoon as the correct object but, lacking the connection to the left hemisphere, couldn't muster the words to name what it was. This shows, as Sperry put it, that each hemisphere is a "conscious system in its own right."

After Gazzaniga became a professor with his own lab, he carried on the split-brain research with Joseph LeDoux (then his grad student). In one of these experiments, they flashed a picture of a chicken claw to a guy's left hemisphere only. The right hemisphere got a different picture—a snowy cabin scene that the left hemisphere didn't get to see.

The researchers then gave the guy an "association test," laying out another set of pictures and asking him to point to the ones associated with the images he'd just seen. The new pictures included a lawn mower, a broom, a pickax, a toaster, a chicken, and a shovel. As Gazzaniga noted, "the obviously correct association is chicken for the chicken claw and a shovel for the snow scene."

The individual hemispheres did just fine on the test. The verbal left hemisphere put the picture of the chicken claw with the chicken. The visuospatial right hemisphere put the snowy scene together with the shovel.

All good!

Except wait. The researchers then asked the subject to explain why he had picked the items he did—the chicken and the shovel. He—or rather, his verbal left hemisphere, which had gotten the chicken claw picture flashed to it—replied, "Oh, that's simple. The chicken claw goes with the chicken."

But about that shovel...

Now, the left hemisphere had no idea why the right had picked the shovel, *because it never got to see the snow scene.* (All the left brain knew about was what it could see at that moment—pictures of a chicken, a chicken claw, and a shovel.) But amazingly, the left brain immediately came up with a reason for the shovel: It was because the chicken shed was full of poop that had to be cleaned out!

Photo and chicken sweater by Amanda Paul, of the JeanieGreenHens store on Etsy.

This rationalizing by the Interpreter part of the left brain reflects our powerful human need to be (and feel) consistent, coherent, and rational. It seems we will do whatever it takes to get to this place—even if that means just, uh, making chickenshit up.

THE SEVEN DWARFS OF YOU

In a way, the singular Self is a comforting fairy tale about who you are. It would be great if you actually got to be just one character—to play one glorious role (like Snow White, which—tee-hee—also includes bonus sleep sex with The Prince). However, as we've seen, the reality of you is shifting and messy.

Research in evolutionary psychology builds on the neuroscientific findings on the inconsistent "you." Evolutionary social psychologist Vladas Griskevicius and his colleagues find that within what we think of as The Self, we actually seem to have a bunch of different selves, steering us in different directions, driven by competing evolutionary goals.

Griskevicius and fellow evolutionary psychologist Douglas Kenrick named this band of mini-mes our "subselves." (Conveniently, there are seven of them, like the dwarfs.) These seven subselves pop up in response to seven recurring evolutionary challenges: 1. Evading physical harm; 2. Avoiding disease; 3. Making friends; 4. Gaining status; 5. Attracting a mate; 6. Keeping that mate; and 7. Caring for family.

One of these subselves (see #1 above, "evading physical harm") is the "self-protection subself"—a sort of night watchman guarding us against scary and awful things that want to stab, shoot, beat, and/or eat us. This subself is activated by "fear-eliciting cues suggesting physical threat."

As for how this subself helps us avoid harm, Griskevicius explains that "a core strategy evolutionarily associated with successful self-protection is increased safety in numbers." We see this in how animals threatened by predators move together into a big block. Humans feeling endangered band together, too—physically and psychologically. Griskevicius gives the example of people in a chatroom who are made to feel afraid—which makes them "more likely to conform to the opinions of others" in that chatroom.

Another of our subselves (see #5 above) is the "mate-acquisition subself," which the researchers describe as being "primed by real or imagined potential mates." A successful strategy for mate attraction is standing out from the herd—exactly what you don't want to do when, say, there's some creepy killer on the loose.

The researchers ran a study to explore how activating a particular subself might affect the subsequent choices we make. They first showed subjects one of two movie clips. Some subjects saw a clip from *The Shining*, with Jack Nicholson as a crazy mofo chasing people with an ax. The other subjects saw a clip from *Before Sunrise*, with Ethan Hawke and Julie Delpy as two hotties who meet on a European train and fall in love while wandering around Vienna for a day.

Next, they showed the subjects different print ads. Some emphasized that a restaurant or museum was *wildly popular* and that patronizing it was *an opportunity to follow the crowd*. Other versions of the ads emphasized *uniqueness*—how visiting the place would *make a person stand out from the crowd*.

In keeping with prior research on how people react to danger cues versus mating triggers, those who'd been ax killer–primed went for the products and places that were advertised as common and popular—while those who'd been romantically primed went for the ads with the uniqueness angle.

So, clearly, as evolutionary psychologist Robert Kurzban puts it, we aren't so much a singular "I" as we are a shifting "we"—a collection of motivations, systems, and processes, driven by evolution, that pop up as needed to help us survive, mate, and pass on our genes.

WELCOME TO VALU-MART!

The fact that there's no actual "core you" to be "true" to is great news.

This means that you can choose who you want to be and then just act as that person would—even when it is hard or feels scary.

As I've explained, behaviors that you keep repeating become more and more comfortable—until they just become your default behavior. (Yes, it's the ol' brain cells that "fire together wire together.") And yes, it really is that simple: What you do—and keep doing—creates who you are.

But you can't just decide who you're going to be on the fly. You need to map it out in advance. Otherwise, in a moment of conflict, all you'll see is a giant flashing arrow pointing to the easy way out.

The traffic directors for what you do—for how you'll respond in a particular situation—are your values.

Values are the principles you care most about—the guiding standards for your behavior.

To choose your values, forget about how you've gotten in the habit of behaving. Instead, think about the ideal you. What sort of person do you want to be? And what would be the bedrock values guiding that person's behavior?

It might help you to see my top values—which are:

Courage
Wisdom
Kindness/making the world a better place
Freedom/liberty/free speech
Learning/growth
Fairness/integrity/personal responsibility
Honesty (but also judicious honesty)
Perseverance
Gratitude
Humor
Seizing life (my "car crash principle" from chapter 1)

In putting together your own values set, feel free to "steal" any or all of mine that work for you. You can also google "lists of values"; lots of examples will pop up.

However, I do think there are two biggies—two primary values— that we all need, in general and in order to apply the rest of our values. These two are courage and wisdom. Courage allows you to do what you feel should be done, and wisdom allows you to have a sense of what exactly that might be.

So, for example, sometimes the courageous thing—like telling off some jackass in the bank—is the right thing to do. Other times, however, wisdom has to tell courage to put a sock in it—like when the guy happens to be wearing a bunny mask and holding an AK-47.

BE TRUE TO THE SELF-MADE YOU

Initially, it'll feel weird and scary to not just do what you've probably been doing your whole life—folding up like a possessed lawn chair at the first murmur of disagreement from somebody.

To avoid doing this, it helps to shrink your fears to a more manageable size. A number of "cognitive reappraisal" techniques from chapter 11 are good tools for that. But probably the most helpful for standing up for your new values is this advice, from the late founder of cognitive therapy, Albert Ellis: Consider the *worst possible outcome* from being true to your beliefs.

Just think about what you've seen happen when independent types you know have spoken their mind or done the right thing (and never mind whether anybody else approved).

Worst-case scenario, somebody got a little miffed at them. They may have had a tough week or a tough few weeks. But nothing TERRIBLE! or HORRIBLE! happened. No giant claw crept out from the heating duct and yanked them in, nor did they end up friendless, homeless, and airdropped on a deserted island to be the butt of the joke in *New Yorker* cartoons.

Sure, disagreement can be uncomfortable—especially when you're a newbie at it. However, that momentary discomfort is actually a smaller price to pay than the cost of ditching your belief system whenever you're up against anyone more alpha than a houseplant.

Though we ditch our beliefs like this out of fear, it seems we view this type of self-betrayal—in ourselves and others—as a moral failing. Harvard Business School's Francesca Gino and her colleagues find that it brings up feelings of "moral contamination" (whoa!) similar to those that accompany dishonesty.

When the Gino team's research subjects were asked to recall a time they'd gone against their values, they ended up feeling a Lady Macbethian urge to wash (and to use cleansing products like Lysol, Windex, and Crest), along with a longing to engage in morally cleansing acts (do-gooder behaviors like giving to charity).

If this sounds familiar—this need to wash after doing rotten things—it's a finding echoed by other studies, including a handwashing study by embodied cognition researchers Spike W. S. Lee and Norbert Schwarz mentioned earlier in the book.

"Building on this research," Gino and her colleagues write, "we suggest that experiencing inauthenticity results in lower moral self-regard and feelings of impurity, which trigger a desire for physical cleansing and acting prosocially to compensate for violating the true self."

"The true self"?

I know; you're probably thinking, "Yo, Alkon, didn't you just spend most of this chapter telling us there is no such thing?"

And to make matters worse, there's "inauthenticity" in there, too.

We actually need to cut the Gino team a little slack on that. In using "inauthenticity" and the "true self," Gino and her fellow researchers are just going with the accepted social science terminology. However, their actual findings—about the negative effects of violating your personal standards—are right on.

It appears that Kernis and Goldman and other "authenticity" researchers were wrong about what they were actually investigating and measuring. They *thought* it was "authenticity"—this notion of behaving in tune with some "core self" (that you've seen doesn't actually seem to exist).

But as social psychologist Mark Leary noted in a conversation with me, "Evolutionarily, and for our well-being, I can't see any reason why authenticity makes any difference." What other people do want, he said, is for you to be "consistent and predictable and stick to your word."

I think Leary's right. Our longing to be what the researchers describe as "authentic" is really about our evolved need to be—and seem—consistent, reliable, and predictable.

In other words, what ultimately seems to matter is being seen as authentic *in the eyes of others*—because it's essential for them to know whether they can count on you. This makes sense in light of what self-esteem seems to be: our perception of how much or how little other people respect and value us and our feeling about ourselves (feel-good or feel-bad) that comes out of that. This feeling, in turn, motivates our response—doing what it takes to maintain our position if we're popular or, if we're not, keeping a low profile so we won't annoy any social royals into flattening us.

Authenticity, likewise, seems to be a psychological guard dog, protecting us from social ruin. It isn't just a feeling; it's a motivation. It motivates us to behave consistently, reliably, and in keeping with social standards for consistency and reliability, like being true to our word.

Research by Leary with his grad student Katrina Jongman-Sereno supports the notion that social standards play into our sense of authenticity. They find that people rate themselves as more "authentic" when they behave in "socially desirable" ways. Of course, the underhanded stuff we do is just as much "us" as our more fabulous behavior, but Leary and Jongman-Sereno speculate that we benefit socially from believing that the positive things we do reflect the real "us," while we psychologically disown our less admirable qualities and behaviors.

Of course, what we don't quite "know" has less power to hurt us socially. As noted earlier in the book, it seems that we are better at conveying information believably to others if we believe it ourselves. Evolutionary biologist Robert Trivers explains that having "positive illusions" helps us avoid "inadvertent information leakage"—like the fidgeting we do out of nervousness when we're trying to cover something up.

The upshot of these findings is that you've got help from your distorto-vision to accept the chosen you as the real-deal you. This, in turn, should help bolster you to act in line with your shiny new values instead of going with your tired old habits and fears.

THE RED HONEY BADGER OF COURAGE

The honey badger is a tenacious little fucker, as seen in the YouTube video with the hilarious voice-over by "Randall":

"Get away from me!" says the snake. "Get away from me!"
Honey badger don't care. Honey badger smacks the shit out
of it.

Honey badger photo by Richard Toller.

The snake is a king cobra, complete with paralyzing venom and
that creepy expandable jaw. Seriously scary—unless you're a honey
badger. Randall:

> While it's eating the snake—ew, that's disgusting—
> meanwhile, the poisonous venom is seeping through
> the honey badger's body, and it passes out. Look at that
> sleepy fuck. Now the honey badger's just gonna pass out
> for a few minutes, and then it's gonna get right back up and
> start eating all over again, 'cause it's a hungry little bastard.
> Look at this! Like nothing happened, the honey badger
> gets right back up and continues eating the cobra!

I brought up the honey badger because—let's be honest—suddenly
going all New Superhero You in the face of challenges you've spent
years ducking from is no small thing.

So…it might help you to have a symbol—a visual shorthand, like a photo or an object—that reminds you to stand up for the values you chose. You can incorporate it into some anxiety-shooing ritual you do—even just by keeping the photo you choose on your phone and clicking on it for a little courage bolstering before you go into a meeting or hit on some hottie.

This photo I included, by Richard Toller, of the honey badger or a screenshot from the YouTube video might be a good symbol, because this critter's both badass and fun. But, for some people, I suspect a symbol of a human role model for tenacity might work a little better.

You can pick an image from a movie or from your mental catalog of people you admire for their courage. However, if you have trouble coming up with something, I've got a suggestion—a shot of an unassuming little 100-year-old farmhouse in the Ballard neighborhood of Seattle.

This little old farmhouse belonged to a little old lady, Edith Macefield. A company wanted to buy her house and knock it down so they could build a five-story mall. Macefield said no. No, no, no. They eventually offered her a million dollars—well over the little house's value. Macefield kept saying no, and—I just love this—the company ultimately had no choice but to build the mall around her house.

The mall construction foreman, Barry Martin, eventually became friends with Macefield (after she asked him to drive her to a hair appointment). In one of their conversations, Macefield revealed that she wasn't anti-development. She, in fact, thought it was ridiculous that some people in Seattle were trying to preserve a vintage Denny's.

But Edith explained that her mother had died in the house, right on the couch, and it was where Edith wanted to live and die—in her house, on that couch, "not in some *facility*." So she just stood her ground—despite all the pressure. Pressure from the company.

Peer pressure of sorts—from the fact that all the neighbors had sold. And pressure just from looking out the window at all the change around her.

Edith Macefield's house.
Photo by Geoff Loftus.

If a little old lady in a little old farmhouse can put her support-hosed foot down and say no under all that pressure, surely you can, too. So, the next time you order a burger "extremely rare" and it gets delivered just this side of cremated, don't glumly resign yourself to forcing it down. Pull your special symbol out of your pocket, or glance at the photo on your phone of, say, Edith's house stopping all that steel and commerce. Then do what it takes to be a full person instead of a foot-wipe: Wave your server over; remind him of your initial order; and calmly and politely ask for it to be done to your liking.

Again, the first few times you do this sort of thing, you may find it terrifying on the level of crossing a 3,000-foot gully on a fraying rope bridge. However, you should eventually come to see what I've discovered: You don't have to grow up all well-adjusted or join the Navy SEALs to start living with balls. In fact, I'm pretty sure Edith Macefield kept a lavender crocheted pair tucked away in her little old lady handbag.

THEY SHOULD CALL IT WON'T-POWER

The pathetic realities of willpower

The best of intentions often aren't worth a shit.

For example, if anyone knows better than to go facedown into a bunch of sugary carbs, it's my friend Mike Eades.

Mike Eades is formally known as Dr. Michael Eades. He and his wife, Dr. Mary Dan Eades, whose advice on initiating new habits I referenced in chapter 7, are dietary medicine pioneers. They were putting patients on low-carb diets in the '80s—back when conventional wisdom had it that putting a single bite of filet mignon in your mouth might make you have a massive heart attack on the spot.

The Eadeses, however, have long understood that it is carbohydrates—from sugar, flour, starchy vegetables like potatoes, and even apple juice—that cause the insulin secretion that puts on fat (and leads to a platterload of other health problems).

Of course, part of being a diet doctor is being a behavioral guru, and the Eadeses included this little tip for quashing our piggy little impulses in their *New York Times* best-selling book on low-carb eating, *Protein Power*:

> "Unfortunately, one sweet treat usually begs another, and
> the unhealthy devotion to sugar can last a lifetime. The
> good part is that the craving quickly disappears if the

temptation is just ignored. Try it—wait 10 minutes and reconsider."

Smart, huh? This approach—waiting out uncomfortable feelings with the understanding that they'll pass—has worked for me. And former drug, alcohol, and sex addict Amy Dresner has also used it to stay on the sober and narrow.

Well, one day, Mike grumbled on his blog that Mary Dan (aka "MD") had bought a box of chocolates from a kid trying to raise money for some cause: "Why she didn't just give the kid five bucks and say 'keep the candy' I don't know."

MD stuck the box in a drawer—one Mike rarely goes into—where it remained for several months.

One night, MD, who is a fabulous cook, made ribs for dinner. Mike wrote that he felt "full and content" afterward—but "for whatever reason, the knowledge that those candies were there" began to prey on him.

Luckily, he could just take his own advice and wait out his craving.

But Mike confessed: "I opened the box and threw five or six of those suckers back as fast as I could."

THE LITTLE ENGINE THAT CRAPPED OUT

Too frequently, we are all so lame at doing what we should—whether it's standing up to a bullying co-worker or a come-hithering box of chocolates.

That's why Mike Eades is so perfect to spotlight as an example of willpower gone kaput. And though—sure—it's fun to have a snicker at the expert who fails to take his own advice, that's not why I included him. It's because Eades is generally the antithesis of the lazy slacker who spends his days getting derailed by his urges.

The guy not only got through med school, passed his boards, and became a respected doctor and best-selling co-author but also, along with MD, has started a number of successful businesses—some of them internationally successful.

These ventures typically get kicked off when Mike gets curious about something, like when he and MD were staying at a hotel and he had a particularly good pork chop. In fact, it was almost impossibly good. He went down to the kitchen to ask the chef how he did it. Short answer: huge, expensive, gourmet cooking-in-water thinga-majiggie from France. Well, several years of tinkering in le garage d'Eades later, Mike and MD's version for the home, the SousVide Supreme, was in stores around the globe—and even won the prestigious prize for the best new kitchen appliance at some big kitchenware show.

Compare the Mike Eades who put in all the impressive self-control and hard work to become a prize-winning kitchen appliance magnate with the Mike Eades who, in a matter of moments, lost his battle of wills with that box of bonbons.

Striking contrast, huh?

But that sort of self-control fail is actually not surprising—for Mike Eades or for any of us—in light of a number of unfortunate realities about willpower.

Willpower (aka self-control) is the ability to fight off temptation in the moment and cling—like a shipwrecked rat on driftwood—to your long-term goals.

In the war against temptation, you're battling on two fronts: cravings and "avoidings." On one front, you're fighting your urges to throw yourself into all the things you crave that you know are bad for you (or at least less than ideal). On the other front, there are all the adult, responsible tasks you dread but know you *should* do—for instance, going to the gym before your ass becomes eligible to send a delegate to the U.N. You're fighting your urges to *avoid* doing these things.

Of course, as temptation is clawing at you, people will bark that you should "just pull yourself up by your bootstraps!" (or bra straps). By this, they mean, "C'mon, just do the right thing already!"—as if somehow you just *forgot* to want to.

These people are operating under the commonly held misconception that willpower is available to us on demand, in unlimited supply. Supposedly, we just ring up some internal Pink Dot, get a sixer of willpower delivered, and—easy-peasy—stop ourselves from having some cake or some ill-advised sex or whatever.

Yeah, right.

This isn't to say that we *shouldn't* take charge of ourselves and our lives—quite the contrary. But if there's one reliable thing about our willpower, it's its frequent *un*reliability.

One reason for this is that emotion is our psychological advance man—out there way in front of reason. Research by psychologists Daniel Kahneman and Amos Tversky suggests that we have two brain systems, a fast-responding emotional system and a slower rational system that eventually comes around—often after we've mowed through a half-dozen doughnuts or carpet-bombed a relationship out of existence.

Self-control researchers Janet Metcalfe and Walter Mischel describe these fast and slow systems similarly—as "hot" and "cool." Our hot emotional system pops up right away—triggering hunger for food, sex, and other yummygood things and triggering fear and defensive reactions to protect us from things that will eat us or fuck us in a bad way. Metcalfe and Mischel call these reactions "Go!" behaviors, and these hot emotions of ours show about as much interest in consequences as I do in whom the Cleveland Cavaliers traded to the Rams (if those teams even play the same sport, and no, Mr. Copy Editor, please don't ruin my blissful ignorance for me).

The counterpart to our hot system, Metcalfe and Mischel explain, is our cool, controlled cognitive system, which is "crucial for future-oriented decisions" and for succeeding at self-control. And while the wanting, seeking, lusting "Go!" behaviors are driven by the amygdala and its buddies in lower "reasoning," the cool system is "centered primarily in the prefrontal cortex"—the higher reasoning department.

You may be thinking, "Well, okey-dokey, I'll just apply that cool, rational system to all those hot emotional leaps." Unfortunately, it typically isn't that simple. Even when you consciously ring up your rational system—ask it to be a pal and stop you from throwing yourself into that giant bag of Doritos—it will frequently let your call go to voicemail.

Researchers studying willpower have conflicting explanations for why this is. One long-accepted interpretation was social psychologist Roy Baumeister's notion that willpower is a sort of *stuff* in limited supply—a fuel for controlling yourself that gets used up, same as a tank of gas or a bottle of orange juice.

According to Baumeister's *willpower as a limited resource* explanation, on a given day, the more you drink out of your bottle of willpower juice the less you'll have available to you. Yes, this means that every time you override your emotion of "I wanna!" with "I'm not gonna!" you're weakening your resolve to get to your CrossFit class or keep from texting your douchenozzle ex.

And it gets worse, because willpower isn't just "in your head." It's a mental *and* physical response—another example of "embodied cognition," how "our mind is bigger than our brain." Accordingly, being hungry or tired also makes it harder for you to keep from giving in to temptation—including the temptation to avoid making any decision at all. (Meanwhile, bowing out of deciding—just letting things remain as they are—can allow you to feel like you've decided to say no.)

A fascinating example of the effects of being hungry and/or tired on willpower is a study by cognitive neuroscientist Shai Danziger and marketing researcher Jonathan Levav looking at which criminals Israeli parole board judges decided to release and which they stuck back in the pen.

Consider that it's a risk for a judge to parole a prisoner, because the person might reoffend. Judges need to balance public safety with humane treatment—a cognitively demanding endeavor that requires assessing a bunch of facts, making predictions based on those facts, and coming to a fair, reasoned decision. Well, that's how it's supposed to work, anyway.

However, the researchers found that the prisoners who came before the judges *first thing in the morning* were let out about sixty-five percent of the time. In the late morning, just before lunch, the chance of getting paroled dropped to about 20 percent. But right after lunch, the parole rate bounced back up—nearly as high as it was in the early morning. At the end of the day, however... well, a parole-seeking prisoner might as well have remained in their cell.

In other words, getting denied parole seemed to have more to do with the judges' growling stomachs and waning energy levels than the details of a prisoner's case.

Now, we tend to think of an exhausting job as something like farm labor, not the sort of work that's done indoors while seated in a comfy chair. But mentally tiring tasks—tasks that require cognitive energy, like problem-solving and struggling to focus amid distractions*—are big self-control eaters. And, unfortunately, the "problem-solving" that counts doesn't just involve trying to fix the particle beam accelerator at CERN; it also includes using your mental energy at the grocery store to choose just one of the thirty-four slightly different balsamic vinaigrettes.

And here's a cruel one: Grappling with tough emotions also seems to make it tougher to maintain self-control. A study by Baumeister and his colleagues found that getting snubbed zaps willpower, making the just-rejected you more likely to plant your face in a plate of cookies. (Sadly, as I discovered in my medicating-with-brownies

---

*Hello, "open office" idiocy!

phase, this will not smother your sorrows; it will just make them go up a size in pants.)

BRAINS JUST WANNA HAVE FUN

Baumeister isn't wrong that we have problems mustering self-control after we use it—even after we make just one effort to override our "I wanna" with "I'm not gonna." He and his colleagues observed this through experiments involving "sequential tasks"—giving research subjects two willpower-chomping tasks in a row. Over and over, the researchers saw that when people put their willpower into the first task, they had only fumes of restraint left for the second one.

However, where Baumeister does go wrong—as so many social-science researchers do—is in failing to check his *willpower as a limited resource* interpretation against the evolutionary question of "why?" Why would it make any sort of evolutionary sense—as a survival or mating tactic—for our willpower to run out just one task in? As in, if our ancestor Joe Loincloth tried his luck on some hottie one fine Pleistocene morning, upon her rejecting him, no más? No more effort left in Joe's prehistoric OJ jar for the entire day? Meaning no chance of Joe's dragging his ass off to try to spear some dinner? Brilliant. And by "brilliant," I mean "Lights out, and adios forever, Joe's genes!"

Baumeister's idea of *willpower as finite stuff* makes even less sense in light of how when we find ourselves out of motivation for dreaded tasks, we aren't laid flat for *all* activities. In fact, just let somebody suggest something we *want* to do; all of a sudden, our willpower-sapped ass is all el perko for that fun.

The thing is, doing something unfun doesn't burn any more calories than doing the fun stuff. So, since this makes no metabolic sense, what's with the psychological pushback that keeps us from getting on with the next chore?

Well, consider a point evolutionary psychologists make about how we decide which actions are worth taking. Our daily energy is limited; in fact, we have an energy budget, much like a person's grocery budget. (A bottle of Dom and a filet mignon would be lovely, thanks, except for how we'll end up dining on peanut-buttered cracker cutlets for the rest of the month.)

It's our life's traffic directors, our emotions, that tell us how we should allocate our energy budget. These are the same emotions that evolved to be very thumbs-up about our having fun. But don't be misled. They couldn't give a bent fart about whether we're enjoying ourselves.

The feel-good we get from doing fun things reads as a "reward"— a sign that we're engaged in something that's paying off for us. "Paying off" simply means we're seeing some sort of benefit from our actions; we aren't pissing away our energy budget on some hopeless endeavor that could leave us dead and/or a genetic dead end. And yes, our brain's "If it feels good, do it" orientation can easily backfire, since our brain is more likely to say "more, please" to an afternoon in Stonerville than an afternoon in the file room, but evolution sends its apologies for its lack of forethought.

Another problem is that the human motivational system does not like IOUs, which is to say that we are biased toward rewards in the right fucking now. So, when faced with some off-diet yummy that you're longing to scarf down right then and there, the prospect of your looking fuck-a-doodle-do-me in a bikini six months from then is unlikely to be much of a deterrent.

In contrast to the "LET'S PAR-TAAAAY!" emotions that come with fun, there are the unpleasant emotions accompanying activities that require us to go all adultsville and show restraint. Researchers describe these emotions as "aversive." In plain English, when you're straining to keep your snout out of the ice cream, about two tons of "feelshitty" looms inside you. This looming feelshitty, in turn, sends a message to your motivational system—in the form of a big red STOPPPP! sign—at least for any further unfun, willpower-demanding activities.

To break down how this works, when you expend some of your energy on something, your brain is looking out for the both of you, calculating, "Well, what's in it for you and me?" As in, "Hey, if I do all this work to help you not scarf down that entire pie or whatever, what do we get out of it?" And if the answer is "fuck all" or "just this really shitty depleted feeling," can you really blame it for putting its feet up while you debase yourself or light fire to your diet?

However, consider that what's stopping you (from stopping yourself) isn't that you've run out of your supposed bottle of magical willstuff. You're stopped by that "aversive" feeling—the gnawing psychic ache you feel because you aren't showing your brain enough of a return from the unfun activity to make it seem like something worth doing.

This was the conclusion from evolutionary psychologist Robert Kurzban and his colleagues at Penn in their review of the research on willpower. They observed that in a number of studies, subjects' willpower actually got reset (as in, they had more of it for the next task) when they were given a "reward," like a small gift. So, Kurzban and his colleagues explain, when subjects don't have the willpower to carry on with the next disagreeable chore, "it's not 'willpower' that's exhausted—it's that the ratio of costs to reward is too high to justify continuing."

Ironically, one of the scientific papers that led to the Kurzban team's conclusion—a paper with the finding that willpower was reset by a small gift—was co-authored by both psychologist Dianne Tice, Baumeister's wife, and Baumeister himself. Yet, Baumeister either didn't notice or wouldn't admit that *this finding actually disproved his interpretation of willpower as a finite resource*. (This is a perfect example of confirmation bias—our tendency to favor information that confirms what we already believe and ignore evidence that says we're wrong.)

Baumeister's "limited resource" model also did poorly when scrutinized by the math nerd contingent. Psychologists Michael E. Mc-

Cullough and Evan C. Carter and their colleagues found that sample sizes in these experiments were too small to show what Baumeister and others claimed they did. As they put it: "We find very little evidence* that the depletion effect is a real phenomenon."

Other research also supports the Kurzban team's notion of willpower's being driven by a cost-benefit analysis. Consider that a big part of keeping your weight down is making yourself eat moderately. Well, psychologist Martin Reimann and his colleagues found that giving research subjects a tiny gift—just a Happy Meal toy—led them to take a smaller serving of pizza. That's right; your brain, the CEO of You, can be bought off with a promotional plastic toy.

Even more amazingly, these researchers found that the mere *possibility* of getting a prize—winning 10,000 frequent flyer miles, usable on any airline—also motivated the pizza eaters to go for a smaller portion size. Reimann and his colleagues explain that "both food and the prospect of receiving a nonfood premium activate a common area of the brain (the striatum), which is associated with reward, desire, and motivation."

And though the latter reward—the potential for frequent flyer miles—is only a *possibility*, for your brain, it somehow counts as an okay exchange. This may have something to do with how we tend to be optimistically biased about our prospects—seeing our particular glass as at least half-full and probably with a very cold dry martini.

But getting back to willpower, in short:

Willpower is energy for self-control that's "financed" by reward.

---

*The "file drawer effect" also seems to have been an issue with the "limited resource" claims for willpower. It's a scientific misdemeanor of sorts—the term for when researchers file away the studies that don't show the effect that supports their claims (sticking them in a drawer instead of publishing the findings in a journal). The McCullough team crunched the numbers on 68 published studies and 48 unpublished ones in coming to their conclusion that the evidence doesn't support "the depletion effect."

Think of it like having a willpower factory. Sure, it will release more of that super-special self-control energy to you. But sorry; no credit. You'll need to pay upfront. Slip a little something—a little rewardiepoo—to the watchman.

Bribery? Really?!

Now, please don't look too harshly on your bribe-taking nickel-and-dimer of a brain. Remember, it's just trying to act in your best interest—following its evolutionary marching orders to monitor your energy expenditure and see that you don't throw your efforts around unwisely. The good news is that its monitoring system seems to be pretty sensitive—opening up the willpower spigot in response to even the smallest sign that your efforts are being rewarded.

Granted, there are a number of factors that play into whether you'll get that spigot opened for a particular task, like how hungry, tired, or snubbed you feel and the fun-aliciousness of some competing activity on your personal horizon. If, for example, "do my math homework" is merely competing with "do my history assignment," you'll surely need less willpower to dive into those fractions than if the competition were "do my hot study partner."

However, by using the understanding that willpower is really about proving to your brain that you aren't doing something for nothing, you've got a better chance of getting enough mojo released to you to meet some challenge. (This includes social challenges—and going into them with guts instead of going into hiding.) As you'll see in the next chapter, which lays out the "how to" of this, you might just need to give yourself a little something—maybe just a nap or a piece of cheese—to give your brain a sign that you aren't a total idiot in trying to carry on.

— 14 —

WHERE THERE'S A WILL ... THERE'S A BRAIN THAT'S BEEN SLIPPED A COOKIE

How to get the most out of your willpower

Our command center, the human brain, is a marvel of evolution, setting us apart from every other creature on the planet. It allows us to speak, speak French, figure out the moral thing to do, and think about our thinking—all while standing upright and using the really huge September issue of *Vogue* to flatten a mosquito.

Impressive, huh?

Unfortunately, as you saw in chapter 11 ("Your Feelings Are Not the Boss of You"), the human brain is also a bratty, rebellious little shit, pushing you to do the feel-good stuff like getting drunk, having ill-advised sex, and eating cake. (If it's really in achiever mode, it wants more drinks, more sex, and more cake.)

This is a powerful force to combat—especially when you've got emotionally devastating tasks on the agenda, like going over and squeaking out a polite request for your neighbor to stop blocking your driveway with his trash cans.

No, describing that as emotionally "devastating" wasn't a mistake.

Of course, the polite request thing probably isn't a big deal for you if you're reading this book out of curiosity or because you're looking to go from somewhat confident to super-confident. However, if you're a person who's long been a turd under society's shoe, making a reasonable request of a neighbor is an undertaking on a par with standing onstage naked at a charity event so those in attendance can grade your boob perkitude or penis length and girth.

Unfortunately, the research on willpower makes pretty clear that "just use your willpower!" in order to "git 'er done" (whatever *'er* might be) is exactly the wrong advice. Your willpower is more likely to be there for you if it's like my late grandma Pauline's couch—plastic-covered and considered off-limits except on special occasions, like visits by the queen of England to the Detroit suburbs.

In light of that, this chapter has a bunch of tips and insights to help you do all of your socially demanding chores, but without tapping into your willpower—or by tapping into it as little and as efficiently as possible.

TALK LIKE AN ASSHOLE

Assholes use the third person in referring to themselves—like if I'm sitting on your couch and say to you, "Amy would like a piece of cake."

Come on, be honest; if I kept on like that, wouldn't that make you feel just a twinge homicidal?

Well, you don't have to do this sort of obnoxious third-person thing out loud in public, but—incredibly—social psychologist Ethan Kross finds that talking to yourself in non-first-person ways (like in my cake example above) can help you have more self-control. (Another form of this is using "you" rather than "I." For example, in pep-talking yourself, say "*You* can do this"—as in, "You can do this, Amy"—rather than "*I* can do this.")

Kross explains that taking a step back from yourself, even in these small linguistic ways, seems to enhance your ability to take charge of your thoughts and feelings.

This actually makes sense. Consider that it's often hard to know what to do about your own problems but you can be all Socrates Jr. about somebody else's, because you have some "distance" from them.

Kross, writing with one of his co-researchers, social psychologist Ozlem Ayduk, in *Harvard Business Review*, explains that talking in this way also seems to bolster a person's courage—or, as they put it, "pronouns matter when psyching yourself up." They give the example of the young Pakistani Nobel Prize winner Malala Yousafzai, who was asked by TV host Jon Stewart about how she felt when she learned that she was on a Taliban hit list.

She said she was—of course—afraid, but she imagined how she'd respond if she got attacked:

> "I said, 'If he comes, what would you do, Malala?' Then I would reply to myself, 'Malala, just take a shoe and hit him.'"

Researchers Kross and Ayduk believe that the shift she made from "I" to "Malala" wasn't a simple quirk of speech but reflected "something deeper—a process that helped her manage the intense threat that confronted her."

Fascinatingly, there's a powerful conceptual metaphor at work here—this metaphor of "distancing." Recall from chapter 5 that "conceptual metaphors" are called that because they reflect how we *conceive* of the world—with the *structure of our reasoning* coming out of the nature of the body. And right in line with this distance metaphor, when we want to get perspective on something in our physical world, we step back from it—giving ourselves some physical distance. Accordingly, by talking to ourselves as if we were another person— an objective third party—it seems we put psychological distance between ourselves and our "hot" emotional reactions (like cravings and panic).

Self-distancing like this is another form of the calm-the-fuck-down helper known as "cognitive reappraisal"—reinterpreting feelings and situations so they don't take such a big bite out of you. A reappraisal technique from chapter 11 that I find particularly helpful is giving yourself an emotional makeover by recasting anxiety as excitement. Similarly, Kross and his colleagues find that talking about yourself in non-first-person ways helps you see "social-anxiety-provoking events" as "challenging" rather than "threatening."

In other words, when there's some challenge you're facing, it should help to rewrite your inner monologue in the third person: "No, sorry, *Your Name Here*. You don't get to go all fucking pussy-as-usual."

Perhaps you'd prefer to scold yourself using more genteel language. Believe me, my mother would appreciate it if I'd follow your lead. However, I personally find it motivating to "yell" at myself using "bad" language—and it seems to go with the "be ballsier!" territory.

Psychologist Timothy Jay calls swearing "a defining feature of a Type A personality."* Think about it: Swearing feels energizing. Swearwords are aggressive language, used aggressively: "Back the fuck off, shitbag"—as opposed to the mousyspeak of "Excuse me, sir, but if you don't really terribly mind...and you won't hate me forever..."

Swearing also seems to have helpful embodied effects. Psychologist Richard Stephens, who had research subjects stick their hands in ice water, found that swearing seems to increase a person's pain tolerance. Participants who swore were able to hold their hands in the lab's version of Antarctic waters for longer than the other participants. Stephens, in observing the elevated heart rate in the swearing group, points to a fight-or-flight response—the fight kind, in this case—"downplaying feebleness in favour of a more pain-tolerant machismo."

The upshot: If you're trying to move up from beta or worse, it might be a good idea to not only talk to yourself in the third person but also to *shit fuck damn piss hell* yourself wherever you're trying to go.

---

*The claims from the 1950s research on Type A and cardiovascular disease didn't ultimately hold up, but Jay appears to be using this as shorthand for a hostile, aggressive personality.

YOUR BRAIN IS NOT YOUR SERF

My book editor is a sweetheart of a guy. The best character reference for him is actually a photo. He's in a chair at a book launch for one of his other authors. As usual, he's nattily dressed—wearing this beautiful suit and tie and classic antique brown wingtips—and while his author is off signing books, he's holding something for him: "Moochie the guinea pig."

Yet, somehow, my brain kept casting this sweet man as the lead in these recurring nightmares I began having about six months before my book was due. Yes, every night around 3 a.m., there he was—this zombie ax-killer collection agent in those beautiful wingtips, chasing me down the street to get my book advance back because I was so late in turning in my manuscript.

In my defense, though the writing was going slowly, it wasn't because I was spending too much time at the beach or lolling away my afternoons in the local opium den. I just needed more energy for all this science-chewing business. I'd have a few great hours of writing in the morning, when I was really clear and sharp, and then my mind would go fuzzy—and even sort of achy—for the rest of the day. Ugh. It felt like it was rebelling against working.

Well, I'd been making my way through this fantastic textbook on the brain, *Cognitive Neuroscience: The Biology of the Mind*, by neuroscientist Michael Gazzaniga. Through reading it, I got to know the poor brain part I'd been serially abusing—the prefrontal cortex. This is the part right up front that's central to higher reasoning and willpower.

As we've seen in how emotion—from subconscious input from the environment—plays into our decision-making, the prefrontal cortex doesn't work alone. Gazzaniga explains, "Cognitive control requires the integrated function of many different parts of the brain"—meaning it's a symphony orchestra you've got up there, not just a bunch of soloists.

However, the prefrontal cortex (PFC to its friends) *is* the home of a set of mental skills called "executive functions." These are basically mental office managers coordinating the brainwork you need to do (like planning, focusing, remembering, prioritizing, and resisting temptation) in order to achieve your goals.

Cognitive neuroscientist Adele Diamond explains that core executive functions include "inhibition," "working memory," and "cognitive flexibility."

> *Inhibition* is our ability to resist temptations and avoid acting
>   impulsively, which we do by controlling our thoughts, our
>   emotions, our behavior, and where we direct our attention.
> *Working memory*, which showed up in chapter 11, is that
>   "mental whiteboard" that holds a bunch of information we
>   need to kick around in the moment.
> *Cognitive flexibility* is the ability to mentally hop back and
>   forth between different concepts or tasks or adjust to new
>   demands, rules, or priorities.

We use these executive functions in reasoning and decision-making; in focused work, like reading and writing; and in stifling the expression of unhelpful emotions—keeping ourselves from acts of social suicide (and lesser social stumbles).

Now, as I explained in chapter 11, I write to a timer. I also take timed breaks. So I was doing fifty-two minutes of writing, and then, for my seventeen-minute break afterward, I was going online—answering email, scoping out vintage thingamajiggies on eBay, and snarking on Twitter and Facebook.

It occurred to me that, in doing all of this, I was hammering on *the exact same parts of my brain*—the smartypants parts that I needed for my writing. Though I was going on Twitter and eBay for fun, not work, I was still reasoning, making lots of choices, and drawing on my emotional reserve. In other words, my poor brain never got a break.

What an unwitting dumbshit I'd been. That brain ache I kept feeling was my brain telling me, "Fuck you, slave driver." It was a form of that "aversive feeling" we get from expending energy on some willpower-requiring task—in this case, making myself stay in my desk chair and do brainwork instead of, say, lying down on the wicker couch on the porch, throwing back a few glasses of vino, and taking a boozy nap.

So I started taking "stupid breaks"—breaks in which I walked away from the computer and allowed myself to do anything that didn't involve reading or writing or choosing among a bunch of options. My house started to get very clean; my dog started to get very walked; and I stopped feeling like somebody had stripped my mental gears.

However, though I found myself mentally clearer in the early afternoon, I was never as clear and sharp as I was in the early morning. I thought I could maybe bribe my brain—give it "rewards" in the form of snacks and power naps—to get it to front me more energy. Yet still, especially after 3 or 4 p.m., my brain became more of a fleshy gray doorstop.

It's tempting to point the finger at simple fatigue as the reason we can't get it up for willpower-requiring tasks later in the day. However, social neuroscientist Michael Inzlicht, whose findings on willpower dovetail with the Kurzban team's conclusions, told me that there's an important distinction between fatigue and sleep deprivation.

Inzlicht explained that when we are *sleep-deprived*, all we want to do is sleep. Period. Bottom line. Case closed.

However, when we are *fatigued*, we can be motivated to do other things if the payoff—that reward thingy again—is good enough.

So—as I noted in the previous chapter about what we are and aren't "el perko" for—you might feel too fatigued to sit down at the kitchen table and start doing your taxes yet have no problem locating the energy to put in fourteen hours straight playing *Grand Theft Auto*.

I had a hunch that for most people, it's probably better to do things requiring mental or emotional effort earlier rather than later in the day. Inzlicht agreed. He feels that there are probably multiple reasons for this. However, the one that makes the most sense to him comes out of research on circadian rhythms (our body's internal twenty-four-hour clock, controlling sleep cycles and related bodily functions, such as cell regeneration).

As Inzlicht put it to me in an email, "Our body has natural phases of more or less vigor (due to daily hormonal fluctuations), and typically, peak vigor is experienced in the morning hours. Now this is not true for everyone, with 'night-people' ('owls') feeling more vitality toward the end of the day."

The time of day that's best for you to do things is called your "chronotype." Cognitive neuroscientist Angel Correa and his colleagues explain that there are three main kinds of chronotypes: morning people ("larks"), people in the middle (who get no cute bird name), and night people (those "owls" Inzlicht mentioned). For most people (the non–night owls), as the day goes on, it gets tougher and tougher to summon the mental energy to perform difficult tasks—those requiring cognitive or emotional control.

However, I suspect that it's more than our coloring outside the margins of our biologically ideal work time that turns our cognitive ability to mush.

Research on mice by neuroscientist and physician Maiken Nedergaard and her colleagues found that the brain basically accumulates neural garbage throughout the day—the same way you accumulate physical garbage (like a Slurpee cup, Taco Bell wrappers, and the envelope from some FedEx package you got). These neurotoxins piling up include beta-amyloid, which has been associated with Alzheimer's disease.

There *is* a janitor who can come dispose of your neural garbage—

cerebrospinal fluid—only there's a problem: Your brain cells (neurons) are too big during the day to let it through. However, at night, when you sleep, your brain shrinks, and channels open up within it— allowing the cerebrospinal fluid to finally do its job and get rid of all the neural crap you've accumulated.

So, regarding my late-in-the-day slowdown, maybe it comes partly out of the neural trash that's piled up. You probably aren't very efficient (or happy) doing your job in a junked-up workspace; maybe your brain balks at it, too.

Happily, this research on neural trash disposal joins a lot of other research on the brain to point to some ways that might help you work within your brain's limitations to make the most of the willpower you have.

THE EARLY BIRD GETS THE WILLPOWER

As I came to see—and in keeping with the old saying "Eat your frogs first"—it's probably best to do your cognitively and emotionally toughest tasks as early as possible. (Of course, if you're an "owl" or one of those midday chronotypes who didn't get a cutesy bird name, you should figure out what time of day "as early as possible" actually is for you.)

Behavioral economist Dan Ariely explains in a Reddit Ask Me Everything how people piss away their first few hours of the day:

> One of the saddest mistakes in time management is the propensity of people to spend the two most productive hours of their day on things that don't require high cognitive capacity (like social media). If we could salvage those precious hours, most of us would be much more successful in accomplishing what we truly want.

You might also keep in mind that smarty-pants tasks eat up the energy you'd use for socially challenging things you need to accomplish. As psychologist Daniel Kahneman puts it, "Both self-control and cognitive effort are forms of mental work"—that apparently draw on the same energy source. So, if you need to hit somebody up for a job or a favor, maybe do that before you do four hours of complicated re-engineering on some nitwit co-worker's spreadsheets or some other odious, cognitively demanding task.

YOUR WILLPOWER IS LIKE A MOB EXTORTIONIST

If your brain has role models, one of them has to be that movie cliché mob guy—the one who comes into the corner grocery store once a week to pick up his paper bag of cash.

As we've seen from evolutionary psychologist Robert Kurzban, paying off our brain—giving it a show of "reward" like a snack, a nap, or...yes...masturbation—seems to be a way to convince it that it isn't an idiot to release more energy to us for the next cognitively or emotionally demanding task in our lineup. However, this only goes so far, and the time of day and the wear and tear you've already put on your willpower may have an effect.

Recall that diet doc and low-carb expert Mike Eades gobbled those chocolates in the evening. Had he been staring them down in the morning—before he'd gone through a full day hammering on his prefrontal cortex—he might've tossed them in the garbage instead of down the hatch.

MORE CHOICE IS BETTER—EXCEPT WHEN IT ISN'T

Choice is a good thing, right? The truth is, we're mentally unprepared for the massive level of options we have at every turn in modern life, having evolved in an environment where the, uh, headwaiter was more likely to present choice on the level of "Sir, can I bring you the grubs or the grubs?"

Making choices—especially from a slew of alternatives—is a sneaky hijacker of the energy you need to take on socially stressful missions. Every time you make a decision, you're hitting up your prefrontal cortex for another serving of energy—even if you're simply deciding what to have for breakfast on one of those deli menus that's twenty-four pages long. (Yeah, I'm talking to you, Jerry's Deli!)

Recognizing this, I eat the exact same breakfast every day. I just grab the fixings out of the refrigerator automatically; there's no cognitive energy that goes into choosing what to eat.

You can even avoid choice-making in getting dressed—as the late Steve Jobs did by wearing the exact same outfit every day: a black mock turtleneck, jeans, and New Balance sneakers.

And, finally, though we're considered "higher life-forms," we sure do have some lower impulses. In fact, as we've seen, to be human is to be a whiny little snot—intent on getting out of whatever adult, responsible thing that we're supposed to do.

Because of this, it sometimes helps to remove any possibility of choice from the equation, using what I call "roboting." This is my name for things I make myself do no matter what—giving myself no choice in the matter—like doing 10 pushups and 10 situps every time I make a cup of coffee (which I do about five times a day).

This has had a pretty fabulous effect. Though I've spent my days for the past few years moving between the bed, the computer, and the refrigerator, this coffee-cize thing (combined with my low-carbing since 2009) has transformed me into somebody who looks like she belongs to—and actually goes to—a gym.

A few elements were essential in making my pushup/situp sequence an ironclad must-do. First, I made my environment remind me to do it. Next, there was what I told myself and how I behaved in response.

First, the environment thing.

I learned from psychologist Art Markman about using the environment to support the creation of a habit. In *Smart Change*, he explains that we design our bathrooms to support our habit of brushing our teeth. We have toothbrush holders built into the sink, or we'll put our toothbrush in some kind of holder near the sink. So, standing in your bathroom in the morning, you see your toothbrush and you brush your teeth.

But consider the poor neglected package of floss lying around your bathroom somewhere. There are reasons we don't floss, Markman concedes, like in how it's kind of yicky to stick your fingers in your mouth and how the benefits from flossing come in the long term. However, he explains, "perhaps the most important problem is the floss container itself." The packages are not very attractive, and they don't come in a uniform size and shape. "As a result, it's not clear where to put it in your bathroom." Floss gets stuck in the medicine cabinet or dropped in a drawer—where it's (conveniently) easy to forget.

I've changed that—and started flossing—by buying a toothbrush holder that fits both my toothbrush and Gregg's and the floss.

As Markman observes, "Your environment is a powerful driver of what you do. Because your habits involve a consistent mapping between the environment and behavior, your habits are activated by the world around you. Do not assume that behavior change is a purely internal structure."

Understanding this is what led me to tag the new exercise habit I wanted to develop to something I already do throughout the day— make that next cup of coffee. This gives it a distinct place in my life in a way the loosey-goosey, floating "I should do these exercises daily" would not.

There were two more parts to integrating my new habit into my coffee-making process—what I told myself and what I did.

What I told myself: The situps and pushups are a necessary
    step in making coffee—meaning that I could no more
    avoid doing them than I could avoid pouring hot water on
    the grounds.

What I do: I act like I believe what I told myself—that there will be no next cup of coffee for me without pushups and situps—and I never let myself skip doing them.

It took just a few days of this—maybe a week—before the pushup/situp thing was pretty well woven into the coffee-making behavioral chain in my mind. There's no forgetting, no internal negotiation about how I "should" do it. After I hit the switch on the electric teakettle, I just robot right down on the rug and get to it.

Of course, if you work in an office, it might be a little awkward to drop and "gimme 10" on the cold linoleum every time you grab a cup of coffee in the break room. However, you can come up with similar rules and behavior strings for yourself to advance changes you're trying to make—like, say, whenever you buy yourself a fancy coffee, you have to talk to a stranger, and not just the one who says, "That'll be $7.28, please."

THE PROBLEM WITH NEW YEAR'S RESOLUTIONS IS THAT THEY'RE PLURAL.

People fail to follow through on their New Year's resolutions because they make, oh, ten of them. Unless you were bitten by a radioactive worm or are the progeny of space aliens, you have a normal (and, frankly, rather weakly) human prefrontal cortex. So, take the advice of Roy Baumeister and *New York Times* science reporter John Tierney, in their book, *Willpower*: "Make *one* resolution and stick to it."

Yes, it's enough to be trying to improve your confidence. In fact, it's a pretty huge fucking deal. You'll be more likely to succeed at it if you aren't also dieting, quitting smoking, and trying to go from scrawnydude to world heavyweight champion while launching a tech startup.

PLANNING IS THE MOTHER OF ACCEPTING CHALLENGES
LIKE A PERSON INSTEAD OF A POTATO

It's helpful, before you're in the thick of things socially, to consider the ways you commonly go limp. This allows you to put some fore-thought into how you'd *like* to behave—like by expressing an opinion when your friends are talking politics, making a case for your ideas at work, or having the guts to say "I don't know."

The flaw in this idea of preplanning, of course, is that, in the heat of the moment, it's easy to wimp out of whatever you planned to do. A strategy originated by economist Thomas Schelling may help you avoid doing that. It's called "precommitment," and it involves prearranging to make it hard (or impossible) to duck out of your goal.

Say, for example, that you're a woman with self-worth issues—manifesting in an inability to say no to casual sex, despite how it always leaves you feeling all angsty and the only orgasms you ever have from it are those you fake.

As I advised a girl who wrote in to my advice column with this problem, you could do things that make you too embarrassed to get naked with a guy, like wearing ratty granny panties and—in permanent marker across your stomach—writing something come-hither-y, like "Got herpes? (I do, and I love to share.)"

But you may not have to take such drastic measures. Because of our evolved concern for reputation, peer pressure is a powerful precommitment tool. You rev it up by telling others what you plan to do or avoid doing and asking for their watchful eyes and support. That's another thing I suggested to this girl—bringing in her friends to cheer her on in sticking to her plan and, in case she gets seriously tempted, to keep her out of bars and on the clothed and narrow.

BE YOUR OWN SURVEILLANCE STATE

Increasingly, your right to privacy and other civil liberties are treated as annoyances to be ignored—like by those three federal agents warrantlessly recording you from the "Heating and Cooling" van outside your house.

However, acting as your own tiny personal surveillance state—monitoring yourself to track your progress in achieving your goals—is a good thing. In fact, social psychologists Roy Baumeister and Brad Bushman call behavior monitoring a "key ingredient" in self-control—one that "often presents the best opportunity for immediate improvement" in your ability to stick to your goals.

Monitoring involves looking at your behavior and then holding it up to your standards to see how you're doing. This sort of attention—forcing yourself to judge how well you're hitting your marks—appears to be more motivating for staying on task (or getting back on it) than mere good intentions.

There are habit-monitoring apps to help you log your progress and show you all the days on the calendar on which you met your goal. (Search for these in the app store by typing in "habits" and/or "New Year's resolutions.") You can also go old school and just make big red X's on a calendar.

Having visible evidence of your progress—those colorful daily, weekly, and monthly blocks of success—is especially motivating. The power of the tangible ties back to "neural reuse" from chapter 4—the theory that our mental ability to understand things seems to come out of our physical experience of the world. Physical representations, including the 2-D kind in pictures, seem to make abstract ideas easier for us to grasp—that is, to understand. (And yes, "grasp" making "understand" easier to, uh, grasp is an example of this.)

Of course, it can be tempting to ditch the monitoring after you've had a bit of success in sticking to a new goal. Amy Dresner used a monitoring app to help herself stay vapeless for fifty-four days, but then she got cocky and deleted it. In days, she was back on the "pen."

Dresner explains that without the app, her sense of accomplishment about quitting became "sort of amorphous." She says, "I just didn't have the pride I did when I was counting off the days."

ABS OF SELF-CONTROL

Remember bidirectionality—how there's a two-way street between behavior and emotion? Well, it shows up in research by marketing professor Iris W. Hung, who finds that—as she puts it—"steely muscles can lead to a steely resolve."

Really.

Try something: Right at the moment you're doing some dreaded social chore, clench a muscle—your biceps, your fist, or your calf muscle—whichever works for you. In Hung's experiments, she found that this helped the participants muster the willpower to do all sorts of unpleasant tasks.

However, there is an important caveat, and it's that doing the muscle clench *in advance* of your activity (as a sort of "the more the better" attempt at self-control) may backfire on you—diminishing your willpower instead of amping it up.

And though muscle clenching can help you have willpower, this isn't to say you should go all mini-Hulk to speak your piece at the neighborhood council meeting and then throw your muscles back in storage for the next six months. Exercise is a powerful self-control booster. Cognitive neuroscientist Adele Diamond notes that a number of studies find that "aerobic exercise robustly improves prefrontal cortex function" and the executive functions. For example, one of these studies, by neuroscientist Laura Chaddock-Heyman, finds that children who are more aerobically fit outperform their less fit peers in self-control.

Of course, if you've got some important plans for your willpower on a particular day, consider that you might not want to tax it by dragging your ass out for a run. At the very least, it might be a good idea to do your exercise at the end of the day—and because acts of drudgery feel even drudgier then, maybe do it at a gym with a lot of hotties so you have an ulterior motive yanking you there.

FLOPPING TALL

If you have a deep fear of failure, it probably keeps you from even trying a lot of things—including those that might help you overcome your deep fear of failure.

We've all heard people sing the praises of failure: *Failure is the best teacher!... The real failure is when you stop trying...* blah, blah, blah.

These things aren't just overly shared Facebook memes. They are also true.

That's why it's important to get okay with failing.

Being helped by your setbacks—or at least not so hobbled by them—starts with reframing your thinking on goals. To do that, consider the difference between being *goal-oriented* and *goal systems–oriented*.

A *goal* is simply a result you're aiming for. It's a singular target, meaning that it's a win-or-lose, all-or-nothing proposition.

A *goal system*, as explained by social psychologist Arie Kruglanski, is a network of "interconnected goals." That sounds complicated. But to explain it another way, a goal system is a goal family—including all of your goals' brother, sister, auntie, uncle, and cousin goals. And looking at your goals in these terms gives you a big cushion from your failures.

I'll let *Dilbert* cartoonist Scott Adams explain.

I first encountered this goals-versus-systems thinking in his book *How to Fail at Almost Everything and Still Win Big*. In it, he writes, "In the world of dieting, losing twenty pounds is a goal, but eating right is a system. In the exercise realm, running a marathon in under four hours is a goal, but exercising daily is a system."

He explains that a goal is "a reach-it-and-be-done situation, whereas a system is something you do on a regular basis with a reasonable expectation that doing so will get you to a better place in your life."

Having a system makes individual failures, like blowing your diet one night, easier to digest. These individual failures are just small bummers within the bigger picture.

"To put it bluntly," Adams writes, "goals are for losers.... For example, if your goal is to lose ten pounds, you will spend every moment until you reach your goal—if you reach it at all—feeling as if you were short of your goal. In other words, goal-oriented people exist in a state of nearly continuous failure that they hope will be temporary. That feeling wears on you. In time, it becomes heavy and uncomfortable. It might even drive you out of the game."

Perhaps even worse, with a goals approach—as opposed to a goal-systems one—even when you reach one of your goals, you still lose. Sure, Adams says, "you celebrate and feel terrific..." and then, the kicker: "...but only until you realize you just lost the thing that gave you purpose and direction."

PART THREE

—

Putting It All Together

RISE AND SPINE

Grow a backbone and put the damn thing to work

Okay, it's time for you to make mojo out of that nojo—that perpetual "No. Nuh-uh. I can't" that wells up in you when life presents you with some social challenge.

And remember where doing this can ultimately take you:

- To quitting your lifelong position at Loserhood Inc.—and having your reflexive ("go-to") response be standing up for yourself and what's fair.
- To being able to seize opportunities that present themselves to you instead of shrinking from them because you dread (gulp!) revealing yourself to other human beings.
- To having love. To having a relationship with someone who's your equal, who's with you because they love you and not because they're hoping to bleed you dry before they move on to the next sucker.
- To having real friends and real friendships—the kind where you've got your friend's back and they've also got yours (and not just when they need a surface to write on).
- To generally having people's respect—though they might not agree with you. And if they don't, to being okay with

that instead of wishing you could, say, curl up like a bug
and be put out of your misery by the hoof of a passing cow.

In part 2 of this book, "The Building Blocks of the New You," you
read a lot of stuff about how we're wired, why we behave as we do,
and how to calm the fuck down. All of that was prep for the stuff in
this last section of the book—the advice on how to stand tall, march
out there, and finally live like the foot instead of the football.

As for how you'll transform yourself, the answer comes out of that
line from chapter 3, "The mind is bigger than the brain."

What this "mind is bigger than the brain" thing ultimately means—
in practical terms—is that your body and your behavior are your gym
for turning yourself into the new you. Just like in a real-life gym, you
have to do your reps. That's really all it takes to transform yourself—
from "Dismissed!" "Disrespected!" "Disenfranchised!" to somebody whose mere presence sends the message, "*Dis* is not a person
you should screw with."

NO MORE SLUMPTY DUMPTY

Your grandma was onto something in nagging you to stand up
straight.

Consider that the CEO has different body language than the shy
intern.

The "large and in charge" posture of highly successful business
honchos is right in line with the metaphor of *power* as *bigness*—for example, "Big Brother," "big man on campus," and the big ape being
the alpha.

When somebody's confident, they feel entitled to take up space.
In fact, they may pretty much "own the place," dominating whatever
space they're in—like by putting their hands behind their head, lean-
ing back in their chair, and putting their feet up on the desk. By
stretching out like this, they are taking up *a lot of space*—much more

than they'd take up sitting normally at a desk—though it's unlikely they do this consciously.

Contrast these confident space-seizers with people who lack confidence. The latter types tend to sit and move in ways that reflect shame, submissiveness, and a need to be *smaller*—hanging their head, hunching their shoulders, and taking up as little space as possible. (If nobody notices them, maybe they can live to mouse another day.)

A much-talked-about 2010 study (later found to have problems in methodology) by social psychologists Dana Carney and Amy Cuddy and management researcher Andy Yap looked at whether using the body language of the powerful might make a person feel and act more powerful. They put subjects through a series of experiments—after having them spend two minutes holding "expansive" postures they called "power poses," reflecting some of the body language you see in power brokers, like that hands-behind-the-head/feet-on-the-desk sprawl.

Other subjects were assigned "low-power" postures—taking up as little space as possible—like standing with their arms and legs crossed and their hands hugging their body.

The researchers reported that the group who'd done the power broker-type poses experienced empowering psychological, biochemical, and behavioral changes. The details? The power posers said that they *felt* more powerful afterward. They were more willing to make a risky bet in a subsequent gambling test, and they showed "elevations in testosterone" and decreases in the stress hormone cortisol. This hormonal change is noteworthy, Carney, Cuddy, and Yap explain, because previous research has found that powerful people show lower cortisol levels and also because higher testosterone levels both "reflect and reinforce" dominance.

Woo-hoo, huh?

But there was a problem.

A team of researchers, led by Swiss psychologist Eva Ranehill, did what's known as a "replication"—a redo to see whether research findings reproduce—of the power poses research. The Ranehill team, disturbingly, found that power posing had "no effect on the hormones and risk tolerance in a large sample of men and women."

How could this be?

Well, psychologists Joe Simmons and Uri Simonsohn, who critique research methodology on their blog, *Data Colada*, noted that the initial power poses study had too few subjects (only forty-two, while Ranehill had 200).

Epidemiologist and stats guru Sander Greenland talked to me about why the number of subjects in a study matters, explaining that "a study that's too small can easily display effects that aren't real. What you see could just be due to chance or 'noise,' like if you flipped a coin five times and, for no real reason at all, it came up heads on four of the tosses." He noted that "small studies can also easily miss real effects."

In statistics-speak, Greenland explained, "a small study is said to be *underpowered*."

Uh-oh. So, forget the idea that posture has an effect on emotion?

No. Because there are plenty of studies that show that it does—including the Ranehill study.

The Ranehill team's experiments did replicate one of the three findings from the Carney/Cuddy/Yap study. They found that power posing had "a significant effect" on subjects' "self-reported feelings of power." This alone is a big deal, because if you feel more powerful, you're likely to act more powerful—more self-possessed and more comfortable with asserting yourself. And these feelings should be reflected in your voice, your breathing, and how you move.

The missing effects on testosterone in the Ranehill study were puzzling, considering that plenty of other studies suggest that behavior and even experience—especially those related to power, competition, and dominance—affect testosterone levels. For example, research by sociologist and engineer Allan Mazur, among others, finds that winning increases testosterone while losing stomps it down.

And anthropologist Lee Gettler is among the researchers who've found that becoming a dad is associated with decreased testosterone—which makes sense, considering that the "Eat my sword, Spartan wussy" hormonal profile of the gladiator isn't exactly conducive to long afternoons of coochie-schmoopie-poo with the baby.

So, why did the Ranehill team not see any increase in testosterone from power posing? Well, maybe despite the prior body of work associating testosterone and dominance, "expansive" poses just don't do whatever it takes to get testosterone out of bed.

This is a possibility. And I looked for other possibilities, as well.

I pored over the Ranehill paper and the "supplemental material" with the details on how they conducted their study. I noticed that their methodology differed from the original study's in a number of possibly meaningful ways. For example, subjects in the Ranehill study were instructed on how to pose by a computer, not a human.

The subjects in the Cuddy/Carney/Yap study, on the other hand, had an experimenter there in the room with them, helping them with their pose and even touching them—putting a (fake) "electrocardiography lead" on their calf and left arm, explaining it as a "sensor."

Whatever, right?

Maybe not.

Because I look at research through an evolutionary lens, I'm attuned to what social animals we are—how our behavior is affected by the presence of an audience or even just thinking about having others' eyeballs on us.

Consider that we're not confident in a vacuum—not all "Ho-ho-ho, am I ever the shit!" when nobody's around. Our confidence—or lack of it—is a reaction. It comes out in response to other people around us.

To explain the apparent problem with the Ranehill replication another way, consider social psychologists Joseph Cesario and Melissa M. McDonald's work on "context." They contend that for research to tell us anything real and meaningful about our psychology and behavior, it needs to consider the body "in context," because context shapes how we think and behave.

Context, in simple terms, means the circumstances at hand—what situation a person is in (for example, the physical environment and the social environment). This notion that our thinking (our *cognition*) is *grounded* in context—shaped by the *situation* we're in—is called "grounded cognition" or "situated cognition," and it's supported by countless findings from across psychology, in addition to Cesario and McDonald's research.

Cesario and McDonald explain that the context dictates what behaviors are *possible*—or optimal. So, for example, whether you are motivated to go get a hammer or a fork depends on the context—whether the thing on your coffee table in need of your attention is a loose nail or a piece of cheesecake.

Cesario and McDonald also note that the *meaning* of a particular behavior is defined by the context. Take the meaning of lying on your stomach—lying "prone." Cesario and McDonald explain, "In the context of a fight, lying prone indicates submissiveness, whereas in the context of the beach, lying prone indicates relaxation."

Clearly, studies that don't reasonably approximate a real-world context are deeply flawed, no matter how many subjects they have—failing on giving us a realistic account of how humans are likely to feel and behave in the real world. In fact, they omit *the* most behavior-determining part of the picture. As evolutionary psychology research emphasizes, our genes motivate us to act *in response* to things and situations we encounter in our environment. In ev psych terms, our responses are "domain-specific," not "domain-general," meaning that the domain—the situation we're in—shapes our preferences.

Recall that there is no singular self and we have no consistent set of standards, preferences, and practices good for all occasions. Instead, we have shifting context-dependent motivations to help us adapt to the challenges or opportunities of a particular situation—like whether it calls for getting it on or getting away from a guy who looks ready to go all crazymofopants on us with an ax.

Yes, that's a reference to that study from chapter 12 in which subjects watched either a romantic movie clip or a clip of the ax-wielding Jack Nicholson in *The Shining*. Remember that the mating-primed subjects—those who had watched the romantic clip—went for the place advertised as unique (all the better to stand out from the competition), while those who had been danger-primed by *The Shining* opted for the "wildly popular" establishment (all the better to duck into that crowd and keep the arms and legs they came in with).

This brings me to a bit of bad news—but not to worry; I show in the next chapter why you actually don't need to worry about it.

The thing is, unlike the tidily AMAZEBALLS!!! conclusions about human behavior you see in clickbait "science" online, actual science is kind of messy.

Accordingly, consider that there are (ugh!) some context-related complications with the simple notion of "stand up straight and you'll rule the world!" Say, for example, that some evening, things aren't going so well for you socially. Well, in a study by social psychologist Keith M. Welker and his colleagues, subjects who struck an "I own the place" pose and then got snubbed felt much worse from their snubbing than subjects who'd slouched.

And say you're trying to project a self-assured ease while chatting at a cocktail party. Standing all expansively Aryan and proud like one of those "Übermenschen" in the Nazi propaganda pic *Triumph of the Will*...well, let's just say that people will not be laughing with you.

So, I'm sorry to say...regarding these power poses findings, it's a tangled ball of yarn we're left with. This means that until a bunch more research is done, the conclusion on power poses is basically that Facebook relationship status: "It's complicated."

However, what I can tell you—once again—is that there's a body of research that finds that a confident posture is an integral part of behaving confidently.

BOD IS YOUR CO-PILOT

In trying to make sense of the body's role in confidence, I went back to metaphor. Confidence comes out of feeling powerful—feeling like you have the goods to tackle what's in front of you (meaning that you have a reasonable expectation of succeeding).

But beyond *feeling* powerful, social psychologist Dacher Keltner and his colleagues define *being powerful* as being free to do what you want and being able to control other people through doling out or withholding material goodies and social resources. Material goodies are things like food, money, gifts, and a job you give or take away. The social resources are things like "knowledge, affection, friendship, decision-making opportunities, verbal abuse, or ostracism."

Understanding this, consider the metaphors for power. They're all upward and outward. Power is *big*. Power is *up* (a *lofty* position, being *on top* of a situation, having control *over* somebody). And power is *forward motion*. (When you're powerful, you go toward things—*approaching* what you want—as opposed to shrinking from things.)

The word "approaching" might remind you of "neural reuse" from chapter 4. This is the notion that evolution did the thrifty thing and built human emotions on an already existing base—the approach-avoidance impulses of tiny organisms: "Go toward that particle thingy! Looks yummy!" or "Eekers, get outta here before you end up dead!"

As we've seen, the older brain mechanisms that drive *motion* seem to be redeployed in us for *emotion*, but, as psychologist and neuroscientist Michael L. Anderson puts it, "without losing their original functions."

Well, the late psychologist Jeffrey Alan Gray explained that we also seem to have *predispositions* for approach or avoidance—meaning that we have overall tendencies to be drawn to new experiences and people (*an approach system*) or to be fearful and err on the side of backing away (*an avoidance system*).*

APPROACH   **AVOID**

In fact, it seems that we each probably have either a more approach-oriented or a more avoidance-oriented personality. To fully understand what that means, it helps to understand what personality is. Personality researcher William Revelle explains personality as a pattern—over time—of feelings, thoughts, and desires (goals) that shapes how you behave and, in fact, how you are *predisposed* to behave.

Psychologists Andrew J. Elliot and Todd M. Thrash, who research approach and avoidance as dimensions of personality, explain that each of these temperaments has roots in "a broad network of neurophysiological mechanisms." In other words, this is yet another confirmation that these predispositions aren't just thinky things; they involve the body. For example, they note that "approach and avoidance mechanisms are operative in the spinal cord, the brainstem,

---

*In case you're interested in the history: Back around 1970, psychologist Jeffrey Alan Gray came up with the theory that we have two different systems guiding our behavior—the behavioral approach system and the behavioral inhibition system. ("Inhibition," of course, is just a slightly fancy researcher term for avoiding things.) So, yeah—that's approach and avoidance. Forward and reverse.

and the cortex, and involve both neurotransmitter and hormonal activity."

Elliot and Thrash explain that though these temperaments of approach or avoidance direct how we think, feel, and behave—leading us to respond in pretty consistent ways—there's hope for breaking out of our patterns.

They explain that we can adopt "goals" that go against our underlying temperament, "overriding initial inclinations and redirecting behavior."

In a word (or so): Ya. Hoo.

We really don't have to be lifelong prisoners of who we've been.

SHIFTING OUT OF REVERSE

I once had a car—that pink 1960 Rambler—that, for a while, only turned left. I tried a number of measures to get it to turn right again, such as squinting really hard when I came to a corner. I found this surprisingly effective, but only at giving me a brain freeze-style headache. Eventually, however, fixing the problem with my car ultimately took the intervention of a guy in greasy coveralls who understands how this turning business plays out under the hood.

Likewise, in your efforts to remodel yourself, understanding the mechanics of approach and avoidance should help you shift more smoothly into an orientation that's more "Forward ho!" than "Forward? NOOOOO!"

OUR AVOIDANCE SYSTEM

Our avoidance system is our "Back away from that!" system—our behavioral guide in response to all manner of scary, negative, frustrating, dangerous, and stress- and sob-inducing stuff. It's the system of pessimism and powerlessness.

Social psychologist Keltner and his team note that this system comes with its own special brain chemistry, featuring, among others, the stress-response hormone cortisol and the neurotransmitter nor-epinephrine (aka noradrenaline, a big participant in revving you up for fight-or-flight).

To give you an overview of how this system works, say you're about to go after something—some tasty-looking berries on a bush, some person you'd like to date, that ball of yours that got kicked into Creepy Guy's yard.

However, your avoidance system goes, "Yoo-hoo! Ass-for-brains! *Really?!*"—getting you anxious that things aren't going to end well for you. And this, in turn, puts you and your motivation in reverse.

In other words, your avoidance system is a *shrink!* system, a *make yourself smaller!* or *hightail it outta there!* system—right in keeping with all the metaphors of powerlessness.

Granted, hightailing it out of there sometimes makes sense. Explaining what goes on in your mind between "Hmm, I'd like to ask that girl out" and the response "Run! Run like the wind!" psychologist Jeffrey Alan Gray and his colleague neuroscientist Neil Mc-Naughton explained that our brain does "risk assessment" when we have conflicting goals. This starts with weighing the benefit of our getting whatever we're going after against the likelihood that we'd get squashed doing it.

This, in turn, drives how we respond—i.e., as McNaughton put it to me, whether we go "big and bold and driving forward; small and panicked and rushing to the exit; or checking all the options, dithering or chewing (our) nails and often then backing away."

Over time, if you generally respond in fraidy ways, it reinforces the fraidy response as your habitual response. (Yes, for the 113th time, it's that neurons "that fire together wire together!" thing.)

To be able to respond differently—to be more willing, for example, to take on social risks—you need this system to sit the fuck down so you can have your approach system be your go-to response.

OUR APPROACH SYSTEM

Our approach system is our "Go get it!" system—guiding us to pursue goals and "reward" (stuff in our environment that's valuable for survival and reproduction). Approach is the system of optimism and opportunity.

If approach had a language, it would be cheerleader-ese, like "You can do it!" and "Bring it on!"—spurring you to go forward. Yes, throw yourself into that job opportunity, that chocolate frosting, that orgasm at the end of the sex rainbow.

The postures that go with approach are, of course, the *BE BIG* ones—the ones that show that you feel entitled to take up space. Entitled—but not angrily entitled. Big, powerful people are relaxed about taking up space. They don't even think about it. For them, it's just the natural thing to do.

The essential neurochemical in approach appears to be dopamine. For a thumbnail of how it works—as neuroscientist Wolfram Schultz explains it—dopamine neurons "predict and detect rewards" and "label environmental stimuli" as rewarding.*

Or, more simply put, dopamine is the neurotransmitter involved in wanting, seeking, and "go get that fabulous thing right now, you fabulous person!" Okay, so maybe dopamine doesn't come right out and call you a fabulous person as it's pushing you to go after fabulous, rewarding things, but it might as well. It's part of the brain chemistry of the optimism that fires you up for all of the big, bold opportunity-seizing it urges you to do.

It's helpful to keep in mind that approach is a *motivation* (as is avoidance)—and more than that, it's a motivational *system* (with all

---

* To clean up from all the hyperbole about dopamine that you've likely read, seen, and heard in mainstream media, here's a bit from my science-based advice column: *Though dopamine is still widely known by its outdated nickname, the "pleasure chemical," research by neuroscientist Kent Berridge suggests that it doesn't actually give you a buzz (as opioids in the brain do). It instead motivates you to do things that might—like eating cake, smoking a doob, and making moves on that girl with the hypno-hooters.*

the interconnectivity a system entails). Social psychologist Jennifer Lerner, with Keltner, makes the point that emotions trigger "a set of responses" (in our physiology, behavior, attention, and judgment) that allow us to "deal quickly" with problems or opportunities that pop up.

Research by Keltner, with social psychologists Deborah Gruenfeld and Cameron Anderson, supports the notion that habitually responding a particular way—in approach or avoidance mode—leads to an overall tendency to respond that way. This means that your *Go forward!* or *Pull back!* tendency spills over into your emotions, actions, perceptions, beliefs, and decision-making.

One of many examples of this spillover effect comes from Cameron Anderson's research. Anderson finds that powerful people seem to have emotions that are more positive—in addition to having a better overall mood—whereas those lacking power are more likely to feel like rewarmed crap. (Not exactly how the researchers put it, but you get the idea.)

Keltner and his colleagues also note that being more powerful also "increases sensitivity to rewards"—both social ones (like approval) and material ones (like food and money). In simple terms, if you're powerful, you're likely to be the first to spot that twenty-dollar bill fluttering in the bush. Maybe that sounds a little crazy, but it has to do with how an approach orientation is associated with sharpened attention to rewards—chemically sharpened, through "increased dopamine." (Research by neuroscientist Kent Berridge suggests that dopamine drives desire—or, as he puts it, *wanting*—zeroing your attention in on things that could prove rewarding so you'll giddyup and go get them.)

Keltner and his team additionally explain that being powerful may lead you to be "less cognizant of others." This isn't to say that power gives you vision problems, making it hard to spot the mailman. It just means that powerful people don't spend a half-hour gnashing over what somebody will think of them before having a thirty-second conversation about whether to go with the blue-bordered name tags or the red.

Ultimately, the research suggests that there's a whole team of *approach* perceptions, emotions, and behaviors that work together and gin one another up.

Yup. Power is a package deal.

I suspect that it works this way, at least in part, because of the brain's attempts for energy efficiency. Recall that your brain tries to be thrifty—whether it's building on old machinery for new purposes or it's just doing its thing day to day. Cognitive scientists talk about how the brain is "expensive" to run.

It doesn't like to expend energy on things it's already figured out. So it automatizes, meaning that it brings out the emotional/behavioral combo that's worked for you in the past. This means that the more you take what we could call "the *approach* approach" and the more that it works for you, the more it becomes your default motivation.

Yes, what I'm saying is that by repeatedly behaving as an "approacher" would, you can set yourself up—emotionally, bodily, and behaviorally—to *become* an approacher.

To understand what the brain mechanics of this might be, let's upgrade the cliché "It's like learning to ride a bike" to "It's like learning to fly a drone." The first time you take the thing up, you're seriously wobbly at operating it. Determined as you are to get a glimpse of somebody having sex, you can barely keep the thing from coming to a watery end in the neighbor's Jacuzzi.

This awkwardness of yours continues for a while, and you have to look at your hands and struggle to remember what worked. But as you keep sending the thing up, your hands just start "knowing" what to do. And—wow—before long, you find yourself violating multiple local, state, and federal laws with aplomb!

BE A SPACE INVADER

It is important to get in the habit of sitting, standing, and moving like the confident, comfortable-in-your-skin person you want to be.

In general, that is.

This means that when you're at your desk or walking down the sidewalk—that is, when you aren't in the hot seat—it's good to remind yourself to sit, stand, and walk tall instead of small (and actually do that).

However, there's a problem with making power postures and speech a "must-do" for, say, some important conversation with Mr. Big Guy.

Silently reminding yourself to maintain some new posture while you're also speaking differently *and* remembering what you need to tell somebody will probably cause too much of what psychologist John Sweller calls "cognitive load." This amounts to mental overload—giving your working memory more than it can juggle all at once. That's when you can easily slip into what I call Babblish. (You've got all the right words; they just take it upon themselves to show up wherever the fuck they want in your sentences.)

Another problem is "leakage." This (as seen in chapter 9) describes inconsistencies that show up in how you're presenting yourself—sometimes in your words and often in your body language. So, for example, you can be standing tall and expansive, but if you're trembling and sweating as you speak, it's like your body is calling "BULLSHIT!" on the confidence you're trying to project.

But the good news about these "large and in charge" postures is that you don't have to be all do-or-die about remembering to do this one and that one in the moment. That's because—in the next chapter—I explain how to fire up the approach system as a whole instead of fussing with each individual part.

Still, because it is important to know what to do with the individual parts, I'll give you a few guidelines that you can use at times when you aren't under a lot of pressure.

And to simplify this further, the overriding guideline in most of these is just two words: BE BIG.

Being big means taking up space.

You do that in a number of ways:

BODY

- Stand up straight, or at least sit up straight.
- Pull back your shoulders, and push out your chest.
- Hold your head up (meaning look straight ahead instead of down like it's your life's work to find lost change).
- Don't fiddle around with your hands, hair, and clothes.
- And—taking context into consideration—at times when it wouldn't be utterly ridiculous, stand with your feet apart and your hands on your hips, kind of like you're surveying all the workers in that factory you own.

If you try this, I think you'll see that it really does feel like you're in charge of something, even if it is only the Ikea bookcase (aka "Svensquatch") that your attempts to put together previously led to your taking two mental health days off work.

VOICE

Being vocally big doesn't mean talking in a booming voice—all "HANDS UP! GET ON THE FUCKING GROUND!"—like you're trying to save the hostages or something.

Being vocally big just means speaking like you "va bien dans sa peau"—which, translated somewhat literally from the French, means that you "go comfortably in your skin" (as opposed to sounding like you want to unzip it, step out, and run away screaming).

So...

DON'T SPEED

You take up space with your voice by speaking slowly—which suggests that you feel entitled to take up time.

I'm guilty of speaking fast—both because I have a lot of rushing thoughts and because, underneath it all, I still sometimes worry that people will try to escape before I finish what I have to say. Okay, some may. But many more are likely to want to if I speak so fast it sounds like somebody's playing me back at double-speed.

What really helped me slow down is hearing myself speaking on my weekly podcast.* You can do the same by recording yourself with the voice memo feature on your phone. Then, before you go out to some social event, remind yourself to try to speak slowly.

BREATHE

Breathe from your diaphragm, not your chest. To understand the difference, try this: Talk. Put your hand under your ribs. When you're breathing from your diaphragm, you'll feel it moving.

SPEAK; DON'T SQUEAK

Speaking—as opposed to squeaking or croaking out what you have to say—is another way to be big. A great resource for this is a slim little book by Hollywood voice coach Dr. Morton Cooper, *Change Your Voice; Change Your Life.*

Cooper, whom I saw for a couple of very helpful sessions, explains that many of us don't use our optimal pitch, meaning the one that we'd have if we stripped away the fear and speaking tics. In *Change Your Voice*, he explains how to find it. To do this now, go back up the page

---

* My speed before I worked on slowing down would have been appropriate had I been on fire and trying to tell you the location of the suitcase nuke and the train with all the Nazi gold before I turned into a pile of ash.

here and read some lines, and then respond to anything with which you agree with a "spontaneous and sincere" *umm-hmmm*. Do this with a "rising inflection" and with your lips closed.

Cooper writes that, by doing this, the sound you produce should be "your right voice"—your "natural pitch." To check whether you're doing it correctly, he explains that you should "feel a slight tingling or vibration around the nose or lips." If your pitch is too low, you'll feel "too much vibration in the lower throat and little, if any," in the mouth/nose area. He advises that you keep doing the "umm-hmmm" until you feel the tingling sensation around the lips and nose.

DON'T FILL EVERY NOOK AND CRANNY OF AIRSPACE

Show the courage to allow open spaces in conversation—silences between sentences or even big pauses when you're thinking about what to say. This allowing silences business is scary for some of us, but just try it a few times and you'll see that nobody will fill those silences with jeering about what a slow-witted idiot you are.

GET TOASTED

No, I'm not suggesting you try to drown your speaking fears in vodka. The rotten little fuckers would just bob right back up again.

To get some practice at speaking, try a forum where you'll be encouraged out of your terror rather than shunned for it, like the nonprofit group Toastmasters (toastmasters.org). They have local clubs all over the world. Members practice speaking and get tips and encouragement from other members. You can read rave reviews of local Toastmasters groups on Yelp. You'll see how it has helped numerous people (including my friend and former assistant Lydia) not only pry themselves out of being terrified but get good at speaking, too.

EYES

There's this idea that if you're powerful, you look directly into somebody's eyes when you're talking to them and that if you look away while you're talking, loser-ino!

Um...not quite.

Granted, looking down while you're talking is a sign of guilt, shame, or submission, so you should see that you unglue your eyes from your shoes while you're making your case. However, this isn't to say you should maintain creepy, unbroken death-stare eye contact as your conversational M.O.

Research by psychologist Gwyneth Doherty-Sneddon finds that we look away when we're talking for two reasons. Either we're self-conscious—from, say, fear of failure—or we're thinking about what we're about to say. In other words, looking away is natural (and perhaps even a sign that you're thoughtful), which is why plenty of people who feel pretty damn confident do it, too.

Also, as former FBI profiler Joe Navarro and psychologist Marvin Karlins note in *What Every BODY Is Saying*, a strong, direct gaze doesn't communicate just one emotion. It's a feature of a number of mental and emotional states, including love, hate, curiosity, and having seriously scary intentions (à la "If I cut you into small pieces, I can fit most of you just under the ice cube rack in my freezer").

Navarro and Karlins explain that we figure out which emotion is being conveyed by looking to context—meaning that we rely on "other facial displays that accompany eye gaze behavior," such as a tightened jaw and compressed lips (which suggest dislike) or "a relaxed smile" (which suggests somebody likes us and feels comfortable with us).

But, again, you can't be all frettypants about where your eyes are going without putting a big dent in your overall mojo. Though it's good to understand these points about eye contact, once you get more confident overall, the eye contact of a confident person will just be there as a ride-along.

THE LOOK OF FEELING COMFORTABLE

Confidence is a form of comfort, so if you want to come off as confident, you need to come off—and *be*—comfortable, down to the clothes you're wearing.

Consider the "Hollywood slob."

There's something to be said for how, back in the '90s, Hollywood bigwigs started dressing like they were waiting to get an emergency call to clean out somebody's garage. This was followed by tech honchos like Mark Zuckerberg going around in "power hoodies" and movie stars showing up to premieres in flip-flops.

I'm not suggesting that we all slob down. (In fact, I hate all of this slobbery and personally go way in the other direction.)

But beyond how feeling physically ill at ease can make you feel emotionally out of sorts, business consultant Olivia Fox Cabane notes in *The Charisma Myth* that wearing an uncomfortable piece of clothing, like an itchy sweater, and then yanking at the collar and squirming to try to get comfortable can effectively make you come off as a loser. The same goes for wearing too much clothing and then getting all hot and sweaty or forgetting your sunglasses and squinting in the bright sun.

In short, dress uncomfortably and say "Bon voyage!" to your charisma.

The problem is that we can read people's expressions of physical discomfort as emotional discomfort. So, using the example of the squinting, Cabane explains that "your face will show the same reaction to discomfort from the sun as it would to feelings of anger or disapproval" from another person. This also goes for the fidgeting or sweating.

This means that it's important both to dress comfortably and to take any other steps you can to be physically comfortable. So, eat before you meet; don't go to a meeting hungry. And allow enough time to get there so you can keep your cool—as opposed to arriving in a frazzled rage, brimming with hate for drivers who don't get that green means "go," not "examine your arms for cancerous moles."

Cabane even advises taking comfort into account when choosing the location of a meeting (if you have a choice in the matter)—considering things like temperature and noise level. Of course, there will be times when you just can't help but feel uncomfortable for one reason or another—if your clothes are trying to strangle you, your allergies are turning your nose into a no-breathing zone, or you're seated in a restaurant chair that feels like a repro from Inquisition days.

When you do feel out of sorts like this, say so. Cabane advises being quick to point the finger at the offending object making you hot or squinty or whatever. The goal in this is possibly heading off others from misinterpreting your physical discomfort as emotional tension (which might lead them to believe you're either deeply troubled or deeply troubled about being there with them).

RAISE YOUR RIGHT ARM. NO, YOUR OTHER RIGHT ARM.

As I mentioned about all these body moves—standing up straight, talking a certain way, etc.—it's good to practice them when you aren't under a lot of pressure. And come on—don't beat yourself up after you march in to make your case to the VP but, feeling a stab of fear, instead direct all your arguments to the tips of your shoes.

You put yourself out there, and that's something.

Remember, this is a process.

As you do the stuff I suggest in the next chapter, you'll *feel* what it's like to go out into the world as a confident person. And as you start doing that more and more, the cool thing is that the right postures and all will just come along.

ROCK 'N' ROLE!

Time to slip into somebody more comfortable

Tragically, some loves are not meant to be. Romeo and Juliet. Tristan and Isolde. Blankie and me.

Blankie was my very first love.

But before I tell you what brought us together, a little background on me.

I am the eldest of three girls. By the time the third—my sister Caroline—came into the picture, my parents were more relaxed about the whole *caring for another human being!!!* thing. In fact, they were pretty much all, "Caroline, go play chicken with the traffic while Mommy makes dinner."

But with me, because I was the first, it was, "OMIGOD, DIAPER RASH! SHE'S GOING TO DIE!"

Yes, as you may have guessed, "Blankie" was my baby blanket— this stained, woolly pink square I dragged everywhere with me as a toddler, often sucking on one of the ends.

Before long, I was no longer a toddler, but I was still dragging Blankie around.

These nervous new parents of mine kept flashing on mental snapshots of the adult me, caught *in blanket delicto*—walking down the aisle clutching Blankie or coming into some business meeting trailing the thing behind me and then teething on a corner.

Something had to be done.

One day, I woke up, and my dingy pink beloved was gone. "MOMMMMM!"

My parents blamed Dy-Dee Diaper Service. For the record, Dy-Dee is in the business of cloth diaper delivery, not stealing mangy comfort items from children, despite the hefty prices these surely command on the black market.

I was heartbroken. Traumatized. Like, to the point where, at around age twenty-five, I called my mom and again asked about Blankie—despite how memory generally isn't my strong suit. (I once said to a guy, "How *do* I know you?" and heard, "Uh...we slept together.")

As I was writing this chapter, I phoned my mother in Michigan and again asked about Blankie. Uh...you know...just out of curiosity.

"I think we hid it," she said. "I know we hid it." She just had no idea where. Grrr.

Truly, I do understand that my mom and dad meant well; they were simply doing the best they could as terrified young parents. However, I was just a little slow to let go—like I was a little slow to stop wetting the bed. I inevitably would have ditched the thing of my own accord and never given it another thought.

Of course, that's just what happens in life—we "put away childish things"—especially when we start wanting to be kissed by a boy and realize that...yikes...there's a tattered pink field of barbed wire and land mines standing between us and a long, dreamy make-out session with someone who is not our pillow.

To be fair, there *were* some things from childhood I didn't "put away"—namely, my fearful, suckuppy ways of relating to other people. In fact, over time, these became a template for me—my model for how to relate.

Granted, these behaviors had been *adaptive*, meaning they protected me from physical and emotional harm back when I was a bullied little kid with no friends. But as I got into new social circles in my late teens and early 20s, my behavioral template started to be *maladaptive*—a mismatch with these new environments, much like the sugar lust that kept us from malnutrition in ancestral times but now keeps many of us from being able to fit both ass cheeks into a single airplane seat.

Unfortunately, I couldn't see that the shrinking, submissive way I was behaving was making things worse for me—sending little pings out to the world signaling to everybody that I was someone to disrespect, to kick around, to ignore.

Now, I think we're all prone to just keep doing what we've been doing—neglecting to ask ourselves whether our go-to behavior still makes sense. Personally, it didn't even occur to me that there might be another way. That's probably because the bootlicky way I behaved didn't just seem like behavior; after years of repetition, it seemed like who I was. I didn't yet understand that I could just act differently—and keep acting differently—and, through that, make my escape from my long social exile and have a nice, big life.

P.S. Mom, next time you're in the basement, could you please check those boxes behind the furnace?

TRAINING WHEELS FOR THE SELF

Testosterone appears to do a number of jobs, including reducing anxiety and depression and improving spatial abilities. But testosterone is best known as the hormone of the gladiators—the biochemical brew behind "Go slay them and tear out their livers!" (aka Casual Disembowelment Friday).

Remember, from the beginning of the previous chapter, the claim that power postures raise your testosterone—the one that got tagged with the science cooties of "failure to replicate!"?

Let's pretend that twelve different research teams ran replications of the power poses research, complete with the most airtight methodology ever, and every one of those teams found, "Holy crap! These postures actually do pump up people's testosterone like crazy!"

There's still a problem: If you aren't *already* the gladiator type, that elevated T would be pretty meaningless. Basically, it would just make you a loser with higher testosterone. You'd have no idea what to do with it. Or, putting this in practical terms, you wouldn't be psychologically set up to storm out into the world and make use of it.

Understanding why this is starts with understanding that there's a whole host of stuff that goes into starting to become confident—including calming down through applying reason to your overblown fears and cutting yourself some slack through self-acceptance and self-compassion. For your confidence to be believable to other people, you need to display the body language of confidence. And, as I explained in chapter 8, because confidence is a predictive thing—a feeling of how you'll do *based on your prior performance*—it would help if you had some successes from acting gutsy stacked up (kind of like how it's easier to make money if you're already rich).

Putting these elements (and others) together piece by piece while in some social situation *is* a huge and unwieldy job—a confidence-eating job. Just as you're remembering to shore up one area, you're forgetting to shore up a bunch of the others. And as you witness yourself bombing on multiple fronts, up comes self-loathing to finish off whatever tiny buds of confidence you came in with. (Welcome to Clusterfuckville, Population: You.)

To actually go out into the world with confidence, you need to bypass the need to hit all of these individual marks at once. I've come up with a way for you to do that—and it's by test-driving *the whole package* of what it means to go around as a confident person. This is what I was doing in my brief stints "being" somebody else—typically my boss, coolly confident Kathy, the TV commercial producer.

Yes, I'm telling you that the way to start your transition to the new confident you is to spend some time as the old confident somebody else.

This person *already* has all of the individual bits of confidence pulled together into a confident whole. This eliminates, for example, the need for you to work really hard to calm yourself while you're interacting with other people. First of all, you temporarily aren't "you." Also, the confident person already is calm. You just need to engage with the world a few times as that confident person to experience the benefits of being calm and the stance and bodily sensations that go with.

I call this "training wheels for the self."

As I explained in chapter 2, using this "training wheels" method is how I started my climb out of loserhood. I later came to see that it was pretty much the social stylings version of crime writer Elmore Leonard's advice to aspiring writers—to imitate a writer they admire as a steppingstone to developing a style of their own. (When Elmore was starting out, he actually used to retype a paragraph or two of Hemingway and then come up with the next paragraph in the same style to get in gear to write some of his own stuff.)

I just did my practice runs here and there for a few minutes at a time—for example, interacting with a guy at the deli or some seat hog on the bus. However, a few of these little forays were enough to show me that I was on the right track. In stepping out of my scaredy-pants ways and standing up for myself (using the psychological airbag of doing it as somebody else), I started to have something I'd never had before: hope.

My hope came out of noticing that when I was playing life as Kathy, I was treated differently. I felt different. And I saw that nothing terrible happened to me. And out of all this, something very important became clear to me about my lifelong social suckage: *I* was not the problem; it was just the way I had *behaved*.

I began to think I might be able to have a very different life if I used my role-playing experiments as a launchpad for engaging with people as me—the full-on, unshrinking version. We'll get to the "how-to" of being able to do that—"exposuring yourself"—which is Part Two (of a two-step process). But first, here's a little more about

Part One—this "training wheels" thing: How to impersonate your way to becoming the real you.

PART ONE
CREATING THE TEMPORARY NEW YOU

Yes, really—the way to start your transition to the new confident you is to spend a little time as the old confident somebody else.

WHO SHOULD YOU BE?

Do as I did and pick somebody you admire for the way they go about life with self-respect and confidence—ideally somebody who stands up for themselves, their beliefs, and what's fair.

This can be some person you know, some person you just know from the movies (George Clooney being an obvious choice if you're a dude), or some fictional movie or TV show character. (Sorry, fellow bookworms. Don't pick a character from a novel, because merely imagining how they speak and move isn't enough. You need to call up mental video clips of them actually doing that stuff.)

HOW OFTEN?

No, you don't have to go around acting like this person 24/7. In fact, you may just need to do it once or twice for a few minutes—or maybe a handful of times—over a week or a few weeks.

Maybe that sounds unbelievable, but I'm guessing that you'll see pretty quickly that your life can be different—that if you behave like you're "somebody," that's how people treat you. This prediction comes out of my own experience—and believe me, I'm not some emotional prodigy. My optimism is also supported by somewhat-forgotten research on role-playing in therapy published by clinical psychologist George A. Kelly back in 1955.

Kelly explained that we have expectations—preconceived notions—about how life's events (especially interactions with other people) will play out for us. In response, we have set ways of behaving that we automatically fall into, which Kelly calls our "roles."

The reason for this comes out of something I've discussed a bit in this book—how our energy-conservationist brain goes on automatic so we don't have to think out every single situation we're in from scratch. Our mind identifies patterns—situations that show some similarities with situations we've dealt with before—and directs us to just do what we did the last time around.

This does save cognitive energy. Yay, right?

However, Kelly explains the problem with this: We're unthinkingly acting as if our expectations are correct. But maybe they're wrong. Maybe they made sense at one point but don't anymore.

Kelly advised that when some area of our life isn't quite working for us, we should look at it as a scientist would. In other words, when we have some belief about how some situation or behavior will play out for us, we should consider it a hypothesis—a guess only—to be tested through action. Kelly advocated doing this through role-playing as somebody else.

In Kelly's version of role-playing for therapists and their clients, the therapist writes a character for the client to play for two weeks—somebody who approaches life in less self-defeating ways. The client rehearses this role with the therapist at first and then does "field trials"—going out into the world and seeing how life treats them when they're acting like somebody else. This role-playing allows them to do what I did—to "experiment with new behaviour...while protected by 'make-believe,'" as British psychology professor David Winter puts it in explaining Kelly's work.

Kelly saw that when patients tried on someone else's persona for just two weeks, it exploded their long-set expectations about what was possible for them or likely to happen. This, in turn, allowed them to incorporate new behaviors that worked better for them.

I think you might not need two weeks—not if you climb into a real person's persona rather than a made-up one. Because you're "playing" an existing person, you also mimic their voice and body language. This gives you a far more powerful "vehicle"—one empowered by how "the mind is bigger than the brain."

All in all, I just put on my Kathy persona about five times over a period of a few weeks for maybe a minute or two, standing up for myself in little day-to-day life situations. As soon as I saw (and felt) the kind of positive response I got from speaking up in Amy-as-Kathy mode, it set off ye old cartoon lightbulb in me—spotlighting how differently I got treated when I acted like a person instead of a crumb.

From this, I recognized that the assumption I'd been running on for so many years was wrong. People didn't treat me like shit because some tribunal had sentenced me to eternal loserhood; it was because I'd been acting as if that were the case. In fact, my shrinky self-protective behaviors were mainly protecting me from having the life I wanted.

What I needed to do was clear: act as I did when I was interacting with people as Kathy, but do it as me. And then I just started doing that—standing up for myself, making my case, and the biggie: even asking people to do things for me. (Previously, I would have crawled naked through a gauntlet of alligators on a juice fast to keep from asking to briefly borrow a co-worker's pen.)

P.S. If you're one of those who need more than a few times doing this role-playing thing, don't take it as yet another sign that you suck. Take it for what it—objectively, self-acceptingly!—actually is: just a sign that you need a little more time.

WHO SHOULD YOUR GUINEA PIGS BE?

People you've known for a while have perceptions of you that are pretty fixed. In time, you should be able to change how some or many see you and relate to you by consistently showing them that your days of rolling over and playing dead are *fini*. (Some people's perceptions will be harder to change than others'—for example, those of your family, since they've known you in meek mode for, like, forever.)

However, while you're in your training wheels period, go off and practice on strangers. This has the added benefit of removing some of the potential cost from your practice runs. The guy in the Macy's returns department isn't part of your social circle. If you do something dipshitty when you engage with him, you'll be momentarily embarrassed, but he won't be there at your Monday morning staff meeting, making it the first order of business to tell everybody what a turdpiece you are.

WHERE AND WHEN?

Sure, you could go to a mall for an afternoon and practice on various people you encounter. But maybe that turns this into some big, horrible homework assignment that you'll never get around to. It also doesn't give your mind a chance to mull over each experience before you crowd it out with another and then another.

So, consider doing what I did. I just spontaneously seized opportunities to engage with strangers as they came up in my day-to-day life—times when my default behavior would have been knuckling under. I instead threw on my Kathy persona, and—whoa, holy crap—I found myself getting treated with respect.

THE FAKERY WILL SET YOU FREE

Perhaps you're worried that this "training wheels" thing will turn you into some creepy fake person—an imposter, a fraud. Don't worry. It won't. Your practice persona is just temporary. You're simply borrowing somebody else's manner and behaviors and using them as a launching pad for your own.

And technically, yes, when you wear somebody else's persona out into the world, you are deceiving people, but that doesn't make you a douche. Motivation counts. You aren't role-playing in hopes of separating some fool and their life savings. You're just trying to coax up the long-submerged you. Basically, you're looking to live more honestly... to live with guts, as the full-blown you... which is a pretty admirable purpose—and one you can (and should) feel pretty great about.

PART TWO
EXPOSURING YOURSELF

This is the part where you go out there as you and start doing what you're afraid of.

Challenging your fears through action like this is basically do-it-yourself "exposure therapy."

Formal exposure therapy is pretty much what it sounds like: a therapist repeatedly *exposing* a patient to something they're irrationally afraid of (like spiders, riding in elevators, or social rejection) so they can see that their fear is unfounded. Helping them declaw their fear allows them to stop avoiding the thing they've been afraid of, so, for example, they can finally take the elevator to their new office on the 110th floor instead of hoofing it up 220 flights of stairs.

Exposure therapy has roots in experiments back in the 1890s by Russian physiologist Ivan Pavlov. You've probably heard of the most famous example—about lab doggies and a bell. Food (meat in powder form) was placed in dogs' mouths, causing salivation, which aids in digestion. Next Pavlov paired the presentation of food with the ringing of a bell—ringing the bell just before giving the dogs the meat powder. After repeating this sequence a number of times, ringing the bell alone would cause the dogs to salivate. They salivated in *anticipation* of the food.

This is a wonderful thumbnail of how *learning* works in the brain. The dogs' brains associated the bell with the arrival of food, to the point where the Ding! Ding! Ding! of the bell alone began to read as Food! Food! Food!

Check out the parallel in your life—the social predictions your brain has come to make. If you're like many people reading this book, your mind has paired your asserting yourself in any way with the expectation of a certain consequence: that something socially or maybe even physically terrible will happen to you.

Your habitual mental linking of assertiveness with social (or physical) horribleterribleness has led to a protective way of behaving—a habitually groveling way of conducting yourself. Being deferential can sometimes be adaptive. If, say, you're being challenged over a parking space by some sack of steroids in a monster truck, parking a few rows back and walking a few more steps to the store beats walking with a slight limp for the rest of your life. However, deferring in every social interaction doesn't serve you. In fact, it hurts you. Yet, whenever that bell rings—whenever there's some socially demanding task or situation—you go right into auto-mouse.

Thankfully, Pavlov figured out a way to un-ring the bell—that is, to stop the old association from automatically driving behavior—and it is to repeatedly ring the bell and then repeatedly have the expected food be a no-show. The doggy brain observes again and again that the ringing bell is *not* followed by the delivery of something to eat, and in time, the bell ring does not cause any uptick in doggy saliva. This "extinguishing" of the "conditioned response"—that "bell equals dinner!" association—is called "extinction." (Think of it as the meteorite that will take out your behaviorsaurus.)

Extinction is a form of learning. (Psychologists define learning as a change in our behavior that comes out of experience.) In recent years, neuroscientific research by Joseph LeDoux and others has shown how the extinction process plays out in the brain. Consider that your brain's threat detection circuitry—with its band leader, the amygdala—is designed to sound the alarm at things that endanger you. It knows what these things are because you have stored items and situations in memory—marked with some brain code that means "These things are dangerous, you idiot!"

According to studies in LeDoux's lab by his grad student Maria Morgan, it seems that if you show your threat detection circuitry over and over that something it identifies as dangerous actually isn't, it stops sounding the alarm when the thing appears. (Brain nerds, please see the box on the next page for the specifics.) Without that internal siren blasting you out of your skin, you stop reacting to the thing as if it's a threat.

What this means—what you should be seeing from all of this doggy drool/threat detection/dinner bell stuff—is that the problems you have socially aren't mysterious and unsolvable. You, too, can put an end to *your* lifelong social suckage.

You just need to *learn*—as Pavlov's dogs did with that bell that didn't lead to food—that the assumptions you've been living on for all these years are wrong. Ridiculous, even. You'll do this through social exercises (laid out in the next chapter) that show your brain that it needs to unpair social engagement from the expectation that it'll be the death of you. You will see—over and over—that nothing horrible happens and that, in fact, things generally work out better for you when you engage and assert yourself, as opposed to ducking for cover as if North Korea just launched a nuke on the house next door.

CORRECTING OVERBLOWN FEAR RESPONSES
A SIDE TRIP FOR BRAIN NERDS
Your Brain Regrets the Error

Well, truth be told, it's a remorseless motherfucker, but it might be willing to fix it.

Let's pay a visit to our *prefrontal cortex (PFC)*—the evolutionarily advanced front part of the brain that gets called upon for planning, decision-making, and other smarty-pants stuff. The middle part of this—the *medial prefrontal cortex*—is involved in adjusting the amygdala's HOLYSHIT! reaction.

Neuroscientist LeDoux, in *Anxious*, describes the amygdala as "the accelerator"—the driving force—of defensive responses and refers to the lower area of the medial prefrontal cortex (the *ventromedial prefrontal cortex*) as "the brake."

Research by neuroscientist David Euston and his colleagues suggests that the medial PFC is a sort of office manager for our reactions—learning "associations between context, locations, events, and corresponding adaptive responses, particularly emotional response." And clinical psychologist Richard A. McNally, reviewing neuroscientific research on exposure, suggests that the medial PFC "may store long-term extinction memories that inhibit the expression of conditioned fear responses."

Other players in this error correction business include the hippocampus—central to memory and navigation—which helps by differentiating between safe and dangerous situations. There's also the insular cortex, which applies emotional context to bodily sensations, and the anterior cingulate cortex, which has a role in anticipating painful events and making corrections when our expectations are wrong.

— 17 —

SADDLE UP YOUR FEAR AND RIDE
IT LIKE A PONY

Fear is not just the problem; it's the answer

I'm sure there are therapists out there who are all over the latest re-search just moments after it's published. However, when I'm out and about in the world, I usually seem to meet the other kind—those who read their last clinical psych journal article back in 1977 as their ad-viser held them at gunpoint in graduate school.

Recall from the previous chapter that exposure therapy involves challenging your fears through repeatedly throwing yourself into what you're afraid of. The model of exposure therapy that's still widely used by therapists was developed back in the 1980s by clini-cal psychologists Edna Foa and Michael Kozak, with later additions by Richard McNally. A primary goal in this model is reducing fear—in the patient's session with the therapist and between ses-sions.

Obviously, if you have unwarranted fears, fear reduction is *ulti-mately* good. Fear sucks. It feels bad. And it's what has you going about life like a bug about to be squashed—scurrying away instead of living.

However, according to current findings from neuroscience, imme-diately reducing fear seems to be a mistake. In fact, the LeDoux lab research on unpairing fear associations in the brain suggests that fear is actually a powerful tool for learning. It's experiencing fear that will show you that your fear is pretty stupid, which is how you get your threat detection circuitry to untag a thing as something you should be afraid of.

Experiencing fear is also how you come to see that you have the ability to tolerate it and other feel-bad emotions, which is how you keep them from sidelining you.

This is why a newer model for exposure therapy by UCLA clinical psychologist Michelle Craske is so exciting. Craske's model is similar to the traditional approach (and psychologist George A. Kelly's use of role-playing) in how it involves "violating" your "expectancies," the irrational expectations you have about what will happen in a situation.

However, Craske's model takes into account recent findings from neuroscience on how we learn. So, though the *eventual goal* is reducing your irrational fears (same as the goal in the traditional model), the *initial priority* is on *learning*—creating a new, more rational way for you to view the thing you were afraid of *and then* giving that new view some staying power in your mind.

In short, instead of asking the question traditional exposure therapy does—"How can we help you be less fearful?"—Craske's approach asks, "What do you need to *learn*" so you can start living instead of avoiding?

I think it's helpful to break this sort of learning down into three points:

- Repeatedly seeing evidence that what you believe—your association of some thing or circumstance with a particular outcome—is wrong.
- Changing your behavior accordingly.
- Installing the new belief/behavior in long-term memory so you can easily access it when it's behavior time again.

However, there's a problem in making some new behavior your go-to behavior, and it's the competition—the competing older ideas (and all the behaviors that come with).

The older ideas and behaviors have been around a long time, and they have long-established neural networks supporting their continued existence. This makes any new learning pretty fragile in terms of its staying power. This is why feeling afraid and experiencing stark contrasts—the mismatches between what you feared would happen and what actually does—is such a powerful tool for teaching you (and helping you remember) that your fears just don't make sense.

As Craske explained in a psychiatry lecture she gave in Stockholm, "The more the mismatch there is the greater the learning that should take place."

And yes, hypocrisy hunters, there might seem to be a bit of a contradiction afoot in how I explained that role-playing—briefly experiencing conflict while playing somebody else—diminishes a good deal of the fear you'd have if you put yourself out there as you. But remember that this is a two-step process: first role-playing as some confident person you know and then going out there as you after that. (Trust me, you'll be scared as fuck when you do go out there as you.)

And through doing that role-playing as a preliminary step, you solve a problem that often presents itself in exposure therapy: the dropout issue. Many patients drop out of exposure therapy. This is not exactly a surprise, as the practice part of it amounts to stuff like, "Okay, Claustrophobia Girl, please show up to be locked in a tiny closet at 3 p.m. on Tuesday."

Recall from the willpower chapters (13 and 14) that our brain looks um, unfondly, at "aversive feelings"—researchers' term for "feeling like crap"—that come up in the wake of our doing cognitively or emotionally taxing things. So, in doing these exposure exercises, here you are sticking your face in the tarantula pit or whatever and nearly giving yourself a fucking coronary, and for what?

Well, the answer—your incentive for sticking with your "exposuring yourself"—comes out of your little role-playing forays, and it's BECAUSE YOU, FOR THE FIRST TIME IN FOREVER, HAVE HOPE. You see that things can be different for you—different than they've ever been—if you can just start acting differently. And hey, if you're at all like me, you've probably said that you'd "give anything" just to be popular (probably about 65,326 times). Well, doesn't enduring a little passing dread here and there count as "anything"?

DON'T THINK AND DRIVE

Fear and anxiety are not the same thing. However, I've used the terms pretty interchangeably throughout the book—for the same reason I did this with "emotions" and "feelings." (As I explained in chapter 4, I'm assuming you're reading this book to become more confident, not to get a Ph.D. in neuroscience or to open a backyard brain surgery clinic.)

But before we get to fear and anxiety, we should check back in with emotions and feelings—*emotions* being your brain's subconscious responses to goings-on in your environment and *feelings* being your conscious thoughts about them.

Recall from chapter 4 that emotions, technically speaking, are *physical* experiences—your body's split-second subconscious experience of your environment through your senses. This information from your senses (like a fleeting glimpse of sharp teeth) activates parts of your brain (before you're even aware of what you're seeing). It sets off neurochemical reactions that push you to, say, gear up to haul ass before your ass becomes lunch.

Feelings, on the other hand, are conscious, thinky things—your interpretation, in your thoughts, of the environmental input that comes into your brain: "No, dumbshit...those aren't teeth. It's just the sun hitting the log funny. Or is it? Great. Probably about to be eaten by an alligator. I wish I'd told Robert I love him. Wish I'd pursued that Broadway stage career. Wish I'd tried anal."

Understanding the nature of emotions versus feelings is helpful for understanding the difference between fear and anxiety.

Fear, explains neuroscientist Joseph LeDoux, is what we experience when we're *face to face with danger*. It starts beneath consciousness with messages from our senses to our amygdala and other parts of our threat detection circuitry. And though, in response, our body reacts self-protectively, we sometimes don't consciously recognize we're afraid.

Anxiety, LeDoux explains, is a conscious response to *potential threats*—threats that we might face in the future. So, while fear is about threatening stuff RIGHT NOW, anxiety is predictive. It's conscious worry about what could, might, maybe would happen in the future.

We do eventually engage in some conscious processing of our fears—expressed in statements like "Holyshitski! I'm scared out of my mind!" However, this happens in the wake of our physical response to the threat. (Yes, this hearkens back to our old pal William James, back in chapter 3.)

Fear and anxiety *are* our protectors—keeping us alive, unmaimed, and uneaten, physically and socially—so we don't want to ditch them entirely. But it also isn't good for us if they're habitually triggered by things that aren't real dangers—causing us to duck (avoidance mode!) instead of moving forward (yep, the approachie thing). Being overly sensitive like this is like having a smoke alarm that goes off—causing the entire office building to be evacuated—every time somebody walks into the conference room with a piece of burnt toast.

So, in order to be a mover instead of a ducker, you need to recalibrate your fears and anxiety to be more accurate and less crippling. However, both LeDoux and Craske—based on the neuroscientific research—feel it's essential to target "implicit" and "explicit" brain processes separately. This sounds complicated, but "explicit" processes are simply the conscious ones—resulting in thoughts you can verbalize—and implicit ones are the nonconscious, automatic ones.

There's an important reason for separating these. LeDoux explains that the implicit and explicit systems can utilize common resources in the brain, competing with each other and leading to inefficiencies when both forms of processing are called on at the same time. For example, he explains, "if you are attempting to change beliefs in the same session in which you are extinguishing (trying for the extinction of some response), you are asking the brain to learn and store memories in a way that might not be ideal."

According to Craske's research, this divide-and-conquer approach should amp up the effects of your exposure and give it more staying power, over time and in all sorts of different contexts. (More on this in the next section.)

Separating out the doing and the thinking also allows you to make the strongest possible attacks on the three separate "response domains" that psychophysiologist Peter J. Lang observed make up the "database" of fear (or any emotion) in our mind: your conscious evaluations (stuff you can verbalize about your feelings); your behavior (like retreating or avoiding); and your physiological reactions (like a pounding heart and a sweaty face). This three-part model—reflecting, once again, how "the mind is bigger than the brain"—points to why talk therapy alone is such an insufficient and inefficient way of addressing unwarranted fears.

HOW TO PUT YOUR TRANSFORMATION ON TURBO

The advice below should help you make your fear and anxiety recalibration stronger, speedier, and stickier.

But first, a confession. I'm one of those people who, when a book says, "write a bunch of stuff down!" get resentful instead of getting a pen. In case you, too, are one of those people, I'll give you two ways to go about this exposure business—the lazy-ass Amy Alkon way and the more powerful, more efficient way (for anyone willing to pick up a notebook and write shit down).

EXPOSURE FOR LAZY MOFOS

Not surprisingly, when I was in the thick of working on my transformation, I never formally listed the specific things I needed to tackle. (In my defense, I was mousy about everything.) So, even when I was no longer role-playing, I basically used a WWKD (What Would Kathy Do?) model to examine whether braver behavior was warranted in a situation, and then I just gritted my teeth and behaved that way.

You can do that, too. Just look around you for some social challenge—something you don't have the guts to do—and then go fucking do it. Ask that table hog at the busy coffee shop to move their crap so you can sit down. Go chat that girl up—or at least try . . . like Albert Ellis did. And did. And did.

Albert Ellis, the late co-founder of cognitive therapy, was once this scrawny young guy, seriously socially awkward, in part because of his being hospitalized with diabetes quite a bit in his youth. He wanted to pick up chicks, but he was terrified of rejection. He ended up challenging his fear by spending the entire month of August going to the Bronx Botanical Garden and chatting up women—or rather, trying. He approached 130. One hundred of them talked to him. Of those ladies, only one agreed to go out with him, and she stood him up. But the whole experience was an exercise in violating his expectancy— his expectation that something AWFUL would happen to him if a woman rejected him. It kinda sucked when they did, sure, but he saw that he could tolerate "kinda sucked" just fine. Ellis, who was a friend of mine, ultimately became quite the ladies' man.

EXPOSURE FOR PEOPLE WILLING TO WRITE SHIT DOWN

The science-based route, like Santa or Schindler, starts with a list.

Make a list of the social stuff you're afraid of—the things that you'd like to stop shrinking from. This will allow you to target each issue methodically and repeatedly. Concentrating like that is a far more powerful (and much smarter) way to go about this than doing it randomly like I did. (What's that? Am I hearing some of you fellow lazy-asses rummaging around for a pen?)

A few examples of possible items for your to-tackle list:

- Being able to say no—to stuff you don't want to do, to stuff that's unfair, or just for the fucking hell of it, because you finally can.
- Being able to ask for favors.
- Expressing opinions that you know or suspect others don't share.
- Letting people know the real you, even the uncool and embarrassing parts.
- Freely admitting when you don't know the meaning of a word.
- Asking for help.
- Admitting when you're wrong instead of denying it or covering it up.
- Engaging with strangers as if you're worth meeting—like you're about to pass on valuable information, not viral gastroenteritis.
- Responding to a gift or compliment with "Thank you!" instead of hammering the giver with all the reasons that you are undeserving and really just a sinkhole of suck.

Making this list is just step one.

To follow the model for exposure in Craske's research, you'll go through four steps altogether. This is a little queer, but it might help to remember them as List, Consider, Do, and Review. (P.S. I'm to blame for these names, not Craske.)

LIST:

1. List what you would like to do but are afraid of. (You could list just two or three things or even just one to start.)

CONSIDER:

2. Write a line about what you expect to happen if you do each of these things—how you expect people to react to you.
3. On a scale of zero to one hundred, note what you think is the likelihood of that actually happening. *(This one is the kind of thing some readers will skip, but it's helpful for showing yourself how big the gap is between your fears and what actually happens.)*

DO:

4. Do the thing you're afraid of—at least a few times (perhaps three or four times over a few days or a week) so you see the sort of response you get isn't just a fluke.

REVIEW (ideally in writing but at least in your thoughts):

5. Review what actually happened and whether what you expected to happen actually did happen.
6. Review what you learned from the experience—how your expectancy was violated.

As for how this plays out, here's how it went for a guy in one of Craske's studies who was deeply afraid of social rejection and humiliation:

LIST:

1. He said he was afraid to express a professional opinion to a co-worker.

CONSIDER:

2. He expected that if he did this, the co-worker would "stare...contemptuously" at him "and walk away without responding."
3. As for the likelihood of this happening, on a scale from zero to one hundred, he was ninety-five percent sure that this would be the case.

DO:

4. In exposure exercises over the course of a week, he expressed opinions to co-workers four times.

REVIEW:

5. He reported that his expectations were not met. He wrote about what actually happened in one case: "Co-worker responded immediately, agreed with my opinion, and we continued talking."
6. When asked what he learned, he wrote: "Co-workers do not always disregard my opinions."

Hot diggity damn.

YOUR MILEAGE WILL, OF COURSE, VARY

Sorry to sound a bit like one of those car ads where they tell you that you'll get some incredible MPG—and then there's the small print: "at 3 a.m. on highways after a nuclear winter."

However, regarding how much of this exposuring you'll need to do, how often, and for how many weeks or months, well, it's kind of an individual thing. Do these exercises to tackle one particular problem (maybe for a week, maybe for two), and see whether that helps you behave differently in your day-to-day encounters. If you feel like you'd benefit from more exposures, do more.

If you have serious social anxiety—like to the point where you can't even bear strangers' eyes on you—Craske's review of neuroscientific research suggests that your brain is a little slower to learn the lessons of exposure than the average person's. (Basically, going back to that boxed bit for brain nerds in the previous chapter, it seems that your brain's "brake" for anxiety, the ventromedial prefrontal cortex, may be a bit weaker than most people's.)

So, as I noted about the role-playing exercises in the previous chapter, don't feel bad if you need to do more of these exposure exercises than you suspect other people would. We all have our strong points and suckier ones. Remember, what counts are those "small wins"—the fact that each time you go stick your tongue out at your fears, you kill off a bit more of their power to keep you and your life small.

DON'T DO WHERE YOU THINK

Multitasking hurts learning. Recall neuroscientist LeDoux's observation from the research on learning that giving your brain two different things to do at once makes each process less efficient.

As LeDoux and exposure researcher Craske advise, you need to separate the "doing" of "exposuring yourself" from the conscious thinking about it—considering what happened, considering what it tells you about these fears you've been letting run your life, etc.

Basically, this means going out there "dumb" when you're doing these expectancy-violating exposure exercises. And by that, I mean that you shouldn't go into some situation thinking all about what you're doing or why or what it means. Do first, and reflect later (maybe even a day later)—about how some social Cujo turned out to be more of a sleepy teacup Yorkie in some celebritwat's handbag.

KEEP WHAT YOU LEARN

Though Albert Ellis saw results from his, uh, exposuring himself to the ladies, he didn't have today's neuroscientific research on learning to draw from. He might have done more of these exposure exercises each day than is ideal—at least initially—for learning and retaining learning.

An essential component of learning is memory. After all, the greatest insight in the world is meaningless if it's fleeting, like those flashes of brilliance you have in the middle of the night—the ones you swear you'll remember when you wake up but never do. ("Good morning, Miss Einstein. E equals mc next time pick up a fucking pen.")

Research on retaining information by psychologist Robert Bjork finds that "spaced learning"—learning jags with breaks in between—is more effective than "massed learning" (which most of us know as "cramming"). That's because we encode information into memory by first dipping into it and then taking a break from it and then going back and retrieving it from memory (and then repeating the retrievals over time). Retrieval, Bjork explains, is a "learning event." Every time you retrieve something, it burnishes it into your memory just a bit more.

This argument against cramming doesn't just apply to schoolwork. Michelle Craske and her colleagues have found that spaced learning improves results from exposure therapy—improving retention of learning and decreasing the return of fear in later sessions. Neuro-scientist LeDoux explains that spaced learning fosters "memory consolidation"—the conversion, through protein synthesis, of a short-term memory into a persistent long-term memory. Cramming, on the other hand, depletes an enzyme (called CREB) that we need to form these long-term memories.

So, to get the most out of your "training wheels" role-playing sessions, as well as your initial exposure outings (as you), it's a good idea to start by doing maybe just two or three of these jaunts on a Saturday. (Wait to reflect on them until Sunday.) Take breaks in between, and do very little else that would put weight on your brain. By that, I mean just veg afterward—or even sleep. As LeDoux explains, memory formation is easily disrupted several hours after an experience—but that's also when it is more easily solidified. Sleep is when the memory elves really get in there and start hammering out space for your newly created learning in long-term memory.

You may be thinking, "Well, how dumb to wait a day to apply conscious thought to what I experienced." However, psychologist Stefan G. Hofmann explains that neuroscientific research suggests that exposure is a more "cognitively sophisticated process" than researchers had previously understood. Prior to the insights from neuroscience, researchers had incorrectly assumed that exposure only "involves primitive, automatic, and low-level processes" and is "separate from higher-order cognitive processes." However, Hofmann notes that there are six controlled clinical studies that found that *exposure exercises alone*—without talk therapy—led to dramatic changes in thinking.

That said, conscious processing *is* an essential part of being less commandeered by your fears. However, if you let your brain do its thing in the background overnight, then the next day, instead of figuring things out from scratch, you can build on the work it's already done for you.

KEEP THE SURPRISES COMING

After your first exposure session, space out the days between your next sessions. But don't just do them every other day. Instead, stagger the days. As a model for scheduling them, perhaps look to the spider exposure Michelle Craske did with some research subjects—spacing their exposure days out in a 1-2-4-8 pattern. For an example of this: You do some exposure experiments on Monday. Then two days later, some more. Then four days after that. Then eight days after that. Then throw all those numbers in a bag and shake it and let that determine the spread between one day of exposure and the next.

Of course, Craske's 1-2-4-8 spacing out of exposure exercises is unnatural for us—and that's the point. (Most people would just re-sort to the simpler every other day or even every day.)

The thing is, attention is critical to learning, and we pay special attention to things that are novel and hard to predict. They pique our interest. In contrast, when things are the same over and over again, we stop paying attention because we know what to expect.

Craske explains that in doing exposures, it's important to always be raising the experiential stakes because—remember—you have to believe there's a threat at hand in order to violate expectancy. In a podcast with clinical psychologist Jacqueline Persons, Craske said that one way to keep the expectancy level up is to introduce "variability" throughout exposure—varying the length of time a person's doing the exposure, the place they're doing it, and the thing or event they're being exposed to.

So, for example, if you're afraid of spiders, Craske will show you different spiders. That's because if you just see one kind of spider, you will likely be less afraid of that kind of spider but other kinds of spiders will likely still trigger you. Craske will also vary the locations of your spider encounters. You might meet Tito the tarantula on Craske's couch, and maybe Lucy Longlegs will ride down with you in the elevator. Craske explains that variations in exposure like these help you "generalize" what you've learned, so you can apply it when you encounter some new spider in some new place. To borrow from Dr. Seuss, "I do not fear them in a box. I do not fear them with a fox." And that sort of thing.

Varying things up is especially something to focus on after you do your initial violations of expectancy—those days and weeks when you do just a few exercises and, if possible, go home and go to bed afterward. An example of varying things up from Craske and her UCLA colleagues is an assignment they give to socially anxious people: sending them out onto the campus and having them approach thirty "different people, of all different types, and ask them all different questions rather than approaching the same kind of person and asking the same question over and over again."

Craske explains that changing up the encounters like this "enhances the storage of new learning"—more powerfully encoding it and making it more accessible to the person later. Basically, the variation helps beat it into your mind from numerous different angles that no, the horrible thing you expect to happen does not happen. There's also a great reality check by doing this in numbers—by having a sample group of thirty people you approach, not just one.

You should see that sure, you'll sometimes get rejected or blown off. But you don't *always*. This teaches you in the most powerful way—through your own experience—that it pays to go after what you want and that while, yes, rejection sucks, that moment of suckhood quickly passes.

GET COMFORTABLE WITH DISCOMFORT

Running away from what you fear is what gives your fears the power to rule your life. When faced with something that you're afraid of— like speaking up at work or starting a conversation with somebody at a party—you get anxious. This is uncomfortable. You do something to stop feeling so anxious like—for example, keeping your ideas to yourself at work or, at the party, diving into your phone.

Psychologist Stefan G. Hofmann explains, "This is called avoidance. We define avoidance as anything that you do or don't do that prevents you from facing your anxiety." He explains that this has two results. "The first one is that you feel some relief from your anxiety. However, there is also a long-term negative consequence of avoidance: You will always feel anxious in this particular situation. Avoidance preserves your anxiety."

Hofmann has a great avoidance-challenging exposure exercise for socially anxious people—buying a book and immediately returning it. Only, oops—I love bookstores and I don't want people who own them to hate me. So, we'll shift his idea to the grocery store. Go to the grocery store and buy a box of cereal, and then walk toward the exit door but turn around and return it. Like, moments later. And when you do it, don't apologize. Just say, "I need to return this." If they ask why, say, "For a personal reason." And leave it at that.

That's exposure number one. However, Michelle Craske suggests doing "deepened extinction" exercises, raising the complexity and stakes of your expectancy violations and showing yourself that you can tolerate discomfort when things don't work out all that nicely.

So, let's ramp up Hofmann's exercise. The next time around, you again return the cereal, again without apologizing. Only for your reason for return, you say, "I hear voices coming from it. Clearly, this box of cereal is possessed." (This is a version of my wacky therapist pal Albert Ellis's directive to the socially anxious to go to Rockefeller Center at lunchtime and say to people there, "I just got out of a mental institution. Do you know what month it is?")

So . . . what disastrous thing happens when you seem crazycakes? Painful electric shocks administered by a bag boy? Announcement over the supermarket loudspeaker, "Hey, everybody, come look at this batshit loser at the returns desk!"? Or—more likely—an eye roll from the person processing your return?

Sure, you'd prefer applause—or, better yet, no attention paid to you whatsoever. But you will see that the minor negative reaction you'll get won't kill you or cause the spontaneous amputation of one of your arms. Through this, you will see that you were wrong. It isn't HORRIBLE! or TERRIBLE! even if somebody reacts to you unfavorably; it's just momentarily uncomfortable. And you'll see that you can handle momentarily uncomfortable—especially considering what you'll get out of it: on your deathbed, not having to tell people, "I wanted to live life to the fullest, but somebody once rolled their eyes at me, so I hid under the bed for 87½ years instead."

DON'T FORGET THE THINKY PART OF CHANGING

Reviewing what your exposure experiences showed you—through the lens of reason—is the conscious part of learning. In the days and weeks after you do the exposure exercises, think about and even write and talk about what you've learned. Doing this, Craske and LeDoux explain, helps to "consolidate" the new learning—that is, give it more solid placement in your mind, thus giving it more power to be your go-to response.

It's helpful to bring evolution into your reflection—to consider whether various fears you have and the behavior driven by them might be a mismatch with your current environment, perhaps by a million or so years. Take what anthropologist Donald Symons calls "a striking feature of human courtship": the fear of rejection.

Symons notes that this has a powerful effect on behavior—which makes sense, because "sexual/romantic rejection hurts; the memory of being rejected hurts; the thought of being rejected hurts." In fact, we evolved to have rejection hurt. Symons speculates—and I think he's probably right—that this fear may have been adaptive "during the vast majority of human evolution."

During most of human evolutionary history, our ancestors lived in small hunter-gatherer bands. Everybody knew everybody, and everybody knew everybody's business. Or, as Symons puts it: "When Ann the gatherer rejected Andy the hunter's proposition, everyone in their community probably found out about it before long."

Symons explains that the news of Andy's rejection could have diminished his mate value. This may explain why we evolved to find rejection deeply painful; it protected our reproductive interests.

But look around. As I noted in *Good Manners for Nice People Who Sometimes Say F*ck*, we are people who evolved to live in "neighborhoods"—small groupings where everybody knows everybody—but we are now living in these vast strangerhoods, where some of us can go a day or days without running into anyone we know.

So, Symons explains, here's the reasonable way to look at rejection today: "On a modern university campus, with thousands of students and enormous scope for anonymity," a guy who hits on a woman "has little to fear but fear itself."

STAY UNSAFE

While doing your exposure exercises, you should remove what researchers call "safety behaviors," anxiety-reducing coping techniques. For example, there's that guy in Craske's study who was deeply afraid of social rejection. Craske explains that he was "discouraged from fidgeting with his hands, wearing earphones, or bringing a magazine to read as a way of distracting himself during exposure exercises."

Remember, in exposure, discomfort is the point; it's what helps you see that you can stand whatever you've been avoiding, along with showing you (in the most striking ways) that the fears that have been holding you back are stupid. In short, the shittier you let yourself feel the better you're likely to get at going out into the world with confidence—and the faster that's likely to happen, too.

THE CRUTCHES COME LATER

Once you're no longer doing exposure exercises—save perhaps for a pick-me-up exercise here and there (if you need to reinforce that your fears are stupid)—you'll be going out there and doing the brave stuff as you. At that point, you can pull out the "calm the fuck down" helpers you read about in chapters 6 and 7 (on ritual) and in chapter 11 on cognitive reappraisal, including recategorizing your anxiety as excitement and James Pennebaker's "expressive writing" exercises.

But sometimes, you'll need an immediate taming of your fears—like, in ten or fifteen seconds—before some person you need to talk to gets busy talking to somebody else. There's a technique from neuroscientist Matthew Lieberman's research that's particularly handy for that—reducing your fear by putting the emotion you're feeling into words. (You first read about this in chapter 4—that stuff on giving your emotion a name tag.)

As for how you'd do this:

> You could just mumble to yourself about what you're feeling as you're making your way across the room: "Ugh, am I scared to go talk to this dude."

> Better still, incorporate Ethan Kross's research on psyching yourself up through third-person speech: "Okay, Ames, so you're scared to go talk to this dude. Get your ass over there and do it anyway."

> And even better, incorporate findings by Richard Stephens on swearing as a way to increase pain tolerance: "Okay, Ames, so you're scared to go talk to this dude. Get your fucking alabaster ass over there and do it anyway."

As for why this works, it seems there's a sort of seesaw thing going on in the brain. By ginning up the part of your brain that puts thoughts into words—the prefrontal cortex—you reduce amygdala activity and (poof!) reduce your anxious response. Lieberman and his team find that this feeling-labeling business is more effective in diminishing the bodily feelings of fear than simply applying reason to what you're feeling (through reappraising your feelings).

(For more on the specific brain parts at work in this, see the boxed bit, "A side trip for brain nerds," in the previous chapter.)

INVITE YOUR BODY TO JOIN YOU

When you aren't doing your exposure exercises—when you're making your way through the world as you—remember that you aren't a disembodied head.

Look down. Yes, there's a body there. Put it to work. When you've got some social challenge before you, make use of that "shared sink" between your body and your mind that researcher Spike Lee talked about. Take action—physical action, meaning *do* stuff—to ease your stress. Use your secret ritual. Dance yourself into feeling anxiety as excitement. And be sure to take deep breaths.

Breathing slowly and deeply, neuroscientist LeDoux explains, engages the parasympathetic nervous system, which counters our sympathetic nervous system, the home of our fight-or-flight response. I remember the parasympathetic nervous system as the "parachute" system, because it brings you down when you're plastered to the stadium dome by fear. (I first mentioned it in chapter 7, in the mantra meditation section, calling it our body's Department of Chillaxing.)

Most of us probably know about breathing deeply, but here's a calming tip you probably haven't heard: If possible, sit down. Neuroscientist Robert Sapolsky notes that sitting down is a way to "slow down the flow of adrenaline." In his book *Monkeyluv*, he gives this as advice for when you're in a fight with your wife ("Make a rule that you must argue sitting down"), but it might also come in handy when you're just fighting your anxiety.

EXPECT SETBACKS

I won't bullshit you. Though I've gotten to the point where, on a given day, I have like eighty percent superhero confidence, there's part of my old mindset that's still hanging on from my "Hate me; I suck" days.

Depressingly, it turns out that our old associations can get triggered again. As LeDoux explains it, this can happen with the passage of time (especially if you haven't given your learning deep roots in long-term memory). He also says certain kinds of experiences can be particularly triggering, like if there are strong cues in them to your old ways of behaving. For example, maybe you run into somebody you haven't seen for a while—some snobbo who's always treated you like something they stepped in.

But there's actually no need to freak if your old inner Wormo comes back for a visit. Remember that you've got ammunition. Put your fears through the reason grinder (perhaps reminding yourself of your conclusions from exposure); use your body (breathe, baby!); and turn to cognitive reappraisal (like recasting your anxiety as excitement).

SHRINK OR SWIM? WHAT'S IT GONNA BE?

The going *will* get tough. So expect that—and have a little compassion for yourself. But the going will also get rewarding, so expect that, too. And don't forget to cheer yourself for all of your small wins—which, in time, will amount to a really big win. As role-playing researcher George A. Kelly put it: "No person needs to be a victim of his or her own biography."

— 18 —

UNFUCKWITHABLE

If life were fair, the mean girl from high school would get adult acne all over her body.

Obviously, life is anything but fair, but remember the point of this book: You can make things go more in your favor by *choosing* who you're going to be instead of just going along with who you've been.

Chances are, you'll still have "old me" reflux from time to time—that tiny little shithead cabal in your head that sneaks up to whisper, "Oh, come on. Go home. They all think you're a snorebag."

But you've seen that you can choose how you deal with that, too. You can decide that you won't be bullied out of going for what you want. Tell yourself that yeah, feeling uncomfortable or embarrassed or rejected sucks, but it's better than looking back on a life half-lived.

It's gonna be messy. You'll be afraid. You'll make mistakes. But what matters is that you keep making the choice to go out there with your gutsiest self.

As you're doing that, try to remember that courage isn't fearlessness. Courage is going, "Fuck, I'm scared like a little girl…but I'll do it anyway."

KEEP ON UNFUCKING

Below, you'll find a few final tips to help you maintain perspective and patch up any flats you get on the road to Changeville—and beyond:

WHEN LIFE GIVES YOU ASSHOLES, MAKE ASSHOLE-ADE

Misery has been my life coach. And that's a good thing.

This probably sounds like glib after-the-fact bullshit. And, truth be told, there were definitely times—especially as a kid stuck in a small corner of Midwestern suburbia—when I was so crushingly lonely it was like walking around while buried alive.

However, I think that not having even one friend for the first fifteen years of my life—plus knowing how it feels to be left out, kicked around, and used—ultimately made me a more compassionate person. And I'm probably more of a person altogether—stronger, more creative, and more independent—thanks to my childhood stint as the Canterbury Commons subdivision leper.

There's a term for this—for using adversity as a means for growth—and it's called being "antifragile." Nassim Taleb, a risk researcher and former derivatives trader who coined the term, explains antifragile as "the exact opposite of fragile," but he adds that it goes beyond resilience or robustness. "Antifragile" describes the way living things are *improved by stressors*—becoming stronger and more able to cope with difficult, unpleasant, unpredictable stuff that gets thrown their way.

So, a person who's antifragile doesn't avoid criticism; they look for criticism, because it can be a path to improvement—assuming it's coming from wise people, not anonymous assholes on the internet. Then again, why limit yourself? In my experience, if you take the stance of openness to criticism as a means of improvement, you can even get helpful tips from the internet vermin.

I wrote in *I See Rude People* about how a web mob of anony-bullies came after me, posting a slew of awful comments about me on my website ("Are you a man?" "You look like you have a penis") and putting up ugly attack posts about me on their own site.

In one of these posts, they included a photo of me and sneered at how yellow my teeth were. I felt a rush of shame and ran to the bathroom mirror. And yes, they were pretty much Crayola goldenrod—which I guess is what you get for drinking coffee as if it were one of the food groups. But I didn't cry. I zipped right out and got my teeth bleached. Thank you, buttnuggets!

Being able to seek out criticism starts with making peace with making mistakes. Now, I'm not talking about sloppy mistakes, though these can be teachers of a sort, too. As Taleb explains it, being antifragile involves "a love of... a certain class of errors"—the sort that allow us to correct ourselves for the better and to better deal with the uncertainties of life.

Criticism will often come from other people, but you can criticize yourself, too—in healthy ways. I admire Amy Dresner for a practice she does each morning—one she got from AA. She picks out one of these self-improvement flashcards called "character defect cards." These are statements on index cards that she made up from a list of things in herself that she feels need changing. On one side is the character defect (for example, being overly dramatic or reactive or petty), and on the back is the opposite (being rational, balanced, tolerant). The task each day is to be looking for that defect in your thoughts and behavior and then replace it with its better opposite.

Dresner sometimes succeeds at this—but sometimes doesn't. Looking back at how she did with a particular day's card, she says, "I can be hard on myself, thinking, 'Whoa, am I an asshole.' Or I'll recognize 'I wasn't supposed to be reactive today, and I screamed like a banshee at bad drivers.' But then I have to remember that change is slow and I'm human and I'm trying."

What's really helpful in using these cards is something that most of us probably don't do—running through our shortcomings. Putting a spotlight on them like this is the first step to changing them. You can do this without the cards, of course. I do asshole checks on myself as a matter of course—each day or every few days—looking at my less-than-admirable behavior and pledging to myself to do better (and then doing my best to follow through with that). But I think, especially if you're trying to make big changes in yourself, these cards are a great idea.

One thing we tend to forget—especially now, in the age of campus crypussies sniveling that Plato is "triggering"—is that we're *resilient*. We bounce back. In fact, grief researcher George Bonanno explains that, contrary to what many believe, resilience is actually the norm among people. Most people are not so debilitated by tough or even terrible situations that they don't recover from them. However, the grieving people who are most likely to seek out therapists are the small percentage who simply aren't able to recover on their own. Therapists write about grief from the perspective of those patients, leading us to wrongly see being endlessly laid flat by grief as far more prevalent than it really is.

What helps in being or becoming resilient—being able to pull ourselves out of misery and get on with life—is "hardiness." Clinical psychologist Salvatore Maddi explains that "hardiness ... provides the courage and motivation to do the hard, strategic work of turning stressful circumstances from potential disasters into growth opportunities." In his research, he finds that hardiness is made up of three "interrelated attitudes," which he calls the three Cs:

Commitment—a desire to engage with people and life (rather than detach and isolate yourself).
Control—being motivated to take action to make things in your life better "rather than sinking into passivity and powerlessness."

Challenge—a willingness to face stressful stuff and use it as a
learning experience "rather than playing it safe by avoiding
uncertainties and potential threats."

In looking at Maddi's three Cs, I'm reminded of another C: choice.
Even if these attitudes don't come naturally to you, you can choose
to act like they do.

By the way, I would also add one more C to the list: comedy.

For me, a big part of being resilient is humor. I laugh about things
that happen to me and even publicly make fun of myself. In fact, I
try to make a habit of it. Amazingly, telling people what an ass you
are (if you don't cross the line into self-loathing or poor-me-ville)
seems to earn you friends and win you high marks for being enter-
taining at cocktail parties. In fact, it's a "costly signal" to be able to
put yourself down or talk about your humiliations—suggesting that
you have enough social and emotional capital to be flamingly open
about your dipshit-hood.

WOULDN'T YOU LIKE TO NO?

Being true to yourself takes living with boundaries—which means
acting according to what you believe is right (according to your values) instead of checking in with your feelings and asking them what
they'll allow you to do.

This *taking a stand* business will be uncomfortable, especially at
first. The good news is, the more you do it the more comfortable you'll
get doing it. (Yes, it's the ol' neurons "that fire..." blah, blah, blah.)
These tips should also help:

TAKE YOUR TIME TO ANSWER

Unless the question is "Your money or your life?" you can often
delay answering. You can say, "I have to look into that" or "Hmmm,

let me get back to you." Be mindful that after a lifetime of yessing, you'll be prone to respond to questions with an immediate "SURE!!!" "OF COURSE!!!" "WHATEVER YOU WANT!!!" "AND WOULD YOU LIKE A COMPLIMENTARY FOOTBATH WITH THAT?!!!" However, putting off answering gives you an important buffer—the time to decide whether you should do the thing and/or to figure out the optimal way to tell them you won't.

PRACTICE SAYING NO

You can do it. Say it now. "No." "No." "No." Now go say it in the mirror, queer as that sounds, and then go out and practice it on people. Start small. For example: Someone asks you, "Got the time?" Say, "No." And work up from there.

When you are telling somebody no, it's often best to avoid putting a lot of wordage around it—verbal rambling, that is. There's a line I read in personal security expert Gavin de Becker's *The Gift of Fear*: " 'No' is a complete sentence." What this means is that you don't have to go on and on explaining yourself. Doing that tends to make you come off as wishy-washy and weak—giving the person you're speaking to the impression that with a little effort, your *no* can be worn down into a *yes*.

Speaking of which, you should be prepared to slip and say yes when you should have said no. When that happens, don't be mean to yourself. Again, you've had a long habit of yessing. Just resolve to do better the next time.

PRACTICE LETTING ANGER SHOW

Anger is often a sign that somebody is treating us unfairly.

Living with self-respect takes having limits—standards for what is acceptable treatment by other people. When they cross those lines, you owe it to yourself to speak up. It'll be scariest the first time or the first few times, but in time, you'll just start to be a person who isn't in the habit of rolling over for the users and take-take-takers of the world.

BE WILLING TO BE UNPOPULAR

I'm openly libertarian in Venice, California, which is like being a butcher in a bloody apron wandering around a PETA convention. I also tend to get a little miffy when visitors to the hipstertorium that Abbot Kinney Boulevard has become pee on our fences and in our flower beds, making the neighborhood smell like a giant urinal when it rains. When I'm on the porch and I see people unzipping, I shine this very bright night-watchman-in-the-airplane-factory flashlight on them, making them scatter like cockroaches. "Go do that on your momma's front lawn!" I yell after them.

If you start standing up for what you believe, be prepared for it to lead to some changes in your life. You may get dumped by a few people—"friends" who were using you or even real friends who don't take kindly to your brand of politics. This sucks. However, when it's happened to me, I've found that I've replaced these people with new friends who respect me for my views or are big enough to be around somebody they disagree with.

Ultimately, the rewards of living assertively instead of passively—living as the full you (and screw anybody who isn't okay with that)—seem to outweigh the costs. James Baldwin put this well: *"You've got to tell the world how to treat you. If the world tells you how you are going to be treated, you are in trouble."*

NO, IT ISN'T "EAT, PREY, LOVE"

Consider "the scarcity principle." As psychologist Robert Cialdini describes it, we long for what's rare and special and slightly out of reach—what's hard to get, as opposed to what's hard to get rid of.

This is true in business and friendships, but it's especially important to remember in dating and relationships.

As I've pointed out elsewhere in the book, it ultimately won't be enough to just *act* hard to get. (If you really aren't, your desperation will often leak through.) However, acting hard to get *is* a good start. It'll help you see all the benefits, which should help you get started on *being* hard to get.

In the meantime, understanding the principle of scarcity will help you avoid temptation—like when you're just dying to throw yourself at that person you want...to make that call you know you shouldn't...to send that text. (Okay, who are we kidding? To send one...two...three texts with escalating levels of desperation before your date has even pulled out of your driveway.)

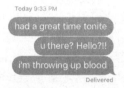

If you're heterosexual, the scarcity principle plays out in somewhat different ways, depending on whether you're male or female. Now, I know this notion is heresy to some as of late—those who insist that the sex differences we see in human behavior are caused by "the patriarchy" and television. (Clearly, those female chimps in the wild who engage in doll play with sticks—observed by primatologists Richard Wrangham and Sonya Kahlenberg—should probably watch fewer Saturday morning cartoons.)

The reality, however, is that research (by evolutionary psychologists David Buss, David Schmitt, and herds of others) finds that there *are* distinct sex differences in who gets to do what in dating—or rather, who gets to do what and have some likelihood of it turning out well for them.

It turns out that which sex does the chasing in heterosexual dating isn't some arbitrary thing. It comes out of what evolutionary biologist Robert Trivers, in 1972, called "parental investment." His theory—borne out in research on humans, insects, and other animals—is that the sex that has the highest cost from sexual activity (the female—in almost all species) will be choosier about whom they mate with than the sex that invests less (which is almost always the male).

Of course, in humans, a woman's the one who gets knocked up and stuck with kids to drag around and feed, while men can just, uh, shoot and leave. So women evolved to be the choosier sex, and men co-evolved to expect that—meaning they're the ones who do the chasing and persuading.

It's sometimes hard for people to accept that these sex differences are still a driving force for us today.

When I explained parental investment in one of my advice columns, a guy in Colorado deemed it "evolutionary psycho-babble," scoffing via email, "Really, hasn't generations of cultural tinkering with gender roles made the biological imperative pretty much irrelevant?"

Actually, no. In a follow-up column, I explained that we're living in modern times with a less-than-modern psychological operating system:

> Women can't just yell at their genes, "Hey, it's 2016, and I'm the VP of a successful startup!" As anthropologist Donald Symons explains, changing any "complex adaptation," like those driving mating psychology, takes "hundreds or thousands of generations."

As for where this leaves us today:

THE SCARCITY PRINCIPLE FOR STRAIGHT WOMEN

The advice for women—in two words: DON'T CHASE!

Men may tell you that they actually like being pursued. And they may. It's flattering, after all. And it's nice to sit back and not have to do any work.

HOWEVER... this does not mean it's a wise idea for you to do the chasing.

Because men coevolved to expect women to be choosy, they appear to have emotional mechanisms that—in the wake of their being pursued by a woman—subconsciously go, "WTF, bro? She can't be all that if she's all over you."

Women will protest, "But my friend asked this guy out, and now they're married, and..." Right. Yes, some women live happily ever after in the wake of asking a man out. The point is, doing it is risky. You can decide to take that risk, but you should do it knowingly, accepting the possible cost. There's a good chance that to a man—subconsciously and perhaps consciously—your pursuit will read as desperation, not as some bold bucking of "archaic" customs.

As a woman, what you *should* do is flirt—which sends a signal to a guy letting him know that you're open to being asked out. In fact, you can even overflirt (and it's probably a good idea if he seems a little clueless or dense). The key, however, is that you DO NOT DO ANYTHING RESEMBLING ASKING HIM OUT. (No, not even asking him to hang out.) No other sneaky shit, either. No throwing a party just so you can invite him or calling him and asking to borrow his biology notes—despite how you won the junior-high science fair when you were only six and he's barely passing the class.

Admittedly, restraining yourself like this feels bad. Remember what eats away at willpower? It's "aversive" feelings, like that shitty feeling that comes up when you really want to call somebody but are doing everything in your power to avoid it.

But let's bring in a little perspective: Though restraining yourself is hard and feels awful, it feels awful *for a little while*. Maybe an hour or a few hours. But, like a fart in the elevator, feelings eventually pass.

If you're having trouble waiting your feelings out, remember from the willpower research what helps alleviate this sort of crappy feeling: reward. It might help to make yourself a deal—a trade, of sorts—that you'll allow yourself something you want (and give it to yourself immediately) if you don't make the call.

Distraction's another helpful tool, and in that tool chest, masturbation's probably a good idea. Alleviate a little tension through rocking your own world and maybe you'll feel a little less of a need to pick up your phone and, um, beg for takeout.

THE SCARCITY PRINCIPLE FOR STRAIGHT MEN

For men, the advice is different: *Do* chase, but do it in a way that's assertive, as opposed to tremblingly desperate.

Healthy chasing involves directness—asking a woman out, not endlessly loitering at the edges of her life and hoping that a freak explosion will blow her into your arms. Oh, and let's be clear: "Asking a woman out" does not mean giving her a scrap of paper with your number on it and mumbling that she should call you sometime. You might tell yourself you're just trying to be polite. However, this is not politeness but pussy behavior in drag as good manners. The right way to ask a woman out is to actually *ask*. Ask for her number, and then call and/or text and invite her out. If she says she's busy, try a few more times, because maybe she really is busy and isn't just blowing you off.

Your first date and maybe the second should be three things: cheap, short, local. No, do not take her out to dinner. You don't buy a pricey meal for a total stranger, and she's pretty much a stranger until you get to know each other. The objective here is to see whether she likes you, not to try to bribe her into it.

Short dates are wise because they give you less time to hang yourself. If you are somebody who's been one shade or another of social reject your whole life, don't expect yourself to turn into Mr. Charmo on your first few times out of your troll cave. Accordingly, instead of planning some epic, eight-hour date of the century, schedule an hour or so for a drink or coffee and have someplace to be afterward (or just claim to and actually leave at the one-hour mark or thereabouts, no matter what).

If you're particularly bad at talking, you might take dates to some place or event—a street fair, a museum, a concert, alligator wrestling. That way, the silence doesn't weigh on you like it does when you're in Starbucks and your mind is screaming: "LOSER! YOU HAVE NOTHING TO SAY!"

Be mindful of the difference between "conversation" and "used-car sales." Your goal should be finding out about her instead of trying to hard-sell her on you. Listen to what she's saying and engage with it. This involves a shift in your usual thinking. Instead of panicking over whether she likes you, you should be considering whether you like her. Yes, really. Do this. Even though it will probably feel weird and wrong. Shifting the focus in this way allows you to come off as *interested* instead of *desperate*.

That said, you should avoid coming off as desperately interested. You can express interest in what she's saying and even some appreciation for things she's done—which is different from complimenting her senseless. No, fawning over a woman is not the yellow brick road to sex. In fact, it strongly suggests that she's your last chance for getting laid that doesn't involve prepayment with Venmo or what would be considered the desecration of a corpse.

After the date, yes, call or text her. Once—the day after, in the afternoon, not twenty seconds after you drop her off. (See the bit above on willpower and restraint.)

The guiding principle here? Leave her wanting more, not less. Make her wonder whether you like her, not whether she should download the paperwork to keep you a hundred feet away from her at all times.

SCARCITY FOR EVERYBODY

In short, whether you're gay, straight, or whatever, less is way, way more when you're hoping someone will value you.

Oh, and count on yourself to fuck this up—at some point to go after some romantic prospect with all the subtlety of a python on a goat.

When you do screw up and go overboard, just write it off and move on. Don't make moping over it or trying to undo it your lifework. Remember, as anthropologist Donald Symons noted in the previous chapter, you aren't living in ancestral times with only three possible partners in your entire hunter-gatherer band. Just pick your sorry ass up and drag it to the next bar, the next town, the next dating site, or whatever.

The bottom line? Absence makes the heart grow fonder, not absence of self-respect.

THOREAU'S MOM SOMETIMES DID HIS LAUNDRY

There's this tendency to romanticize lonerhood, but pretending that you don't need anybody is a weakling's game.

Author Henry David Thoreau is an icon for hermitude and self-sufficiency. However, as Thoreau expert Elizabeth Witherell explains, when Thoreau wasn't championing solitude and his immersion in nature at that Walden Pond cabin, he was pretty much a people person and a community guy, involved in neighborhood issues and the Underground Railroad. In fact, he wrote in *Walden*, "I think that I love society as much as most, and am ready enough to fasten myself like a bloodsucker for the time to any full-blooded man that comes in my way."

We humans evolved to be *interdependent*, meaning we're people who need people—people who *depend* on one another. So, no, being a full person doesn't mean isolating yourself and never asking anyone for anything. Sometimes—like Thoreau, who really did hit up his mom to do his laundry—you're going to need somebody to throw in a load of socks for you.

RUN AND GET HELP

You show that you're a person of value by asking for things, and you also allow people to feel close to you by helping you. (It's especially important to make requests in a relationship—like asking your partner to go to the drugstore to get you the fixins for a NyQuil gimlet when a cold is beating your ass.) Remind yourself that it isn't a sign of weakness to ask for help; it's a sign you're emotionally strong enough to admit that you can't do everything all by yourself. Nor should you have to.

THANK BIG

Misery might "love company," but company generally wants very fucking little to do with misery.

When your life is sucking on some major level, it's easy to just tromp around all grim-faced and snarl at people who've committed horrible crimes—such as existing in your path when you're on your way to work. The truth is, no matter how much your life sucks, you still have something to be grateful for—even if it's just that you aren't being held prisoner in a dark hole with an active cockroach population.

Grateful people seem to be happier people. Research by social psychologist Sonja Lyubomirsky and her colleagues finds people who regularly take stock of what's good in their lives and express appreciation for it—even just to themselves—seem to become happier.

Other research, by psychologist Robert Emmons and his colleagues, suggests that people with high levels of gratitude have lower levels of resentment and envy—feelings that are not exactly social lubricants.

Additionally, social psychologists Sara Algoe and Jonathan Haidt find that expressing gratitude—in your own thoughts and to the person who's done something kind for you—seems to strengthen bonds between people. The gratitude seems to work as a sort of emotional Post-it note, reminding both people in a relationship how good they have it—which is all the more reason to keep investing and keep appreciating.

CHARITY BEGINS NEXT DOOR

One of the fastest, easiest ways to improve your own life and feel better about yourself is going off and helping somebody else.

Lyubomirsky explains that you can get a "cascade" of personal and social benefits from doing this—including insights into yourself, appreciation of how good you have it, new relationships, distraction from your problems, and even increased feelings of what happiness researchers call "well-being."

A pretty amazing example of this increased "well-being" thing comes from a study by behavioral medicine researcher Carolyn E. Schwartz. Five women with multiple sclerosis were trained in "active listening and non-directive support"—providing a kind ear and just reflecting back what another person says without giving advice. These patients then made monthly fifteen-minute calls to a bunch of other MS patients (sixty-seven of them) and basically listened to them complain.

Not surprisingly, this made the patients they called feel better. However, the patients who really, really felt better were the ones making the calls. They found themselves more able to shrug off stuff that bothered them and to cope when their own MS flared up. But the truly amazing finding is that, in terms of overall "life satisfaction," the women doing the listening ended up being seven times happier than the patients they'd been helping.

So, when you find yourself in an extended period of suck, as natural as it feels to just wallow in the bog that is you, it seems counterproductive. As I noted in a TED talk I gave, if you'd rather shrink your problems, maybe ditch 'em for an hour or an afternoon, go find other people with problems, and get busy helping them.

HAVING IT TALL

Life is supposedly short. People have been running around mumbling that for centuries.

The Stoic philosopher Seneca called bullshit on this idea. No, Seneca explained, life is actually not short; "life, if you know how to use it, is long." The problem, explained Seneca, is that we waste a lot of it—that we spend so much of it not really living.

"Really living" doesn't mean being successful at everything you do. It means that you don't let yourself pussy out of going for what you want.

So, instead of fearing that you aren't enough, that you don't have what it takes, put yourself out there. You might not be enough, and you might not have what it takes. But giving it a running try tells you that you need to either shift course or regroup and try again.

In other words, the question you should be asking yourself is not "What if I fail?" but "What if I fail to try?"

Evolutionary psychologist David Buss gave some great advice to one of his grad students, Barry X. Kuhle (who's now a prof himself): "Be bolder than you think you have any right to be!"

Being bold is something you *do*. You may not feel all that bold, and go ahead and acknowledge that, but then *do it*—whatever "it" happens to be. Boldly.

That's the main message I hope you got from this book—that *doing* is the key to *becoming*—to changing from the person you are to the person you want to be and, through that, having the biggest life you possibly can.

So, instead of allowing yourself to spend one more moment ducking from life and hoping things will get better...

Well, I'll put it needlepoint pillow-style:

Today is the first day of the rest of your balls

BIBLIOGRAPHY

Abbreviated, reader-friendly version (Full bibliography online)

Amy Dresner, who gave me invaluable feedback on drafts of this book, suggested a little warning to go with an early version of chapters on embodied cognition and metaphor:

> Please note: If you have had a traumatic brain injury, have been in rehab more than three times, or just aren't that bright, you can just skip ahead to the how-to stuff starting in chapter 6.

With Amy's help (as I laughed off her complaints that William James was about to give her a seizure), I think I've translated the science for this book to the point where it's understandable to normal humans.

Accordingly, being mindful that this isn't an academic book (and not wanting the book to have my full extra one hundred pages or so of bibliography), I'm only including a selected set of sources here—with an eye toward including those that are readable by everyone. I've also included just a few of the scientific books and papers that went into each chapter. (You can find these papers via Google Scholar or—often—on the websites of the professors who have authored them, often sans paywall.)

The entire bibliography—with the over 1,100 references that went
into the writing of this book—is on my site, advicegoddess.com.

PART ONE: You Have What It Takes; It's Just in Hiding

CHAPTER 1: Loserhood Isn't Destiny

DiSalvo, David. "What is Science-Help?" *Forbes*, February 7, 2012.
DiSalvo, David. 2011. *What Makes Your Brain Happy and Why You Should Do the Opposite*. Amherst, New York: Prometheus Books.

CHAPTER 2: Hate Me; I Suck
A coming-of-rage story

Alkon, Amy. 2014. *Good Manners for Nice People Who Sometimes Say F*ck*. New York: St. Martin's Griffin.
Alkon, Amy; Marlowe Minnick; and Caroline Johnson. 1996. *Free Advice*. Dell Pub.
Branden, Nathaniel. 1985. *Honoring the Self: Self-Esteem and Personal Transformation*. Random House Publishing Group.

PART TWO: The Building Blocks of the New You

CHAPTER 3: The Mind Is Bigger Than the Brain
Meet your new BFF, "embodied cognition"

Eighteen of eighty references (see my website for rest)
Barsalou, Lawrence W. 2008. "Grounded Cognition." *Annual Review of Psychology*.
Damasio, Antonio R. 1994. *Descartes' Error: Emotion, Reason, and the Human Brain*. New York: Putnam.
Darwin, Charles. 1872. *The Expression of the Emotions in Man and Animals*. John Murray.
Descartes, René. 1951. *Meditations on First Philosophy*, trans. Laurence Julien Lafleur. Macmillan.
Haselton, Martie G., and David M. Buss. 2009. "Error Management Theory and the Evolution of Misbeliefs." *Behavioral and Brain Sciences*.

Hoffman, Donald D. 2009. "The User-Interface Theory of Perception: Natural Selection Drives True Perception to Swift Extinction." In: Dickinson S. J. (ed.) *Object Categorization: Computer and Human Vision Perspectives*, Cambridge, England: Cambridge University Press.

James, William. 1884. "Mind Association: What Is an Emotion?"

James, William. 1911. "The Gospel of Relaxation."

James, William. 1894. "The Physical Bases of Emotion."

James, William. 1950. *The Principles of Psychology: Volume One*. Dover Publications.

James, William. 1950. *The Principles of Psychology: Volume Two*. Dover Publications.

Johnson, Mark. 2007. *The Meaning of the Body: Aesthetics of Human Understanding*. University of Chicago Press.

LeDoux, Joseph E. 2003. *Synaptic Self: How Our Brains Become Who We Are*. Penguin Books.

LeDoux, Joseph E. 1996. *The Emotional Brain: The Mysterious Underpinnings of Emotional Life*. Simon & Schuster.

Simon, Linda. 1998. *Genuine Reality: A Life of William James*. Harcourt Brace.

Watson, Cecelia A. 2004. "The Sartorial Self: William James's Philosophy of Dress." *History of Psychology*.

Wilson, Andrew D. 2012. "The Embodied Cognition of the Baseball Outfielder." *Psychology Today*.

Wilson, Andrew D., and Sabrina Golonka. 2013. "Embodied Cognition Is Not What You Think It Is." *Frontiers in Psychology* 4. Frontiers: 58.

CHAPTER 4: Meet Your Emotions (the little shits)
More useful than you'd think

Eighteen of 144 references (see my website for rest)

Anderson, Michael L. 2014. *After Phrenology: Neural Reuse and the Interactive Brain*. MIT Press.

Brase, Gary L., and W. Trey Hill. 2015. "Good Fences Make for Good Neighbors but Bad Science: A Review of What Improves Bayesian Reasoning and Why." *Frontiers in Psychology*.

Chandler, Jesse, and Norbert Schwarz. 2009. "How Extending Your Middle Finger Affects Your Perception of Others: Learned Movements Influence Concept Accessibility." *Journal of Experimental Social Psychology*.

Damasio, Antonio. 2000. *The Feeling of What Happens: Body and Emotion in the Making of Consciousness.* Mariner Books.

Dolan, Raymond J., and Patrik Vuilleumier. 2006. "Amygdala Automaticity in Emotional Processing." *Annals of the New York Academy of Sciences* 985 (1): 348–55.

Ekman, Paul. 2007. *Emotions Revealed: Recognizing Faces and Feelings to Improve Communication and Emotional Life.* Owl Books.

Lakoff, George, and Mark Johnson. 2008. *Metaphors We Live By.* University of Chicago Press.

Lakoff, George, and Mark Johnson. 1999. *Philosophy in the Flesh: The Embodied Mind and Its Challenge to Western Thought.* Basic Books.

LeDoux, Joseph E. 2003. *Synaptic Self: How Our Brains Become Who We Are.* Penguin Books.

Nesse, Randolph M. 1990. "Evolutionary Explanations of Emotions." *Human Nature.*

Nesse, Randolph M. 1991. "What Good Is Feeling Bad?" *The Sciences.*

Schachter, Stanley, and Jerome E. Singer. 1962. "Cognitive, Social, and Physiological Determinants of Emotional State." *Psychological Review.*

Shaver, Phillip; Judith Schwartz; and Donald Kirson. 1987. "Emotion Knowledge: Further Exploration of a Prototype Approach." *Journal of Personality and Social Psychology.*

Tomkins Institute, The. 2017. "Nine Affects, Present at Birth, Combine with Life Experience to Form Emotion and Personality." *Tomkins.org.*

Tooby, John, and Leda Cosmides. 1990. "The Past Explains the Present: Emotional Adaptations and the Structure of Ancestral Environments." *Ethology and Sociobiology.*

Tracy, Jessica L., and David Matsumoto. 2008. "The Spontaneous Expression of Pride and Shame: Evidence for Biologically Innate Nonverbal Displays." *Proceedings of the National Academy of Sciences of the United States of America.*

Williams, Lawrence E., Julie Y. Huang, and John A. Bargh. 2009. "The Scaffolded Mind: Higher Mental Processes Are Grounded in Early Experience of the Physical World." *European Journal of Social Psychology.*

Wilson, Andrew D., and Sabrina Golonka. 2013. "Embodied Cognition Is Not What You Think It Is." *Frontiers in Psychology.*

CHAPTER 5: Your Mind Is Also in Your Elbow
Why metaphor matters

Eleven of ninety-six references (see my website for rest)

Baumeister, Roy F., Kathleen D. Vohs, and David C. Funder. 2007. "Psychology as the Science of Self-Reports and Finger Movements: Whatever Happened to Actual Behavior?" *Perspectives on Psychological Science.*

Chandler, Jesse J., David Reinhard, and Norbert Schwarz. 2012. "To Judge a Book by Its Weight You Need to Know Its Content: Knowledge Moderates the Use of Embodied Cues." *Journal of Experimental Social Psychology.*

Cosmides, Leda, and John Tooby. 2000. "Evolutionary Psychology and the Emotions." *Handbook of Emotions.*

Gazzaniga, Michael S. 2008. *Human: The Science behind What Makes Us Unique.* Ecco.

Gottman, John M., and Nan Silver. 1999. *The Seven Principles for Making Marriage Work.* Harmony.

IJzerman, Hans; Marcello Gallucci; Wim T. J. L. Pouw; and Sophia C. Weiβgerber. 2012. "Cold-Blooded Loneliness: Social Exclusion Leads to Lower Skin Temperatures." *Acta Psychologica.*

Lakoff, George, and Rafael E. Nunez. 2000. *Where Mathematics Comes From: How the Embodied Mind Brings Mathematics into Being.* Basic Books.

Lee, Spike W. S., and Norbert Schwarz. 2012. "Bidirectionality, Mediation, and Moderation of Metaphorical Effects: The Embodiment of Social Suspicion and Fishy Smells." *Journal of Personality and Social Psychology.*

Pinker, Steven. 2009. *How the Mind Works.* Norton.

Schwarz, Norbert. 2012. "Embodiment in Social Psychology."

Wilson, Vietta E., and Erik Peper. 2004. "The Effects of Upright and Slumped Postures on the Recall of Positive and Negative Thoughts." *Applied Psychophysiology and Biofeedback.*

CHAPTER 6: Eat Shit and Die
The power of ritual

Nineteen of forty-two references (see my website for rest)

Alcorta, Candace S., and Richard Sosis. 2006. "Why Ritual Works: A Rejection of the By-product Hypothesis." *Behavioral and Brain Sciences.*

Atlas, Lauren Y., and Tor D. Wager. 2013. "Expectancies and Beliefs: Insights from Cognitive Neuroscience." *Oxford Handbook of Cognitive Psychology.*

Doidge, Norman. 2007. *The Brain That Changes Itself: Stories of Personal Triumph from the Frontiers of Brain Science*. 62–63. Penguin Books.

Gennep, Arnold van. 1960. *The Rites of Passage*. University of Chicago Press.

Giblin, Chris. 2017. "10 Most Interesting, Superstitious Rituals of Professional Athletes." *Men's Fitness*.

Gino, Francesca, and Michael I. Norton. 2013. "Why Rituals Work." *Scientific American*.

Legare, Cristine H., and Andre L. Souza. 2012. "Evaluating Ritual Efficacy: Evidence from the Supernatural." *Cognition*.

Legare, Cristine H., and Andre L. Souza. 2014. "Searching for Control: Priming Randomness Increases the Evaluation of Ritual Efficacy." *Cognitive Science*.

Malinowski, Bronislaw, and Robert Redfield. 2007. *Magic, Science and Religion, and Other Essays*. Kessinger.

Norenzayan, Ara. 2015. *Big Gods: How Religion Transformed Cooperation and Conflict*. Princeton University Press.

Norton, Michael I., and Francesca Gino. 2014. "Rituals Alleviate Grieving for Loved Ones, Lovers, and Lotteries." *Journal of Experimental Psychology: General*.

Plassmann, Hilke, and Tor D. Wager. 2014. "How Expectancies Shape Consumption Experiences." *The Interdisciplinary Science of Consumption*.

Rosenberg, Jennifer. 2017. "The Story of the Jonestown Massacre." *ThoughtCo. com*.

Schatz, Carla J. 1992. "The Developing Brain." *Scientific American*.

Wager, Tor D., and Lauren Y. Atlas. 2015. "The Neuroscience of Placebo Effects: Connecting Context, Learning and Health." *Nature Reviews Neuroscience*.

Wegner, Daniel M., and Daniel B. Gold. 1995. "Fanning Old Flames: Emotional and Cognitive Effects of Suppressing Thoughts of a Past Relationship." *Journal of Personality and Social Psychology*.

Wegner, Daniel M., and Sophia Zanakos. 1994. "Chronic Thought Suppression." *Journal of Personality*.

Zell-Ravenheart, Oberon, and Morning Glory Zell-Ravenheart. 2006. *Creating Circles & Ceremonies: Rituals for All Seasons & Reasons*. New Page Books.

Zhang, Yan, Jane L. Risen, and Christine Hosey. 2014. "Reversing One's Fortune by Pushing Away Bad Luck." *Journal of Experimental Psychology*.

CHAPTER 7: Souplantation for the Soul
Make your own daily rituals!

Nine of twenty-five references (see my website for rest)
Benson, Herbert. 2013. "Why You Should Meditate—Meditate Every Day." *Esquire.*
Bormann, Jill E. 2005. "Frequent, Silent Mantram Repetition: A Jacuzzi for the Mind." *Advanced Emergency Nursing Journal.*
Goyal, M., S. Singh, and E. M. S. Sibinga. 2014. "Meditation Programs for Psychological Stress and Well-Being: A Systematic Review and Meta-Analysis." *JAMA Internal.*
Grossman, P., L. Niemann, and S. Schmidt. 2004. "Mindfulness-Based Stress Reduction and Health Benefits: A Meta-Analysis." *Journal of Psychosomatic.*
Krisanaprakornkit, T., W. Sriraj, and N. Piyavhatkul. 2006. "Meditation Therapy for Anxiety Disorders." *The Cochrane Collaboration.*
Lowenstein, Daniel. 2008. "Foreword." In *The Mantram Handbook*, 3–10. Nilgiri Press.
Metcalf, O., T. Varker, D. Forbes, and A. Phelps. 2016. "Efficacy of Fifteen Emerging Interventions for the Treatment of Posttraumatic Stress Disorder: A Systematic Review." *Journal of Traumatic Stress.*
Radvansky, G.A., and D.E. Copeland. 2006. "Walking through Doorways Causes Forgetting: Situation Models and Experienced Space." *Memory & Cognition.*
Raichle, M.E., and A.Z. Snyder. 2007. "A Default Mode of Brain Function: A Brief History of an Evolving Idea." *Neuroimage.*

CHAPTER 8: Self-Esteem Is Not What You Think It Is
The irrelevance of whether you like you

Seventeen of 166 references (see my website for rest)
Barkow, Jerome H., John Tooby, and Leda Cosmides (eds.). 1992. "The Adapted Mind: Evolutionary Psychology and the Generation of Culture." 627–37. Oxford University Press.
Bateson, M., D. Nettle, and G. Roberts. 2006. "Cues of Being Watched Enhance Cooperation in a Real-World Setting." *Biology Letters.*
Baumeister, R.F., and M.R. Leary. 1995. "The Need to Belong: Desire for Interpersonal Attachments as a Fundamental Human Motivation." *Psychological Bulletin.*

Branden, Nathaniel. 1998. *A Woman's Self-Esteem: Stories of Struggle, Stories of Triumph*. Jossey-Bass Publishers.

Branden, Nathaniel. 1995. *The Six Pillars of Self-Esteem: The Definitive Work on Self-Esteem by the Leading Pioneer in the Field*. Reprint. Bantam.

Durso, G.R.O., A. Luttrell, and B. M. Way. 2015. "Over-the-Counter Relief from Pains and Pleasures Alike: Acetaminophen Blunts Evaluation Sensitivity to Both Negative and Positive Stimuli." *Psychological Science*.

Eisenberger, Naomi. 2014. "Social Pain." *Edge.org*.

Eisenberger, N. I. 2010. "The Neural Bases of Social Pain: Findings and Implications." *Psychosomatic Medicine*.

Henrich, J., and F. J. Gil-White. 2001. "The Evolution of Prestige: Freely Conferred Deference as a Mechanism for Enhancing the Benefits of Cultural Transmission." *Evolution and Human Behavior*.

Hill, S. E., and D. M. Buss. 2006. "The Evolution of Self-Esteem." In *Self-Esteem Issues and Answers*, edited by M. H. Kernis.

Kirkpatrick, Lee A., and Bruce J. Ellis. 2002. "An Evolutionary-Psychological Approach to Self-Esteem: Multiple Domains and Multiple Functions." In *Blackwell Handbook of Social Psychology: Interpersonal Processes*, edited by G. J. O. Fletcher and M. S. Clark. John Wiley & Sons.

Leary, M. R. 2005. "Sociometer Theory and the Pursuit of Relational Value: Getting to the Root of Self-Esteem." *European Review of Social Psychology*.

Leary, M. R., and R. F. Baumeister. 2000. "The Nature and Function of Self-Esteem: Sociometer Theory." *Advances in Experimental Social Psychology*.

Leary, M. R., E. S. Tambor, S. K. Terdal, and D. L. Downs. 1995. "Self-Esteem as an Interpersonal Monitor: The Sociometer Hypothesis." *Journal of Personality and Social Psychology*.

MacDonald, Geoff (Ed); Jensen-Campbell, Lauri A. (Ed). (2011). Social pain: Neuropsychological and health implications of loss and exclusion (pp. 53–78). Washington, DC, US: American Psychological Association.

Webster, Gregory D., and Lee A. Kirkpatrick. 2006. "Behavioral and Self-Reported Aggression as a Function of Domain-Specific Self-Esteem." 32 (October 2005): 17–27.

Zahavi, Amotz, and Avishag Zahavi. 1997. *The Handicap Principle: A Missing Piece of Darwin's Puzzle*. Oxford University Press.

CHAPTER 9: Jeer Pressure
What shame actually is and how to beat it

Ten of thirty references (see my website for rest)

Beilock, Sian. 2011. *Choke: What the Secrets of the Brain Reveal about Getting It Right When You Have To.* Free Press.

Benenson, Joyce F. 2014. *Warriors and Worriers: The Survival of the Sexes.* Oxford University Press.

Krasnow, M. M., L. Cosmides, E. J. Pedersen, and J. Tooby. 2012. "What Are Punishment and Reputation For?" *PloS One.*

Miron, A. M., and J. W. Brehm. 2006. "Reactance Theory—40 Years Later." *Zeitschrift Für Sozialpsychologie.*

Ryan, R. M., and E. L. Deci. 2000. "Self-Determination Theory and the Facilitation of Intrinsic Motivation, Social Development, and Well-Being." *American Psychologist.*

Smith, R. H., J. M. Webster, and W. G. Parrott. 2002. "The Role of Public Exposure in Moral and Nonmoral Shame and Guilt." *Journal of Personality.*

Sznycer, D., J. Tooby, and L. Cosmides. 2016. "Shame Closely Tracks the Threat of Devaluation by Others, Even across Cultures." *Proceedings of the National Academy of Sciences.*

Tybur, J. M., and D. Lieberman. 2009. "Microbes, Mating, and Morality: Individual Differences in Three Functional Domains of Disgust." *Journal of Personality and Social Psychology*

van Vugt, M., and J. M. Tybur. 2015. "The Evolutionary Foundations of Status Hierarchy." In *The Handbook of Evolutionary,* edited by DM Buss. Wiley.

Zahavi, A., and Avishag Zahavi. 1999. *The Handicap Principle: A Missing Piece of Darwin's Puzzle.*

CHAPTER 10: You Suck. Or Do You?
Confidence, assertiveness, and the Self sisters
(self-compassion, self-acceptance, and self-respect)

Twelve of eighteen references (see my website for rest)

Alkon, Amy. 2014. *Good Manners for Nice People Who Sometimes Say F*ck.* St. Martin's Griffin.

DeWall, C. Nathan. 2013. *The Oxford Handbook of Social Exclusion.* Oxford University Press.

Kirkpatrick, Lee A., and Bruce J. Ellis. 2002. "An Evolutionary-Psychological Approach to Self-Esteem: Multiple Domains and Multiple Functions." In *Blackwell Handbook of Social Psychology: Interpersonal Processes*, edited by G. J. O. Fletcher and M. S. Clark. John Wiley & Sons.

Kraus, Michael W., and Wendy Berry Mendes. (2014). Sartorial symbols of social class elicit class-consistent behavioral and physiological responses: A dyadic approach. *Journal of Experimental Psychology: General*, 143(6), 2330–2340.

López-Pérez, B., T. Ambrona, and E. L. Wilson. 2016. "The Effect of Enclothed Cognition on Empathic Responses and Helping Behavior." *Social.*

Neff, K. D. 2016. "Does Self-Compassion Entail Reduced Self-Judgment, Isolation, and Over-Identification? A Response to Muris, Otgaar, and Petrocchi." *Mindfulness.*

Neff, Kristin. 2017. "Definition and Three Elements of Self Compassion." *Self-Compassion.org.*

Patoine, Brenda, and Martha Bridge-Denckla. 2010. "What's the Real Deficit in Attention Deficit/Hyperactivity Disorder?" *Dana.org.*

Shapiro, Susan. 2007. *Only as Good as Your Word: Writing Lessons from My Favorite Literary Gurus.* Seal Press.

Slepian, M. L.; S. N. Ferber; J. M. Gold; A. M. Rutchick. (2015). The Cognitive Consequences of Formal Clothing. *Social Psychological and Personality Science.*

Van Stockum, C. A., and M. S. DeCaro. (2014). Enclothed Cognition and Controlled Attention During Insight Problem-Solving. *Journal of Problem Solving*, 7(1), 73–83.

Womack, Rebecca. 2016. "Enclothed Cognition: The Effect of Attire on Attention Task Performance." *Samford Undergraduate Research Journal.*

CHAPTER 11: Your Feelings Are Not the Boss of You
It's not what you feel; it's what you do

Fourteen of sixty-three references (see my website for rest)

Bandura, A., and D. Cervone. 1983. "Self-Evaluative and Self-Efficacy Mechanisms Governing the Motivational Effects of Goal Systems." *Journal of Personality and Social Psychology.*

Beilock, S. L. 2008. "Math Performance in Stressful Situations." *Current Directions in Psychological Science.*

Brooks, A. W. 2014. "Get Excited: Reappraising Pre-Performance Anxiety as Excitement." *Journal of Experimental Psychology: General.*

Buckner, R. L., J. R. Andrews-Hanna, and D. Schacter. 2008. "The Brain's Default Network." *Annals of the New York Academy of Sciences.*

Gortner, E. M., S. S. Rude, and J. W. Pennebaker. 2006. "Benefits of Expressive Writing in Lowering Rumination and Depressive Symptoms." *Behavior Therapy.*

Goyal, Madhav; Sonal Singh; and Erica M. S. Sibinga. 2014. "Meditation Programs for Psychological Stress and Well-Being: A Systematic Review and Meta-Analysis." *JAMA Internal Medicine.*

Griskevicius, Vladas, and Noah J. Goldstein. 2006. "Going Along versus Going Alone: When Fundamental Motives Facilitate Strategic (Non) Conformity." *Journal of Personality and Social Psychology.*

Gross, James J., and Robert W. Levenson. 1997. "Hiding Feelings: The Acute Effects of Inhibiting Negative and Positive Emotion." *Journal of Abnormal Psychology.*

Lyubomirsky, Sonja; Lorie Sousa; and Rene Dickerhoof. 2006. "The Costs and Benefits of Writing, Talking, and Thinking about Life's Triumphs and Defeats." *Journal of Personality and Social Psychology.*

Sanborn, Mark. 2004. *The Fred Factor: How Passion in Your Work and Life Can Turn the Ordinary into the Extraordinary.* Currency/Doubleday.

Szalavitz, Maia. 2012. "Mind Reading: Jon Kabat-Zinn Talks About Bringing Mindfulness Meditation to Medicine." *Time.*

Wegner, Daniel M., David J. Schneider, and Samuel R. Carter. 1987. "Paradoxical Effects of Thought Suppression." *Journal of Personality.*

Weick, Karl E. 1984. "Small Wins: Redefining the Scale of Social Problems." *American Psychologist.*

"Welcome to MBSR for Penn Students." 2017. *CAPS: University of Pennsylvania.*

CHAPTER 12: Be Inauthentic!

Screw the real you; be the ideal you

Twenty-two of forty-seven references (see my website for rest)

Aronson, Elliot. 1997. "The Theory of Cognitive Dissonance: The Evolution and Vicissitudes of an Idea."

Canli, Turhan; Zuo Zhao; John E. Desmond; and Eunjoo Kang. 2001. "An MRI Study of Personality Influences on Brain Reactivity to Emotional Stimuli." *Behavioral Neuroscience.*

Deci, Edward L., and Richard Flaste. 1996. *Why We Do What We Do: Understanding Self-Motivation.* Penguin Books.

Depue, Richard A., and Paul F. Collins. 1999. "Neurobiology of the Structure of Personality: Dopamine, Facilitation of Incentive Motivation, and Extraversion." *Behavioral and Brain Sciences.*

Ellis, Albert. 2001. *Overcoming Destructive Beliefs, Feelings, and Behaviors: New Directions for Rational Emotive Behavior Therapy.* Prometheus Books.

Engel, Beverly. 2008. *The Nice Girl Syndrome: Stop Being Manipulated and Abused—and Start Standing up for Yourself.* John Wiley & Sons.

Festinger, Leon. 1962. *A Theory of Cognitive Dissonance.* Stanford University Press.

Gazzaniga, Michael S., Richard B. Ivry, and George R. Mangun. 2013. *Cognitive Neuroscience: The Biology of the Mind.* 4th ed. W. W. Norton & Company.

Gino, Francesca, Maryam Kouchaki, and Adam D. Galinsky. 2015. "The Moral Virtue of Authenticity: How Inauthenticity Produces Feelings of Immorality and Impurity." *Psychological Science.*

Goldman, Brian M. 2006. "Making Diamonds out of Coal: The Role of Authenticity in Healthy (Optimal) Self-Esteem and Psychological Functioning." In *Self-Esteem Issues and Answers: A Sourcebook of Current Perspectives*, edited by Michael H. Kernis. Psychology Press.

Griskevicius, Vladas, and Noah J. Goldstein. 2009. "Fear and Loving in Las Vegas: Evolution, Emotion, and Persuasion." *Journal of Marketing.*

Jongman-Sereno, Katrina P., and Mark R. Leary. 2016. "Self-Perceived Authenticity Is Contaminated by the Valence of One's Behavior." *Self and Identity.*

Kenrick, Douglas T., and Vladas Griskevicius. 2013. *The Rational Animal: How Evolution Made Us Smarter than We Think.* Basic Books.

Kernis, Michael H., and Brian M. Goldman. 2007. "Authenticity." In *Encyclopedia of Social Psychology*, edited by Roy F. Baumeister and Kathleen D. Vohs, 79–81.

Kövecses, Zoltán. 2006. *Metaphor in Culture.* Cambridge University Press.

Kurzban, Robert, and C. Athena Aktipis. 2007. "Modularity and the Social Mind: Are Psychologists Too Self-Ish?" *Personality and Social Psychology.*

Leary, Mark R. 2007. *The Curse of the Self: Self-Awareness, Egotism, and the Quality of Human Life.* Oxford University Press.

Martin, Barry, and Philip Lerman. 2013. *Under One Roof: Lessons I Learned from a Tough Old Woman in a Little Old House.* St. Martin's Press.

Paterson, Randy J. 2000. *The Assertiveness Workbook : How to Express Your Ideas and Stand up for Yourself at Work and in Relationships.* New Harbinger Publications.

Skeen, Michelle. 2014. *Love Me, Don't Leave Me: Overcoming Fear of Abandonment & Building Lasting, Loving Relationships.*

Tavris, Carol., and Elliot Aronson. 2007. *Mistakes Were Made (but Not by Me): Why We Justify Foolish Beliefs, Bad Decisions, and Hurtful Acts.* Harcourt.

"The Crazy Nastyass Honey Badger" (original narration by Randall). YouTube video. https://www.youtube.com/watch?v=4r7wHMg5Yjg

CHAPTER 13: They Should Call It Won't-Power
The pathetic realities of willpower

Twenty-two of fifty-four references (see my website for rest)

Ainslie, George. 2013. "Monotonous Tasks Require Self-Control Because They Interfere with Endogenous Reward." *Behavioral and Brain Sciences.*

Baumeister, Roy F. 2003. "Ego Depletion and Self-regulation Failure: A Resource Model of Self-control." *Alcoholism: Clinical and Experimental.*

Baumeister, Roy F., and John Tierney. 2011. *Willpower: Rediscovering the Greatest Human Strength.* Penguin Press.

Carter, Evan C., Lilly M. Kofler, and Daniel E. Forster. 2015. "A Series of Meta-Analytic Tests of the Depletion Effect: Self-Control Does Not Seem to Rely on a Limited Resource." *Journal of Experimental Psychology.*

Carter, Evan C., and Michael E. McCullough. 2013. "Is Ego Depletion Too Incredible? Evidence for the Overestimation of the Depletion Effect." *Behavioral and Brain Sciences.*

Carter, Evan C., Eric J. Pedersen, and Michael E. McCullough. 2015. "Reassessing Intertemporal Choice: Human Decision-Making Is More Optimal in a Foraging Task than in a Self-Control Task." *Frontiers in Psychology.*

Danziger, Shai; and Jonathan Levav. 2011. "Extraneous Factors in Judicial Decisions." *Proceedings of the National Academy of Sciences of the United States of America.*

Eades, Michael R., and Mary Dan Eades. 2000. *The Protein Power Lifeplan.* Warner Books.

Hockey, G. Robert J. 1997. "Compensatory Control in the Regulation of Human Performance under Stress and High Workload: A Cognitive-Energetical Framework." *Biological Psychology.*

Inzlicht, Michael; and Brandon J. Schmeichel. 2012. "What Is Ego Depletion? Toward a Mechanistic Revision of the Resource Model of Self-Control." *Perspectives on Psychological Science.*

Kahneman, Daniel. 2011. *Thinking, Fast and Slow.* Farrar, Straus and Giroux.

Kool, Wouter; and Matthew M. Botvinick. 2013. "The Intrinsic Cost of Cognitive Control." *Behavioral and Brain Sciences.*

Kurzban, Robert. 2010. *Why Everyone (Else) Is a Hypocrite: Evolution and the Modular Mind.* Princeton University Press.

Kurzban, Robert; Angela Duckworth; and Joseph W. Kable. 2013. "An Opportunity Cost Model of Subjective Effort and Task Performance." *Behavioral and Brain Functions.*

Kurzban, Robert; Angela Duckworth; and Joseph W. Kable. 2013. "Cost-Benefit Models as the Next, Best Option for Understanding Subjective Effort." *Behavioral and Brain Functions.*

Markman, Arthur B. 2014. *Smart Change: Five Tools to Create New and Sustainable Habits in Yourself and Others.* Perigee.

Metcalfe, Janet, and Walter Mischel. 1999. "A Hot/Cool-System Analysis of Delay of Gratification: Dynamics of Willpower." *Psychological Review.*

Mischel, Walter. 2014. *The Marshmallow Test: Mastering Self-Control.* Little, Brown and Company.

Reimann, Martin; Antoine Bechara; and Deborah MacInnis. 2015. "Leveraging the Happy Meal Effect: Substituting Food with Modest Nonfood Incentives Decreases Portion Size Choice." *Journal of Experimental Psychology: Applied.*

Schultz, Wolfram. 1998. "Predictive Reward Signal of Dopamine Neurons." *Journal of Neurophysiology.*

Sharot, Tali. 2011. "The Optimism Bias." *Current Biology.*

Tice, Dianne M., Roy F. Baumeister, and Dikla Shmueli. 2007. "Restoring the Self: Positive Affect Helps Improve Self-Regulation Following Ego Depletion." *Journal of Experimental Social Psychology,* no. 43: 379–84.

CHAPTER 14: Where There's a Will...There's a Brain That's Been
Slipped a Cookie
How to get the most out of your willpower

Twenty-three of eighty-four references (see my website for rest)

Adams, Scott. 2013. *How to Fail at Almost Everything and Still Win Big: Kind of the Story of My Life.* Penguin Books.

Ariely, Dan. 2015. "Dan Ariely, Reddit AMA." *Reddit.*

Ayduk, Ozlem; and Ethan Kross. 2015. "Pronouns Matter When Psyching Yourself Up." *Harvard Business Review.*

Chaddock, Laura; Kirk I. Erickson; Ruchika Shaurya Prakash; and Michelle W. Voss. 2012. "A Functional MRI Investigation of the Association between Childhood Aerobic Fitness and Neurocognitive Control." *Biological Psychology*.

Correa, Ángel; Tania Lara; and Juan Antonio Madrid. 2013. "Influence of Circadian Typology and Time of Day on Temporal Preparation." *Timing & Time*.

Diamond, Adele. 2013. "Executive Functions." *Annual Review of Psychology*.

Duckworth, Angela L., Tamar Szabó Gendler, and James J. Gross. 2016. "Situational Strategies for Self-Control." *Perspectives on Psychological Science* 11 (1): 35–55.

Francis, Zoë, and Michael Inzlicht. 2015. "Proximate and Ultimate Causes of Ego Depletion." *Self-Regulation and Ego Control*.

Hung, Iris W., and Aparna A. Labroo. 2011. "From Firm Muscles to Firm Willpower: Understanding the Role of Embodied Cognition in Self-Regulation." *Journal of Consumer Research*.

Inzlicht, Michael, and Brandon J. Schmeichel. 2013. "Beyond Simple Utility in Predicting Self-Control Fatigue: A Proximate Alternative to the Opportunity Cost Model." *Behavioral and Brain Sciences*.

Inzlicht, Michael; Elliot Berkman; and Nathaniel Elkins-Brown. 2016. "The Neuroscience of 'Ego Depletion' or: How the Brain Can Help Us Understand Why Self-Control Seems Limited." *Social Neuroscience*.

Jay, Timothy, and Kristin Janschewitz. 2012. "The Science of Swearing: Association for Psychological Science." *Association for Psychological Science*.

Jessen, Nadia Aalling; Anne Sofie Finmann Munk; Iben Lundgaard; and Maiken Nedergaard. 2015. "The Glymphatic System: A Beginner's Guide." *Neurochemical Research* 40 (12): 2583–99.

Karpowicz, Phillip; Yong Zhang; John B. Hogenesch; and Patrick Emery. 2013. "The Circadian Clock Gates the Intestinal Stem Cell Regenerative State." *Cell Reports*.

Kross, Ethan; Emma Bruehlman-Senecal; and Jiyoung Park. 2014. "Self-Talk as a Regulatory Mechanism: How You Do It Matters." *Journal of Personality*.

Kruglanski, Arie W. 2003. "Goal Systems Theory: Integrating the Cognitive and Motivational Aspects of Self-Regulation." *Motivated Social Perception: The Ontario*.

Lara, Tania; Juan Antonio Madrid; and Ángel Correa. 2014. "The Vigilance Decrement in Executive Function Is Attenuated When Individual Chronotypes Perform at Their Optimal Time of Day." Edited by Virginie van Was-senhove. *PLoS ONE* 9 (2): e88820.

Markman, Arthur B. 2014. *Smart Change: Five Tools to Create New and Sustainable Habits in Yourself and Others.* Perigee.

Nedergaard, M. 2013. "Garbage Truck of the Brain." *Science.*

Schelling, Thomas C. 1978. "Egonomics, or the Art of Self-Management." *The American Economic Review.*

Schwartz, Barry. 2004. *The Paradox of Choice: Why More Is Less.* Ecco.

Smith, Jacquelyn. 2012. "Steve Jobs Always Dressed Exactly the Same. Here's Who Else Does." *Forbes.com.*

Xie, Lulu; Hongyi Kang; Qiwu Xu; Michael J. Chen; and Yonghong Liao. 2013. "Sleep Drives Metabolite Clearance from the Adult Brain."

PART THREE: Putting It All Together

CHAPTER 15: Rise and Spine
Grow a backbone and put the damn thing to work

Thirty-six of 110 references (see my website for rest)

Amir, Dorsa, and Jerry A. Coyne. 2015. "Guest Post: Pulling the Plug on Power Posing." *Why Evolution Is True.*

Bernhardt, Paul C., James M. Dabbs Jr., Julie A. Fielden, and Candice D. Lutter. 1998. "Testosterone Changes during Vicarious Experiences of Winning and Losing among Fans at Sporting Events." *Physiology & Behavior.*

Carney, Dana R., Amy J. C. Cuddy, and Andy J. Yap. 2010. "Power Posing: Brief Nonverbal Displays Affect Neuroendocrine Levels and Risk Tolerance." *Psychological Science.*

Carney, Dana R., Amy J. C. Cuddy, and Andy J. Yap. 2015. "Review and Summary of Research on the Embodied Effects of Expansive (vs. Contractive) Nonverbal Displays." *Psychological Science.*

Carver, Charles S. 2006. "Approach, Avoidance, and the Self-Regulation of Affect and Action." *Motivation and Emotion.*

Carver, Charles S., and Teri L. White. 1994. "Behavioral Inhibition, Behavioral Activation, and Affective Responses to Impending Reward and Punishment: The BIS/BAS Scales." *Journal of Personality and Social Psychology.*

Cashdan, Elizabeth. 2003. "Hormones and Competitive Aggression in Women." *Aggressive Behavior.*

Cesario, Joseph, and Melissa M. McDonald. 2013. "Bodies in Context: Power Poses as a Computation of Action Possibility." *Social Cognition*.

Cooper, Morton. 1984. *Change Your Voice; Change Your Life*. Macmillan.

Cuddy, Amy J. C., Caroline A. Wilmuth, and Dana R. Carney. 2012. "The Benefit of Power Posing before a High-Stakes Social Evaluation" (working paper, Harvard Business School).

Cuddy, Amy J. C., Caroline A. Wilmuth, and Andy J. Yap. 2015. "Preparatory Power Posing Affects Nonverbal Presence and Job Interview Performance." *Journal of Applied Psychology*.

Depue, Richard A., and Paul F. Collins. 1999. "Neurobiology of the Structure of Personality: Dopamine, Facilitation of Incentive Motivation, and Extraversion." *Behavioral and Brain Sciences*.

Elliot, Andrew J., and Todd M. Thrash. 2010. "Approach and Avoidance Temperament as Basic Dimensions of Personality." *Journal of Personality*.

Fowles, Don C. 2006. "Jeffrey Gray's Contributions." In *Biology of Personality and Individual Differences*, edited by Turhan Canli.

Gable, Shelly L. 2006. "Approach and Avoidance Social Motives and Goals." *Journal of Personality*.

Gelman, Andrew. 2017. "Low-Power Pose Update: Ted Goes All-in." Statistical Modeling, Causal Inference, and Social Science. *www.andrewgelman.com*.

Gelman, Andrew, and David Weakliem. 2009. "Of Beauty, Sex and Power: Too Little Attention Has Been Paid to the Statistical Challenges in Estimating Small Effects." *American Scientist*.

Gibson, James J. 1954. "The Visual Perception of Objective Motion and Subjective Movement." *Psychological Review*.

Goodman, Steven, and Sander Greenland. 2007. "Why Most Published Research Findings Are False: Problems in the Analysis." *PLoS Med*.

Gray, Jeffrey A. 2000. *The Neuropsychology of Anxiety*. 2nd ed. Oxford University Press.

Gray, Jeffrey A., and Neil McNaughton. 2000. "Fundamentals of the Septo-Hippocampal System." In *The Neuropsychology of Anxiety: An Enquiry into the Functions of the Septo-Hippocampal System*, 204–32. Oxford University Press.

Greenland, Sander, Stephen J. Senn, Kenneth J. Rothman, and John B. Carlin. 2016. "Statistical Tests, P Values, Confidence Intervals, and Power: A Guide to Misinterpretations." *European Journal of Epidemiology*.

Hudson, Nathan W., and R. Chris Fraley. 2015. "Volitional Personality Trait Change: Can People Choose to Change Their Personality Traits?" *Of Personality and Social Psychology.*

Ioannidis, John P. A. 2005. "Why Most Published Research Findings Are False." *PLos Med.*

Ioannidis, John P. A. 2007. "Why Most Published Research Findings Are False: Author's Reply to Goodman and Greenland." *PLoS Med.*

Jay, Timothy, and Kristin Janschewitz. 2008. "The Pragmatics of Swearing." *Journal of Politeness Research. Language.*

Junkcharts. 2016. "Reader's Guide to the Power Pose Controversy 3 | Stats-Blogs | All About Statistics." *StatsBlogs.*

Keltner, Dacher; Deborah H. Gruenfeld; and Cameron Anderson. 2003. "Power, Approach, and Inhibition." *Psychological Review.*

Mazur, Allan, and Alan Booth. 1998. "Testosterone and Dominance in Men." *Behavioral and Brain Sciences.*

McCook, Allison. 2017. "'I Placed Too Much Faith in Underpowered Studies:' Nobel Prize Winner Admits Mistakes." *Retraction Watch.*

McNaughton, Neil, and Philip J. Corr. 2008. "The Neuropsychology of Fear and Anxiety: A Foundation for Reinforcement Sensitivity Theory." In *The Reinforcement Sensitivity Theory of Personality,* 44–94.

McNaughton, Neil; Colin G. DeYoung; Philip J. Corr. 2016. "Approach/Avoidance." In *Neuroimaging Personality, Social Cognition, and Character,* edited by John R. Absher and Jasmin Cloutier. Elsevier.

Navarro, Joe, and Marvin Karlins. 2008. "What Every Body Is Saying." New York, NY: Harper Collins.

Ranehill, Eva; Anna Dreber; and Magnus Johannesson. 2015. "Assessing the Robustness of Power Posing No Effect on Hormones and Risk Tolerance in a Large Sample of Men and Women." *Psychological Science.*

Trafimow, David, and Brian D. Earp. 2016. "Badly Specified Theories Are Not Responsible for the Replication Crisis in Social Psychology: Comment on Klein." *Theory & Psychology.*

"Neural Connections: Septo-Hippocampal System—Gray; McNaughton." 2011.

CHAPTER 16: Rock 'n' Role!
Time to slip into somebody more comfortable

AND

CHAPTER 17: Saddle Up Your Fear and Ride It Like a Pony
Fear is not just the problem; it's the answer

Thirty-three of one hundred references (see my website for rest)

Arch, Joanna J., and Michelle G. Craske. 2011. "Addressing Relapse in Cognitive Behavioral Therapy for Panic Disorder: Methods for Optimizing Long-Term Treatment Outcomes." *Cognitive and Behavioral Practice.*

Arch, Joanna J., and Michelle G. Craske. 2009. "First-Line Treatment: A Critical Appraisal of Cognitive Behavioral Therapy Developments and Alternatives." *Psychiatric Clinics of North America.*

Bjork, Robert A. 1988. "Retrieval Practice and the Maintenance of Knowledge."

Bjork, Robert A., and Elizabeth Ligon Bjork. 2006. "Optimizing Treatment and Instruction: Implications of a New Theory of Disuse." In *Memory and Society: Psychological Perspectives*, edited by Lars-Göran Nilsson and Nobuo Ohta. Psychology Press.

Brewin, Chris R. 2001. "A Cognitive Neuroscience Account of Posttraumatic Stress Disorder and Its Treatment." *Behaviour Research and Therapy.*

Cable, Daniel M., Francesca Gino, and Bradley R. Staats. 2013. "Breaking Them in or Eliciting Their Best? Reframing Socialization around Newcomers' Authentic Self-Expression." *Administrative Science Quarterly.*

Cote, Raymond L. 1995. "George Kelly: The Theory of Personal Constructs and His Contributions to Personality Theory."

Craske, Michelle G., Katharina Kircanski, and Moriel Zelikowsky. 2008. "Optimizing Inhibitory Learning during Exposure Therapy." *Behaviour Research and Therapy.*

Craske, Michelle, and Jacqueline Persons. 2014. "Society for a Science of Clinical Psychology—Maximizing Exposure Therapy for Anxiety Disorders." *Recording.*

Craske, Michelle G., Michael Treanor, Christopher C. Conway, and Tomislav Zbozinek. 2014. "Maximizing Exposure Therapy: An Inhibitory Learning Approach." *Behaviour Research and Therapy.*

Didion, Joan. 2008. *Slouching towards Bethlehem.* Farrar, Straus and Giroux.

Foa, Edna B., Elizabeth A. Hembree, and Shawn P. Cahill. 2005. "Randomized Trial of Prolonged Exposure for Posttraumatic Stress Disorder with and without Cognitive Restructuring: Outcome at Academic and Community Clinics." *Journal of Consulting*.

Foa, Edna B., and Michael J. Kozak. 1986. "Emotional Processing of Fear: Exposure to Corrective Information." *Psychological Bulletin*.

Fransella, Fay; Peggy Dalton; and Grant Weselby. 2007. "Personal Construct Therapy." *Of Individual Therapy*.

Geisel, Theodore. 1960. *Green Eggs and Ham, Dr. Seuss*. Random House.

Hofmann, Stefan G. 2008. "Cognitive Processes during Fear Acquisition and Extinction in Animals and Humans: Implications for Exposure Therapy of Anxiety Disorders." *Clinical Psychology Review*.

Hofmann, Stefan G., and Michael W. Otto. 2008. "Session-by-Session Outline." In *Cognitive Behavioral Therapy for Social Anxiety Disorder: Evidence-Based and Disorder-Specific Treatment Techniques*, 216. Routledge.

Kelly, George A. 1963. *A Theory of Personality: The Psychology of Personal Constructs*. 2013 ed. W.W. Norton & Company.

Kelly, George. 1955. *Personal Construct Psychology*. Norton.

Kelly, George, and Brendan A. Maher. 1969. *Clinical Psychology and Personality; the Selected Papers of George Kelly*. Wiley.

Kircanski, Katharina; Matthew D. Lieberman; and Michelle G. Craske. 2012. "Feelings Into Words: Contributions of Language to Exposure Therapy." *Psychological Science*.

Kleim, Birgit; Frank H. Wilhelm; L. Temp; and Jürgen Margraf. 2014. "Sleep Enhances Exposure Therapy." *Psychological Medicine*.

Lang, Ariel J., Michelle G. Craske, and Robert A. Bjork. 1999. "Implications of a New Theory of Disuse for the Treatment of Emotional Disorders." *Clinical Psychology: Science*.

Lang, Peter J. 1968. "Fear Reduction and Fear Behavior: Problems in Treating a Construct." Research in Psychotherapy Conference, 3rd, May-Jun.

LeDoux, Joseph. 2015. *Anxious: Using the Brain to Understand and Treat Fear and Anxiety*. Viking.

LeDoux, Joseph E. 2015. "Psychotherapy as a Learning Experience." *Psychology Today*.

Morgan, M.A., and J. E. LeDoux. 1999. "Contribution of Ventrolateral Prefrontal Cortex to the Acquisition and Extinction of Conditioned Fear in Rats." *Neurobiology of Learning and Memory*.

Morgan, Maria A., Lizabeth M. Romanski, and Joseph E. LeDoux. 1993. "Extinction of Emotional Learning: Contribution of Medial Prefrontal Cortex." *Neuroscience Letters*.

Sapolsky, Robert M. 2005. *Monkeyluv: And Other Essays on Our Lives as Animals*. Scribner.

Tharp, Twyla, and Mark Reiter. 2006. *The Creative Habit: Learn It and Use It for Life: A Practical Guide*. Simon & Schuster.

Tsao, Jennie C. I., and Michelle G. Craske. 2000. "Timing of Treatment and Return of Fear: Effects of Massed, Uniform-, and Expanding-Spaced Exposure Schedules." *Behavior Therapy*.

Winter, David A. 2017. "Fixed-Role Therapy." *Pcp-Net.org*.

"Interview with Peter Lang." 2005. *Society for Psychological Research*.

CHAPTER 18: Unfuckwithable

Nineteen of forty-two references (see my website for rest)

Algoe, Sara B., Shelly L. Gable, and Natalya C. Maisel. 2010. "It's the Little Things: Everyday Gratitude as a Booster Shot for Romantic Relationships." *Personal Relationships*.

Bonanno, George A. 2004. "Loss, Trauma, and Human Resilience: Have We Underestimated the Human Capacity to Thrive after Extremely Aversive Events?" *American Psychologist*.

Bonanno, George A. 2010. *The Other Side of Sadness: What the New Science of Bereavement Tells Us about Life after Loss*. Basic Books.

Buss, David M. 1989. "Sex Differences in Human Mate Preferences: Evolutionary Hypotheses Tested in 37 Cultures." *Behavioral and Brain Sciences*.

Buss, David M. 2003. *The Evolution of Desire: Strategies of Human Mating*. Basic Books.

Buss, David M., and David P. Schmitt. 1993. "Sexual Strategies Theory: An Evolutionary Perspective on Human Mating." *Psychological Review*.

Cialdini, Robert. 1993. *Influence: The Psychology of Persuasion, Revised Edition*. New York: Quill.

de Becker, Gavin. 1997. *The Gift of Fear*. Little, Brown and Company.

Emmons, Robert A., Michael E. McCullough, J. A. Tsang, and J. A. Tsang. 2003. "The Assessment of Gratitude." In *Positive Psychological Assessment: A Handbook of Models and Measures*, edited by Shane J. Lopez. American Psychological Association.

Heitman, Danny. 2012. "Not Exactly a Hermit." *Humanities*.

Hohn, Donovan. 2015. "Everybody Hates Henry David Thoreau." *New Republic*.

Kahlenberg, Sonya M., and Richard W. Wrangham. 2010. "Sex Differences in Chimpanzees' Use of Sticks as Play Objects Resemble Those of Children." *Current Biology*.

Lyubomirsky, Sonja, and Kennon M. Sheldon. 2005. "Pursuing Happiness: The Architecture of Sustainable Change." *Review of General Psychology*.

Maddi, Salvatore R. 2006. "Hardiness: The Courage to Grow from Stresses." *The Journal of Positive Psychology*.

Mead, Margaret, and James Baldwin. 1971. *A Rap on Race*. Lippincott.

Schwartz, Carolyn E., and Meir Sendor. 1999. "Helping Others Helps Oneself: Response Shift Effects in Peer Support." *Social Science & Medicine*.

Seneca, Lucius Annaeus. 2005. *On the Shortness of Life*. Translated by Charles Desmond Nuttall Costa. Penguin Books.

Taleb, Nassim N. 2012. *Antifragile: Things That Gain from Disorder*. Random House.

Thoreau, Henry David. 1854. *Walden*.

INDEX

emotions *(continued)*
  evolution and, 40, 42–45, 90, 123, 165, 196
  feelings vs., 38–39, 226–27
  help and, 257–59
  James and, 27–32, 39
  meditation and, 137–40
  metaphors and, 47, 50–54, 56, 128
  motivations and, 42–43, 74, 90, 123
  pain and, 42, 85–90, 138
  posture and, 40, 56, 192, 207
  power and, 33, 191–92, 196, 201, 253
  putting them into words, 33–34, 38, 131, 241–42
  rituals and, 60–63, 65, 67–68, 74–76, 137–40
  scarcity principle and, 253–55
  self-compassion and, 117, 119
  self-esteem and, 85–92, 94–95
  sets of, 34–37
  shame and, 100–101, 104, 109
  values and, 153–54
  willpower and, 161–63, 165–66, 170, 174, 176–78, 182, 184, 253–54
employment, 10–12, 16, 18, 90, 97, 121, 123, 128, 130, 159, 196, 200, 204, 209–10, 257
  of Alkon, 11–12, 23, 106, 173–75, 177, 205, 213–14, 217
  confidence and, 213, 217–18
  fears and, 232, 238
  rituals and, 62–63, 75–76
  willpower and, 173–78, 181–82
energy, 116, 126, 128, 202, 216
  of Alkon, 13, 16, 173
  rituals and, 61–63
  willpower and, 163–68, 175–76, 178–79
Euston, David, 222
evolution, 30, 70, 98–101, 105, 113, 153, 169, 178, 193–94, 222, 257, 259
  emotions and, 40, 42–45, 90, 123, 165, 196
  fears and, 239–40
  objectives in, 90–92
  scarcity principle and, 251–53
  self-esteem and, 87–92, 94–95

subselves and, 148–50
willpower and, 164, 166, 168, 182
expectations, 110, 112, 186, 196, 216, 220–22, 252, 255
  fears and, 222, 224, 229, 231–32, 234, 236–38, 243
  rituals and, 68–69, 80, 82
exposure, 53, 222, 238
  confidence and, 214, 219–21
  fears and, 223–26, 228–43
expressive writing, 133–36, 241
extinction, 220, 222, 228, 238
eyes, 207–8

facial expressions, 27, 35–36, 39, 44–45, 55, 207–8
fears, 34–35, 37, 40–41, 108, 110, 122, 144, 149, 155, 171, 185, 189, 205, 207, 209, 213–14, 219, 222–44, 259
  actions and, 4, 123–25, 226, 230–34, 237–38
  of Alkon, 13, 124, 211, 214
  avoidance and, 198–99
  breathing deeply and, 242–43
  cognitive reappraisal and, 130–31, 137, 152
  embodied cognition and, 28–31
  exposure and, 223–26, 228–43
  as learning tools, 223–25, 234–37, 239, 243
  rituals and, 60–61, 63, 73–74, 76–77
  self-compassion and, 118–19
  values and, 152, 157
  writing about, 229–32, 241–42
Festinger, Leon, 144
Finzi, Eric, 56
fishiness, 52–53
friends, 30, 50, 103, 143, 149, 156, 182, 189, 196, 250–51, 253
  of Alkon, 4, 6–7, 9–10, 12, 19, 23, 46, 111–12, 124–25, 129, 206, 212, 229, 238, 245, 250
  rituals and, 63, 69–70
funerals, 25, 60, 69–71

Galinsky, Adam, 121
Gazzaniga, Michael, 49, 145–47, 173